THE JACKSON PROJECT

THE JACKSON PROJECT

War in the American Workplace
A Memoir

Phil Cohen

With a Foreword by Si Kahn

The University of Tennessee Press • Knoxville

Editorial Assistant to the Author: Patricia Ford

Library of Congress Cataloging-in-Publication Data

Names: Cohen, Phil.
Title: The Jackson project : war in the American workplace : a memoir / Phil Cohen ;
with a foreword by Si Kahn.
Description: First Edition. | Knoxville : University of Tennessee Press, 2016.
Identifiers: LCCN 2015042382 | ISBN 9781621902430 (pbk. : alk. paper)
Subjects: LCSH: Textile workers—Labor unions—Tennessee—Jackson—
History. | Labor disputes—Tennessee—Jackson—History.
Classification: LCC HD8039.T42 U6418 2016 | DDC 331.89/0477009776827—dc23
LC record available at http://lccn.loc.gov/2015042382

For my daughter, Colie
Always my best angel

CONTENTS

Foreword: A Union Journey   ix
   Si Kahn

The Jackson Project   1

Appendix: Union Leaflets Drafted for the
Jackson, Tennessee, Campaign   347

FOREWORD

A Union Journey

Si Kahn

Union organizers, for the now relatively small number of people in the United States who are still aware that such people exist, tend to be a deeply misunderstood breed. Whether they are paid professional organizers or rank-and-file union activists, their lives have been overly romanticized by Hollywood.

Think of the great Italian movie star Marcello Mastroianni swinging off the train, jumping to the ground as he comes to town for the first time in *The Organizer*. Remember Sally Fields in the film *Norma Rae* as she scrawls "UNION!" on a piece of cardboard, climbs up on a table in the cotton mill where's she's been working for years, and slowly pivots around, holding the sign high over her head for everyone to see. Recall James Earl Jones arriving in Matewan, West Virginia, in the John Sayles film named for the town, on a train filled with African American coal miners who unknowingly have been brought there to break a strike by white miners—and who, upon learning of the situation, promptly leads every single miner who had arrived on the train with him out on strike.

In his revelatory book *The Jackson Project*, Phil Cohen brings it all down to earth. Cohen rose up from membership in the hardscrabble category of the unromantically unemployed, through the gritty ranks of tough, often dangerous jobs, to become a skillful, committed, successful union organizer—and a poetically inspired songwriter.

So it's not surprising that among the most moving and gratifying passages in Phil Cohen's book are those where he describes his own experiences becoming emotionally and politically organized, not simply into a union, but into a new state of consciousness and action. He starts out rough—a white gypsy cab driver in what were, in 1967, some very tough African American neighborhoods: Harlem, Bedford Stuyvesant, the South Bronx, Jamaica Queens. Necessity, risk, danger, anger—these, as any experienced organizer knows, can be an end game, or a starting point.

Those who are poor, exploited, ridiculed, pushed around, paid far less than either they or their labor are worth are always angry. They may come across as polite, quiet, seeking to please, not wanting to offend: "Best employee I ever had." But the anger is always there, underneath the veneer, desperately wanting to break through to the surface and beyond: the rage that life and work have to be so unbearably hard, so wrenching, so wearying, so breaking down of body and soul, draining the sweetness from everything, when with only a little bit of justice, of fairness, of someone looking at you with care and treating you with respect, it could be so much easier.

It can break any of us down, send us whirling off into self-destructive, self-defeating behaviors that may help us get through the immediate situation, but don't do anything to change it. We cannot see the light; we cannot begin to imagine a different life. We do not want the life we have to be as it is, but we do not believe that we have the means—emotional, financial, educational, political—to make our lives other than as they are.

That's what happens when anger becomes the endgame. But that same anger can also be the beginning, the seedbed for action. That's what happened thirty-five years ago to an angry young man trapped in a dead end job named Phil Cohen. Often times the change we want to see begins with us.

This is the starting point for organizing, the moment when anger begins to turn in towards the self-awareness that can, at its best, lead to action. Every good organizer is not only familiar with this dynamic, but works consciously, carefully, strategically to help the people they work with find that place within themselves when, whether they meant to or not, they say, first to themselves and then to others, "Someone's got to do something about this."

If you're going to spend your life trying to play this role, trying to organize workers into unions in the southern United States where Phil Cohen spent most of his long career or anywhere else, it helps if you have gone through that liberating process yourself, and understand deeply the transformative power of that moment, and of the many more moments that stem from it.

The light that broke through for Phil Cohen permeated his work as both a union organizer and songwriter. In his lyrics, he charts working class life with accuracy, deftness, and love. "Cold Wind" is not just a poetic memory of his own early life on the hard streets of New York City, but a chillingly accurate description of what life is like for those who try to stand up but who, without the strength of organization, end up standing alone.

> I followed my dreams down a dead end road
> Where the rainbow ends but there isn't no gold
> I squandered my money abandoned my friends
> Chasing a vision that died in the wind
> Chasing a vision that died in the wind

That's a pretty good description of what it's like for many people an organizer meets upon first arriving in town: Not cheering crowds waiting at the railroad station, not a brass banded welcoming committee with banners and balloons, but workers who are too worn down, brainwashed by management, and scared to even be seen in public with an organizer.

The watchwords of such workers are often phrases like, "Nothing's ever going to change in this town," or "you're not from here, you don't understand how bad things are," or "if I join your union, I'll lose this job. If I lose this job, I'll never find another one." The hardest obstacle to overcome is often, "you've got a job. You don't have to worry about losing yours. No matter what happens here, you've got nothing to worry about. You can always go back where you came from."

In the face of such emotions, why do union organizers like Phil Cohen continue to defy the odds and at times put themselves in harm's way? It is perhaps incongruous, but deeply helpful in understanding this, to reflect upon the Argentinean revolutionary Ernesto "Che" Guevara's most famous quote: "At the risk of seeming ridiculous, let me say that the true revolutionary is guided by a great feeling of love."

That's true not just of revolutionaries but of successful union organizers. Organizing can never be a mechanical, by-the-numbers process. It is of the heart as much as of the head. Workers who have never been respected, honored, understood, cared for on the job, and all too often off the job as well, can tell in the flash of a first meeting how the union organizer really feels about them, whether he's simply doing a job, or whether he is driven by passion and social commitment—and by love for the workers, both abstractly and directly.

But even all this is not enough. There must be empathy, an ability on the part of the organizer to put himself in the shoes of that worker standing there talking to him, covered with cotton lint or coal dust, covered with the weight of too many hours on her feet, too many insults casually tossed at her, too many days without work, too many stresses and troubles at home. And it certainly helps if the organizer has been there himself, maybe even started out there, like Phil Cohen.

Today, workers and their unions stagger under the weight of a relentless, spectacularly funded assault from right wing political movements and multinational corporations. Unions in the United States have seen their numbers and power wrenched away. Collective bargaining for public employees has been outlawed in state after state. Pension plans have been gutted and dumped. Health and safety regulations go ignored and unenforced. *The Jackson Project* takes us back to the era when these forces were first gaining momentum and one union local's fight against them.

It's bad enough that so many of the rights and benefits that unions and their members fought for have been legislated away or given back in exchange for an empty promise that, if you agree to work for less, we just might not close your plant. Millions of jobs that allowed our parents and grandparents to create the possibility of better lives in every sense for us are gone forever, deliberately shipped abroad in the search for greater profits.

It's not just hard times in the mill. There are no mills. In the year that Phil Cohen came South, there were almost one million textile workers in the United States, three quarters of a million of them in North and South Carolina. Today there are almost no textile workers left anywhere in this country. The looms, the cards, the spinning frames still run day and night.

But now they run in some of the poorest countries in the world, where the mill hands work nearly two thirds of the day, six and seven days a week, behind high chain link fences topped by razor wire, patrolled by police and "private security guards," in exchange for the "right" to live in almost absolute poverty and deprivation.

Whole industries that were the bedrock of the industrial working class, the backbone of organized labor, have been scrubbed almost from memory. There is no place in the United States today where iron is smelted into steel, the barges and hoppers of ore day and night pulling up to the mill. The once proud Bessemer ovens of Youngstown have been exploded into dust, along with the dreams of thousands of hard working families.

On the edge of a cliff at the end of the line
A man stands alone and is left to wonder why
For a lifetime of work he's got nothing to show
He's been down all the highways but there's nowhere left to go

Are the lyrics above depressing, hopeless, a sign of the relative powerlessness of working people in the United States today? Or do they simply state an accurate if unwelcome truth: That the economic and social situation of far too many working people in our country has been deliberately driven down as close to the bottom as those in power can make it.

As noted by H.L. Mitchell, one of the founders of the Southern Tenant Farmers Union, which in the late 1930s brought black and white sharecroppers together in one organization, there are "mean things happening in this land." But despite its unflinching hard look at reality, this is at heart a deeply hopeful, inspirational book. It is the story of a significant struggle in what might seem an extremely unlikely place, brought about by courage, by determination, by the traditional "blood, sweat, and tears" of "ordinary" working people, who are never in fact ordinary.

There is no need to recount that story here. In *The Jackson Project*, Phil Cohen has told it as well as such a story can be told. His book seethes with honesty: about work, race, class, pride, risk, honor, power, unions, organizers, organizing campaigns. He is as hard on himself as he is on anybody else—and he can be pretty hard. But at the heart of this book, and of Phil Cohen's life and work as a union organizer, there is celebration, community, empowerment, and love.

> We make the products that America runs on
> The yarn and the cloth and the clothes that you wear
> For so many years we were taken for granted
> 'Till we stood together to get our fair share

If the labor movement is going to endure through the twenty-first century and beyond, it will need more courageous, intense, dedicated organizers like Phil Cohen, who continue to believe and, even more importantly, act on what Ralph Chaplin, poet and organizer for the International Workers of the World, wrote exactly one hundred years ago:

> When the union's inspiration
> Through the workers' blood shall run
> There can be no power greater
> Anywhere beneath the sun
> But what force on earth is weaker
> Than the feeble strength of one
> But the union makes us strong
>
> It is we who plowed the prairies
> Built the cities where they trade
> Dug the mines and built the workshops
> Endless miles of railroad laid
> Now we stand outcast and starving
> 'Neath the wonders we have made
> But the union makes us strong
>
> Solidarity forever, solidarity forever
> Solidarity forever
> For the union makes us strong

All warfare is based upon deception
The general who is skilled in defense
hides in the most secret recesses
of the earth
He who is skilled in attack
flashes forth
from the topmost heights of heaven

—Sun Tzu, *The Art of War*

PROLOGUE

From the Street to the Bargaining Table

Becoming a union organizer or business agent is seldom a childhood ambition. Most veteran union staff didn't start out consciously headed in this direction. Life pushes, shoves, twists, bends, and molds a person until one day they find themselves fulfilling a role not previously envisioned.

The best field operatives in the labor movement often come from difficult beginnings. They took a job in their late teens at a factory, warehouse, garage, or laundry because that was their only option for survival. By chance or fate, they ended up in a union shop. The work was mind numbing and physically exhausting, but they toughed it out one day at a time. Months or even years might have passed before something galvanized them to begin playing an active role in the union.

At that moment a fuse was lit. They fought their way up through the ranks of their local to become president or chief steward. It became as much an incentive to go to work each day as their modest paycheck. Their coworkers grew to trust and respect them, realizing they had the heart to give a damn, the guts to do something about it, and the instincts to make a difference. Eventually, they caught the attention of an international union and were offered a staff position. At least that's the old-school way.

Since the mid-1990s, there has been a growing inclination among union bureaucracies to hire college-educated candidates in the hope of better contending with increasingly sophisticated corporations. These young men and women graduate with a degree in labor studies or political science, and sometimes further their endeavors at the AFL-CIO

Organizing Institute. They are invested with a sense of mission to save the working class about whom, from their own experience, they know next to nothing.

Within a few years they are generally chewed up and spit out in a thousand little pieces. The blue-collar world is rough terrain for which the classroom never prepared them. After licking their wounds, they return to school to become lawyers or professors. A select few, with the most talent and ability to adapt, ascend to join the upper echelons of the organization that hired them. Though their abilities as negotiators and administrators may become formidable, these managers and directors are never fully embraced as one of the people, for they are cut from a very different cloth.

I left home when I was sixteen with a thirst for adventure looking forward and an absence of fond memories looking back. Actually, I was never sixteen. I was eighteen for three straight years because I had to work for a living. It was 1967 in New York City.

A year later, I was reading the want ads in a local newspaper when I came across one that said: "Drivers Wanted. No experience necessary. $30 per day." That was a lot of money back then.

My entrance into the office at the Long Island City garage was memorable. About a dozen men stood around just inside the doorway, joking and hooting as men will do in an industrial setting. One of them was boasting of his sexual exploits at a recent party when an obese gentleman in a sleeveless T-shirt cut in with a profane remark. The group tumbled upon itself with arm punches and howling laughter as if this were the most amusing thing they'd ever heard. Eventually someone noticed me and asked, "What do you want, kid?"

Explaining that I was responding to the ad, he asked to see my driver's license. I willed for him to not calculate from my birth date that I was underage, and he didn't. I was promptly walked into the garage and asked to sit in a car that in some ways resembled a taxi. It had a meter and I was shown how to turn it on and off.

"Go out in the street and make some money," the man told me.

It took me a couple of days to figure out that I had become a gypsy cab driver. Gypsies provide bootleg transportation to neighborhoods where legitimate taxis are afraid to venture.

During the next year, I was employed by several outfits, one of them owned by the mob. I prowled the streets of Harlem, Bedford Stuyvesant, the South Bronx, and Jamaica Queens. Only a handful of other white drivers were doing this. I fought with muggers, drove dilapidated equipment, and was constantly harassed and cited by the "Hack Squad"— NYPD's taxi enforcement division. But at age seventeen, I was making a man's living.

When it came time to renew my driver's license, I had so many outstanding tickets and bench warrants from the taxi police that my application was declined. I descended to life on the streets, migrating between odd jobs and living in a cheap hotel. Over time the owners of the establishment came to know me. I had to my credit the fact that I was intelligent and not a heroin addict. They fired the live-in manager and offered me his position. I was once again earning a decent wage.

Even during this period, I had a willingness and instinct for helping those less fortunate to play the system and survive: concocting elaborate schemes for indigent residents to collect more money from social services, get better health care, and evade fugitive warrants. This was never done for compensation. I simply had an ability to see the landscape in finer detail than most people, and I shared the view.

In 1974 I signed my first union card. The New York City Police Department was making the transition from hard-copy to electronic filing of traffic offences. They lost a lot of data in the process. I was able to pay a lawyer $700 to clear my record, paving the way for a new driver's license.

Now of sufficient age and armed with a clean slate, I obtained a permit to drive legitimate taxis. During this era, the majority of New York taxis were owned by large unionized fleets. New York is a closed-shop state, meaning that union membership is automatic within an organized workplace. While I was filling out my job application, the garage foreman handed me a union card to sign.

The New York City Taxi Drivers Union was everything that gives organized labor a bad name. The sweetheart relationship with employers was transparent, and the grievance process was a sham. Despite this, it was obvious that we were receiving a larger cut of the meter, with better benefits and entitlements, than would have been the case without representation.

Driving a New York taxi during the 1970s was the ultimate existential experience. Fleet cabs weren't equipped with radios. You were trapped in an isolated bubble with your passenger, moving through a sea of chaos. Whether a wealthy executive or psychopathic junkie, whatever transpired between the two of you was without recourse or hope of intervention. Hours of tedium would be interrupted by unexpected encounters that pushed one's survival instincts to the limit.

Fear has a flavor. It is an acrid metallic taste at the back of your tongue. Anyone who has lived with the daily potential for violence knows what I'm referring to. My nights never passed without experiencing this taste.

I was an angry young man attired in T-shirt and jeans, spending much of my evenings driving well-dressed businessmen between airports, hotels, restaurants, bars, and massage parlors. They referred to me as "driver" or "fella" and tried to make small talk. I kept them at bay with monosyllabic responses, like any self-respecting cab driver. I deeply resented these men in suits but also envied them for having a job that paid one to travel.

One night as I made my way through the streets of midtown Manhattan, I had an epiphany. Like all true insights, it was an unanticipated flash that lasted a couple of seconds, yet remained vivid for the rest of my life. I realized that my own values and essential integrity were far more in line with the natural order of things than those of the respectable denizens of commerce who comprised the majority of my clientele. I understood that what I had deep inside was worth infinitely more than their affluence and prestige. It eliminated the need to hate them. It was an important step on my journey to empowerment.

Five years later, I followed the thread of a tumultuous relationship to North Carolina. I'd always dreamed of escaping from New York to a place more rural and close to nature, where one didn't have to walk down the street with hand in pocket, grasping a weapon, braced for confrontation at every turn.

I was utterly unprepared for and shocked by the work environment. Wages were far lower than up north, and the attitude of the workforce was disconcerting. Most working people in New York had an understanding of their basic rights and dignity as human beings. This didn't mean that they weren't exploited, but at least they were aware of it. They became angry and found ways to get back.

I drifted from job to job, surrounded by coworkers who were paid minimum wage, treated like garbage, and yet proud of their circumstances. Grown men were called "son" by people they addressed as "sir," without giving it a second thought. During conversations with friends, I found myself blurting out, "What they need down here are unions." I had no involvement with political or social causes as yet, but the words tore themselves from me time and again.

During the fall of 1979, I landed a job as a city bus driver in Chapel Hill, North Carolina. My years as a "professional driver" had actually counted for something. Chapel Hill is a university town, so the transit system wasn't put off by my longish hair and semi-outlaw persona. I could look in the mirror and once more feel like I had a real job, earning something that resembled a man's wages.

The Transportation Department employed about a hundred drivers and maintenance workers. It also had a union—Amalgamated Transit Union (ATU) Local 1565. The local was utterly worthless. Most southern states have laws that prohibit collective bargaining agreements between municipalities and their employees, meaning you can have a union but not a contract. The ATU thus viewed our situation as a lost cause and provided no service except for collection of weekly dues.

Local 1565 was founded and run by two women who saw the labor movement as their personal hobby. They cherished the symbolism and reveled in the bureaucracy but were clueless when it came to actually helping anyone. North Carolina is a right-to-work state in which union membership is voluntary. Though the shortcomings of the local were readily apparent, I joined at the first opportunity.

While driving a taxi in New York had been dangerous and unpredictable, driving a bus in a university town was stupefying in its boredom. The routes were short and circular, and your speed had to ebb and flow to an exacting time table. An eight-hour shift passed like it was an entire week. I measured my time in seconds and the distance in inches.

Management had no accountability in its treatment of employees. Some were treated fairly; others weren't. The employer wasn't held to any burden of proof in cases of discipline or discharge. Reasonable policies were replaced by the irrationally stringent when least expected. Drivers were fired without cause while the union leadership did nothing to intervene. They held monthly meetings, cackled over their minutes and reports, and engaged in lively debate about the rights of working people.

Over time I came to know and care for some of the senior drivers who had been with the system since its beginning. My most poignant observation was watching the lights slowly flicker out in the eyes of good people, as they gradually succumbed to the grind and capricious whims of others.

I clearly remember my galvanizing moment as if it happened five minutes ago. Drivers were gathered in a semicircle around the garage superintendent as yet another policy change was unveiled. I observed the demeanor of my coworkers, the look on their faces, their body posture. A voice welled up from deep inside saying, *Someone's got to do something about this.*

I scanned the faces and eyes of everyone in the room, trying to recognize who that person might be, so I could approach them afterwards. My gaze finally turned within, and I realized that person was me. At the time, I wished it could have been someone else.

I got myself elected chief steward and took over the business of reorganizing the local and representing employees, leaving the otherwise ineffective president in place as a figurehead to handle uninspiring administrative duties. She resented and opposed my initiatives, but I neutralized her influence whenever and however necessary.

I studied the town's personnel ordinances and grievance procedure, using them in place of a contract. Alliances were forged within the Transportation Board and Town Council. I enlisted support from the Rainbow Coalition and turned the struggles of transit workers into a media spectacle, generating statewide coverage that lasted for years.

Over a seven-year period, the senior management of the Transportation Department and eventually city officials were dragged to the bargaining table. They served within a public arena, and we had acquired the leverage to portray key individuals as either part of the solution or part of the problem. The process of discipline and discharge became accountable, resulting in the reinstatement of terminated employees. Though we still didn't have a contract, the reams of policies and procedures that were negotiated in many ways constituted the equivalent.

During the spring of 1987, a major victory resulted in all the mechanics becoming part of the union. Dramatic health and safety violations, and instances of personal bullying, were brought to light and remedied. The superintendent of maintenance was fired.

The notion started to dawn on me that perhaps I should be doing this for a living. I picked up the phone one afternoon, called the North Carolina AFL-CIO in Raleigh, and asked for the president. I didn't realize it at the time, but the odds against him taking a cold call from a stranger were a million to one; but he picked up. His name was Chris Scott, and I gave him a rapid-fire, ten-minute summary of the last seven years. He offered to schedule a meeting.

A week later, I was sitting in AFL-CIO headquarters. Chris told me, "There are very few people in this world who are natural organizers, but I believe you're one of them." He asked me to prepare a résumé that could be presented with his recommendation to directors within the various unions. Chris also suggested that my local certify me as its delegate to union conferences, so my sphere of connections could be expanded. Within the next several weeks, I made my first appearance on the broader stage of the labor movement, becoming an expected participant at the monthly Central Labor Council meetings in Raleigh.

My daughter, Colie, was two and half at the time and usually attended by my side (or on my lap). It was a familiar context, as she had been joining me at Local 1565 membership meetings since she was eight months old. Her mother and I had recently undergone a difficult separation but remained of one accord when it came to the wellbeing of our child. We had an informal joint-custody arrangement, alternating pickups from day care and keeping her through the night.

During the course of the next year, I received periodic overtures from labor leaders to whom Chris Scott had introduced me. They all involved relocation to the Northeast or Midwest. It was tempting but I wasn't willing to abandon my daughter, though I was sick to the point of revulsion at the prospect of continuing to drive buses. In the spring of 1988, I called Chris to discuss my dilemma. "Let me hook you up with Ernest Bennett of ACTWU," he said.

ACTWU was the acronym for the Amalgamated Clothing and Textile Workers Union, the largest union in the South. It represented a fairly recent merger between the Textile Workers Union of America and the Amalgamated Clothing Workers Union.

Ernest was assistant director of the Southern Region and wanted to get together the next time he was in North Carolina. We met a month later at the Howard Johnson's in Greensboro, where he candidly portrayed the organization for which he worked.

The Southern Region of ACTWU comprised eight joint boards, each with jurisdiction over numerous locals. It had become the focus of national attention during the JP Stevens campaign and memorialized in the movie *Norma Rae*. While this initiative had resulted in the organizing of numerous cotton mills, it had bankrupted the Textile Workers Union, ultimately leading to the merger.

The unromantic truth is that following the glory days of JP Stevens, the Region had fallen into a state of decline and apathy. Many of the joint board managers and staff lacked the competence and determination to withstand membership erosion from right-to-work laws and the incessant onslaught of hostile employers. Bargaining leverage was lost, workers became disenfranchised and uninvolved, while small groups of cronies elected their arrogant and lazy friends to positions of local leadership.

The southern director was a calculating, ambitious reformer in his late thirties named Bruce Raynor. His intention was to revitalize the Region one local at a time by any means necessary. To this end he had hired Ernest Bennett, a freelance community and union organizer, three years before. Ernest became the director of what was referred to as "internal rebuilds."

Rebuilds are one of the most extreme and challenging enterprises within the labor movement. They aren't as straightforward as new organizing drives. An operative is inserted into a troubled local to reorganize from within and shift the balance of power with the company. This means quickly winning the trust of a disillusioned workforce while running a game on the existing leadership until replacements can be trained and elected.

Ernest was interested in the means by which I had transformed my own union local and told me that he hoped to be in touch soon with an assignment. He was sincere and passionate regarding his involvement in the labor movement. Bruce's motivation was far more pragmatic than altruistic. He wanted to take over the national union and needed a strong power base from which to do it. Regardless of his reasons, he had hired Ernest, and Ernest was about to hire me.

A few weeks later I received a phone call. Ernest said, "Okay, we're set. You're going to Andrews, South Carolina." He then gave me an overview of the local and its problems.

"The best I could get for you to start is $325," he told me. This wasn't much more than I was earning as a bus driver, but he went on to explain how expenses were paid. In addition to travel and work-related costs, I would receive a twenty-five-dollar per diem—a tax-free food allowance. What you didn't eat, you kept. I was suddenly about to be earning far more than I ever had in my life, doing something I cared about.

Ernest stressed that I was being sent into a "hardcore situation" and wanted my assurances about being able to handle it. I was genuinely unconcerned. My whole life had been a hardcore situation.

On July 5, 1988, I drove down an intricate web of two-lane roads to Andrews. All things considered, I'd fared well in being assigned only four hours from Chapel Hill. It would be possible to return home every other weekend for three days. The objective for which I'd held out had been achieved: a job within the labor movement that kept me close to Colie.

Andrews was a poor, backwater community about thirty miles from the coast. There were two traffic lights, and the hub of social activity was a recently constructed Hardee's. Within forty-eight hours, I was situated in a small apartment overlooking the union hall.

Local 1900 consisted of nine hundred hourly workers engaged in the manufacture of T-shirts and panties, employed by Oneida Knitting Mills at three factories. The knitting plant produced fabric and cut patterns for two sewing facilities which pieced together the garments. The union was in total disarray after years of incompetent administration that management had exploited. It was barely maintaining majority status, with membership hovering near 50 percent.

The local had been serviced for years by James Johnson, manager of the South Carolina Joint Board. Ernest had thoroughly briefed me about this man. He had worked for Con Edison in New York and been a shop steward for twenty years before his wife convinced him to return to her roots in South Carolina, where he got a job at Oneida. Appalled by the wages and working conditions in a nonunion southern mill, he had jumped head-long into the fray when union organizers showed up at the plant gate. James had "risen like a fireball" during the campaign, been hired once the contract was signed, and promoted shortly thereafter to manager.

Ernest portrayed him as someone who had ascended through the ranks too quickly, becoming complacent and more enamored of his position than its responsibilities. He considered James an adversary and was concerned about my working relationship with him.

I decided to form my own opinion at our first meeting. James was actually quite congenial. He loved the union but not quite as much as good food and pretty women from the local who saw him as a big shot.

"Look, this is a chance for us both to look good," I told him. "I'm aware that with everything you've had to do managing the Joint Board, you couldn't possibly have had time to address all of the Oneida local's problems. Give me a free hand, I'll knock some heads together, and I'll turn the local into something that will make your whole Joint Board shine. In the end, I don't care how much credit you take for it. You'll be the king and I'll be your knight."

James found this to be a magnificent arrangement, and we got along famously.

The local president, Ron Talbert, was functionally illiterate. On its own, this reflected a cultural tragedy common to rural, Old South communities. But a person with these limitations was ill-equipped to represent hundreds of people under the terms of a collective bargaining agreement he could barely read or comprehend. Ron tried to compensate with belligerence and swagger. He was the textbook example of an unqualified leader, elected year after year by a handful of friends, while everyone else ignored the elections.

Document boxes containing grievance files were placed on my desk. There were over fifty cases dangling in limbo between the various steps of the process. Half of them lacked contractual merit, but the rest represented serious issues that should have been resolved months or even years before. One of my first tasks was to conduct private meetings with each of the local officers and shop stewards, secretly making profile notes and rating them on a one-to-three scale.

I met with a young steward from the Cutting Department named Anthony Coles, whose involvement in the local had nearly ceased. He had long ago lost faith in the bargaining process but was thoughtful and intelligent, with a clear grasp of what needed to be done. He was indignant but not hotheaded. Within five minutes I recognized him. He was the future president of Local 1900.

Over the coming months, an entirely new infrastructure emerged within the local union. There were numerous vacant positions, and it was easy to define a role for the right people. I trained and developed an alternative tier of leadership, slowly transferring control of the local over to them. Workers were organized in mass demonstrations of support behind major group issues, leading to dramatic resolutions and policy changes from the company. The most reviled members of management were discredited in the process and eventually replaced. Two hundred fifty-three workers joined the union, bringing the membership to 88 percent.

Hundreds of members turned out to vote at the local elections, and Anthony became president in a landslide. A shop steward named Loretha was elected vice president—the first female officer in the history of Local 1900. Ron Talbert never knew what hit him.

Early in the campaign, I became involved with a sewer named Stacie, the drop-dead gorgeous, hottest girl in town admired by every guy over the age of fifteen. She became a steward at the sewing plant, using her charm to help build union support among its workers.

Once established in Andrews, I began periodically returning with my daughter. She hung out with me at the union hall and off-shift workers were happy to babysit while I visited the plants. The membership became mesmerized by little Colie, with her wavy blond hair, sparkling blue eyes, and mischievous laugh. They referred to her as "a blessed child."

The Oneida campaign was a perfect storm. It made my bones and established the foundation for my career in the labor movement. Both Anthony and Loretha went on to be hired by the union.

In March 1989, I drove back to North Carolina at the conclusion of the project to rest, regenerate, and spend time with my daughter. Like the secret agent in an old spy movie, I awaited the phone call that would tell me where I was going next.

CHAPTER 1

I lived in an old farmhouse about ten miles south of Chapel Hill—a refuge of peace within a lifestyle of conflict. One afternoon, the phone rang.

"I've lined up your next project," said Ernest. "It's at the Buster Brown plant in Chattanooga. The membership is down to 33 percent, and I think the company is getting ready to try and decertify us. We really need you there."

He provided details of a meeting scheduled in Knoxville with Mark Pitt, manager of the Tennessee Joint Board.

Once again, several days after speaking with Ernest, I was on the road, this time headed west on I-40. I believed in pacing myself to be effective when it mattered most. I left a day early and took a hotel room in Black Mountain, a picturesque town in the Smoky Mountains about thirty miles east of Asheville.

The meeting wasn't until the following evening. I slept without setting an alarm and made a leisurely exit from the hotel. My mind was cloudy, and everything seemed surreal as I packed my bags. Andrews had been my whole universe for nine months. Each day had been so densely packed that it felt like several years. Suddenly this reality and the intimacies I had found within had vanished like a glimmering soap bubble pricked with a pin.

I drove along the winding mountain passes through Asheville and beyond, where the interstate once again straightened into never-ending monotony. The "Welcome to Tennessee" sign finally loomed to my right, inciting the rush I always experienced when crossing a state line for the first time. I pulled onto the shoulder to commemorate the moment and stepped out of the vehicle, feeling my shoes touch the ground and breathing the air deeply.

I proceeded with the remaining two-and-a-half-hour journey, turning into the parking lot of a Waffle House on the outskirts of Knoxville as dusk fell. Ernest and Mark had just arrived and were sitting at a table.

Mark was a slender man with stooped shoulders and short black curly hair that was starting to become speckled with traces of white. His dry and matter-of-fact monotone contrasted sharply with Ernest's effervescent and passionate demeanor. He was clearly very intelligent. Ernest had a stocky but not very muscular build and was nearly bald. One wouldn't have guessed that both men were only a year or two older than my thirty-eight years. I stayed in shape through daily exercise, was learning to eat healthy, and made a point of getting enough sleep when possible. Neither of these directors embraced such disciplines.

Following an hour of discussion about the situation at Buster Brown, Mark mentioned that he was also having serious problems with a textile plant in Jackson. Local 281 was a runaway train. Membership had declined to a third of the workforce with multiple new exits each week. The company was also in serious financial trouble. Mark had gotten the workers to accept concessions that management claimed were necessary to stay in business. I sensed that workers had been pressured to comply in a manner which failed to maintain their confidence. It was eventually decided that Buster Brown could wait and I would be assigned to Jackson. I asked where it was.

"About six hours west of here, off of I-40," Ernest nonchalantly replied.

My heart skipped a beat up into my throat and then sank to my stomach. I was being sent to perhaps the most remote outpost of the Southern Region—thirteen hours from my daughter. My expression remained deadpan and my eyes betrayed no emotion.

"Sounds like a plan," I said. "Give me directions and all the contact info when we get to the hotel."

Ernest had flown to Knoxville so we drove in my vehicle to the accommodations he had chosen.

"I like working with you," he confided.

When I asked why, he thought for about thirty seconds and then said, "You go the extra mile . . . and you're hungry. You remind me of myself when I was starting out."

I became distracted and missed an exit which was quickly corrected through an illegal U-turn over the median. "Look out Tennessee. Phil's just arrived," Ernest chuckled under his breath and continued the briefing.

The plant in Jackson was a historic facility, built in 1906 by the Bemis Bag Corporation with a union local dating back to 1938. A Pakistani investor named Humayun Shaikh had acquired the business nine years earlier and renamed it Tennessee Textiles.

The mill had originally manufactured yarn from raw cotton, which was then woven into cloth for burlap bags, a common agricultural commodity during the first half of the twentieth century. As the product became obsolete, production shifted to rolls of unfinished cloth for sale within the apparel and other textile markets.

There were currently 387 hourly employees, reflecting a significant downsizing that had occurred over the years. Even before the era of free trade agreements, the output of American textiles was diminishing in the face of foreign competition. The company had been struggling for months to successfully consummate its sale to new owners.

One of the accommodations the union had offered was the postponement of all 1988 vacation wages until the end of the year. Management and union officials had assured employees that the delay was necessary but payment could be expected before Christmas. Each worker was owed between one and four weeks' salary, depending on seniority. The deadline had passed four months ago, and the company remained in default, further diminishing the union's credibility. This had become the most volatile group issue in the plant.

The local had been serviced for years by a business agent named Eddie Cox, whom Ernest described as lazy, not very smart, and a heavy drinker. He made a monthly pilgrimage to Jackson, sat in on grievance meetings, but then did little to follow-up with resolution. I asked Ernest why the union didn't simply let him go.

"It's not that simple," he responded. "Eddie was once president of his own local, at an old Celanese plant, and his way of handling things seemed to work in that situation. When the plant shut, he was hired into a position for which he wasn't really qualified. He's been with us for over twenty years. What are we supposed to do? Where could he go if he lost this job? He'd probably end up pumping gas somewhere."

We arrived at the hotel and continued our meeting in the lobby until midnight.

"I know you like to hit the ground running and take a plant by storm," Ernest cautioned, "but that's not going to work here. It's going to take time before these people trust an outsider. The wild card will be the new owners. The company has refused to provide any details about who they are. If it turns out we can work with them, the project goes in one direction. If not . . . then we'll have to deal with it.

"For now, work your way into the local and build relationships. Identify the major issues and do what you can to resolve them. But don't get too far out in front of the people or you'll lose them."

There is an ethic within the labor movement that a moment spent not serving the cause is a moment when one doesn't deserve to be alive. A dedicated staff member is expected to be available 24/7. I had never bought into this. Instead, I believed that by nurturing oneself and staying fit, an organizer kept his edge and presented his best to the field. Most union representatives adopt the lifestyle of a businessman. I tried to live like an athlete.

Ernest's flight wasn't until late morning, and with nothing more to discuss, it made sense to sleep in. I wanted to start the next leg of my journey feeling rested and arrive in Jackson with my wits about me.

At 7:00 a.m. there was a knock, followed by pounding on my door. I knew it was Ernest but decided to ignore him and try to fall back asleep. The effort was unsuccessful so I showered and dressed. Upon opening the door, I found a note attached by tape. It was a page-long diatribe from Ernest, cussing me out for not responding. When we encountered each other at checkout, he asked, "Where the hell did you go? I knocked on your door earlier this morning."

"I was in the shower," I told him. "I must've not heard you."

"Oh, okay," he grunted, and let it go.

We had a cordial parting at the Knoxville airport, and I found my way back to the interstate. Jackson is in West Tennessee, about two thirds of the way to Memphis coming from Nashville. I periodically stopped at pay phones to make introductory calls and schedule my first meetings. I arrived exhausted, with my nerves frayed. It wasn't how I had wanted to begin the assignment, but that's how it was. I took a room at the Ramada Inn.

Mark had contacted the personnel director, casually informing her that I would be assuming the duties of the local's business agent. It's not unusual for unions to reshuffle workloads, so there was nothing about this call to raise an alarm.

My first meeting in Jackson was on March 30 at 1:00 p.m., with Local President Percy Ray Long. Local 281 owned a rather nice union hall in a residential neighborhood of old mill houses, which is where we introduced ourselves. It was apparent from the beginning that this was a good man with a serious drinking problem. Percy had one of the more high-end jobs at the plant, as a loom fixer in the Weaving Department. He was a black man about my age, with a once-muscular build that hadn't fully deteriorated due to the physical demands of his work. His hair and mustache showed premature streaks of grey.

Percy seemed genuinely pleased to make my acquaintance. Mark had apprised him of my arrival shortly after the meeting in Knoxville. "It's about time the International sent in someone like you," he said. "The union is in really big trouble and it's getting worse each day."

Percy went on to talk about the vacation pay issue and how he felt that management was trying to bust the union. He raised numerous other concerns as well but I was only able to take disjointed and fragmented notes. This was an off-shift day for Percy. He displayed the rambling and unfocused demeanor of the functionally intoxicated.

"Have you found yourself any Tennessee pussy yet?" he inquired.

I explained that I had only arrived the previous night.

The portrait of an innocuous-looking man in sport jacket and tie hung on the rear wall of the large meeting area.

"Who's that?" I asked.

"He was one of our former business agents back in the late 1940s," Percy answered. "He got shot during a strike."

"How'd that happen?"

"He knocked on someone's door, and they met him with a shotgun. And then they blew him away."

Members of the Local 281 Shop Committee and Executive Board began entering the hall at 4:00 p.m. These two bodies comprised the central leadership core of old textile locals. The Shop Committee sat at the table during grievance meetings and contract negotiations while the

Executive Board handled administrative duties. It wasn't uncommon for an individual to serve on both, and each of them acted as shop steward within their department and shift. (Stewards were front-line representatives within their immediate work areas.)

Collective bargaining agreements allow for the local leadership to be excused from work to attend meetings. The union reimburses earnings through a process known as "lost time." Those who were leaving work under this procedure were all present by 4:05. The others straggled in over the next half hour. I shook hands and introduced myself to each one as they entered the room.

Vice President Georgia Bond arrived at 4:15. Mark had made a point of warning me about this officer, characterizing her as a hothead militant, whose influence should be limited. I took this under advisement while deciding to keep an open mind. Georgia had wavy black hair, sharp piercing eyes, and a pleasant smile. Her presence didn't put me off during this first encounter.

The ten local officers arranged folding metal chairs so that we sat in a circle. The group included a Shop Committee member named Reverend Donald Vandiver. His demeanor exuded a level of confidence and composure. It's not uncommon in the rural South for ministers of small congregations to preach on Sunday and earn their living in a factory during the week. Donald worked as a fixer in the Carding Department and was the only white member of the group.

During the late 1980s, the demographics of the average southern textile plant were approximately two-thirds black and one-third white. There was usually a disproportionate ratio of black to white employees among union members, especially within the leadership. Black workers were inclined to view the labor movement as an extension of the civil rights movement, while many of the whites, in the longstanding tradition of the Old South, tended to identify with the Caucasian management structure. It would be necessary for each constituency to feel well represented if the local was to be reunified. I decided to keep my eye on the preacher.

Once the committee was assembled, Percy opened the meeting by asking us to rise while Reverend Vandiver said a word of prayer, a common practice in southern locals. I introduced myself to the group and explained my reason for being in Jackson, asking them to discuss the most serious issues at the plant, as well as the sentiments of their coworkers and management.

Everyone began speaking and shouting at once, ranting about various concerns while at the same time reiterating that the situation was hopeless and that "the union can't do nothing about it."

"Day by day, the union keeps steady losing ground!" one of the voices declared.

They turned on each other, arguing and screaming, some gesturing wildly. I tried to interject several times but was cut off and drowned out.

An older man, wiry of build and wearing denim overalls with a straw hat, periodically leapt to his feet, flapping his elbows against his side and bellowing, "Caw, caw, caw! Caw, caw, caw!" I had no idea regarding the meaning of this proclamation.

I finally stood, put my foot up on the chair, and said, "SHUT THE FUCK UP!"

All chatter ceased and a dead silence filled the room.

"Do you want to have a union, or do you want to just keep on complaining while the company walks all over you?" I asked. "It's up to you. It's your local. If you don't want to work with me, that's fine. I'll call the union and they'll be happy to send me somewhere else tomorrow. But if you want to save your local and build it into something you can be proud of, you're going to have to trust me.

"I am not Eddie Cox or Mark Pitt, so as of now, you're done blaming me for what they did. I am not some college boy who decided to save the working people. I am working people. I was the leader of my own local for eight years, and it was in worse shape than this one when I got there. I'm a specialist in fighting the worst companies and I'm here to help you fight this one.

"You don't know me. You've been lied to and given false hope before. Some of what I'm saying you're not going to be able to believe until time goes by.

"What you've got to do right now is look me in the eyes, and then look into your hearts, to the place where God, or your own inner voice, or whatever it is you most believe in speaks to you. Ask that voice if you can trust me. If the answer is 'no,' then I'm out of here. But if the answer is 'yes,' then starting right now you have to work together, follow my plan, and do what I ask of you, because I've been in this situation before and this is what I do."

I gazed out at the committee, scanning from face to face as they stole glances at each other and at me.

Percy finally spoke up. "I may hate to admit it, but I think we've got nothing to lose. The union's sent in this man to help us and we should at least give him a chance."

Heads began to nod. Georgia said, "If this man's really here to fight, then I'm with him."

Hollis Wade, the man in the straw hat, put his hands on his waist and stared thoughtfully at the floor.

"This is your local and your town, and I have a lot to learn from you," I said. "But I can only learn what I need to know if you give it to me in a way that I can wrap my mind around and make sense of.

"I'm going to ask you questions and if you have an answer, raise your hand and I'll call on you. One person speaks at a time and they have the floor until they're finished. If you disagree with what they're saying, wait your turn. No one gets interrupted.

"Management may be a bunch of selfish bastards but they are professionals. If you want to fight them and win, you're going to have to learn how to act like professionals yourselves. The way you were all fighting among yourselves when the meeting started, the division among the workers, that plays right into management's hands. As long as we're fighting each other, we can't organize and become strong enough to fight them."

Heads once again began to nod. Hollis raised his head and looked me in the eyes. Donald murmured "amen" under his breath.

I began asking targeted questions to identify and flush out the primary issues, writing as the committee members spoke and discouraging outbursts of emotion and personal opinion.

"It's not that as a human being I don't care what you think and feel," I said, "because I do. But thoughts and feelings don't win grievances and arbitrations. Evidence does. I've come to town with a gun, but I need you to give me the bullets."

It appeared to me that this was the first time any of them had been spoken to so candidly or interviewed in this manner by a union representative. Everyone remained at the hall much later than expected. Some periodically excused themselves to call home and apologize to their spouses. I ended the meeting by stressing that everything we discussed needed to stay among ourselves for the time being: "Resist the temptation to talk about this with the folks in your department and even your families. You can say that you've met the new union rep and he seems to know what he's doing, and let it go at that."

"But the company's laughing at us," said Georgia. "We've got to let them know that we're going to stand up and we're not going to put up with this anymore!"

"If we do that, the campaign will be over before it starts," I said. "For right now, this is a covert operation. We have a lot of work to do until we're ready to fight. The longer we can keep this a secret, the stronger we will be when we choose the moment to let things rip. The company will never know what hit them."

"So you're saying that the company and the scabs get to keep on laughing at us?" asked Hollis.

"I hope so, until the day we smack the grin off their faces."

As I lay in bed that night, I reflected on how my girlfriend in Andrews had given me an invaluable gift. She taught me how to dress as a union rep. Stacie was fastidious about her own appearance. She was not conceited or aloof but did take quiet pleasure in being the town's most sought after girl. Stacie would arise at 4:30 each morning to spend an hour and a half in the bathroom, making certain that her clothes, makeup, and hair were just right. When she walked down the aisles of the sewing plant, she expected all heads to turn.

My preferred look had always consisted of jeans, boots, and a leather jacket in total disregard of fashion trends. Before leaving for South Carolina, I'd scraped together a meager collection of what I thought were appropriate clothes for the business world.

Once the campaign was underway, over a hundred Oneida workers began showing up for the monthly union meetings. The largest segment of the workforce consisted of women who worked at the sewing plant. The night after each meeting, Stacie would share with me how the girls had critiqued each item of my attire. She would admonish me with remarks such as, "They all loved what you had to say, as always, and they thought your shirt was cool this time, but how can I say this, they didn't think much of those pants and shoes."

Stacie told me that the girls wanted to see their union rep dressed in a manner that was professional but still down to earth. He should look like someone who conducted business with corporate vice presidents, but not like a "suit" the average person couldn't approach. They needed to identify with and be able to look up to him at the same time.

Stacie began to accompany me on trips to the shopping mall, and within a few months, my work ensemble had evolved into a business-casual mode consisting of a traditional dress shirt with collar, khakis, and a nice pair of laced shoes. Loud colors and golf shirts simply weren't me. I kept the beard and mustache, but my longish hair was now better styled.

It felt like the passage through an initiation the night that Stacie, lying beside me in a skimpy negligee, smiled and said, "The girls thought you looked really cool today! They approved of everything you wore."

I awoke the next morning at the Ramada Inn and selected a pin-striped shirt and beige trousers from my closet. Having met with the local leadership, it was now time to begin introducing myself to management. It was critical that they perceive my arrival as a routine transfer, that I was in town in an administrative capacity, not as an organizer. I grabbed a quick breakfast and drove to the mill for an appointment with Personnel Director Byrnice Butler.

All factories segregate their front office section from the manufacturing area. It's climate controlled and comfortable, in stark contrast to the overbearing noise, fumes, and seasonal extremes of temperature that lie just down a corridor, through heavy metal doors.

Byrnice was a rotund, fairly congenial woman in her late forties who had been with the company for many years. Though not overtly hostile to the union, she obviously held it in subtle contempt. The personnel director gave me two documents her secretary had neglected to mail, listing the names of employees who had decided to revoke their membership.

She was nonchalant in handing the papers across her desk, but I could sense an aura of complacent satisfaction. Instead of referring to the union as ACTWU, both letters began, "The following employees wish to withdraw their membership from the ACTWA." Byrnice had been dealing with the union for years, and she was far from illiterate. It was a casual gesture of disdain.

I began the meeting by inquiring about the state of the business, assuming control of the discussion in a way that would inspire her to relax and provide information. Byrnice talked about the mill's serious cash-flow problem and her expectations that the plant would be sold within the coming months. This opened the door for me to raise the vacation pay issue. She assured me that the plant manager was looking into it and would get back with all of us shortly. I addressed the matter sufficiently to imply that I fully understood its history and legal implications but not to foreshadow the imminent escalation of the union's response.

We turned our attention to several terminations that were part of the grievance caseload. Byrnice expressed confidence that the company had thoroughly reviewed its position and acted correctly. I told her I would further study the files before commenting. She then shared with me that a number of years ago, a young organizer had been assigned to run a membership-building campaign. He had "stirred things up quite a bit" and put out leaflets referring to her by name, complete with caricatures lampooning her weight.

I said it was my practice to communicate with workers through printed materials but not in a manner which made things unnecessarily personal. Byrnice asked if I would allow her and the plant manager to review my leaflets before distribution.

"To the same extent that the two of you plan to have me review your employee memorandums before posting," I answered.

I left the office after a couple of hours, feeling that my objectives had been accomplished. Byrnice understood that I wasn't one to trifle with but didn't perceive me as a threat.

I expected to spend a solitary and boring weekend at the Ramada, making follow-up calls to committee members and filling out my expense report. I was in a first-floor room facing the parking lot in a motel style building.

Few environments are more sterile and less nurturing than a hotel room. A night alone in a hotel on business is not the same as being on vacation with your family. I now understood why so many businessmen in my taxi had requested assistance in finding a prostitute. While this hadn't become part of my lifestyle, my judgments and perspective mellowed considerably.

At nine o'clock on Saturday night I was in my lounge clothes, feeling somewhat dazed and numb by confinement and lack of activity. My guard was down as I searched in vain for something worth watching on television until I was tired enough to fall asleep.

There was a pounding on my door that quickly repeated itself. My heart rate accelerated and I instinctively went into defensive mode. "Who is it?" I shouted through the door.

"It's me, Percy."

I opened the door to encounter the local president, nicely dressed in a sport jacket and reeking of alcohol. I had no alternative but to invite him into my room. The last thing I wanted was force myself into work mode and relate with a drunken Percy, but there he was.

"I just came from seeing one of my honeys," he slurred. "Mmmmmm, that pussy felt good!"

He raised his fists like he was grabbing onto something and began to gyrate his hips. "I kept moving real slow, in and out, in and out. I wanted it to last forever . . ."

He looked up to see if I was impressed. *This is going to be a really wonderful night,* I thought to myself.

Percy decided it was the ideal time to show me about town and suggested we take a ride in my car. I got dressed and obliged. We drove around the streets and highways of Jackson for several hours. I couldn't understand most of what he was talking about, but Percy didn't seem to know the difference.

Jackson could best be described as a small city surrounded by rural countryside, rather than a town. It had a moderate industrial base for its size, and the largest demographic was lower-income working class. It was a drab and Spartan environment with little culture and few amenities. The population was large enough for the hard-drug world to have made its inroads.

In a state of relief and exhaustion, I dropped Percy by his car in the Ramada parking lot at 2:00 a.m. and returned to my room, furious at the front desk for having given out its number. Standard procedure is to call a guest, informing them of a visitor in the lobby. Once the campaign heated up, such sloppiness by the hotel staff could have serious consequences.

The union hall was a one-story brick building with a small lawn in front. One entered through a foyer and passed a second set of doors into a large meeting area with a wooden stage at the far end. The desk reserved for the union representative was located off to the side. I situated myself on Monday morning, found some letterhead, and wrote an introductory letter to the plant manager, Paul Poston. A shop steward or union member who noticed my car out front came in periodically to engage me.

The committee arrived promptly at 4:00 p.m. This session began with their silence and full attention. They had spent the weekend reflecting on my words and returned to the union hall with a sense of anticipation that redress, for which they had abandoned all hope, might suddenly be at hand.

The group assured me they had been discreet during the intervening days, sharing just enough with coworkers to arouse their curiosity. This was precisely what I had hoped for because it set the stage to begin engaging the membership.

The workforce was assigned within a seven-shift "continuous operation"—standard at many textile facilities. Larger departments were divided into four twelve-hour shifts with day and night crews, working three days on, followed by three off, plus alternating Sundays. The schedules rotated through the weekly calendar, distributing workdays evenly over time. The remaining departments operated on three eight-hour shifts.

I proposed a series of shift meetings held around the clock to accommodate the various schedules, starting a week from Wednesday in the evening and running through Sunday morning. The recording secretary held up a generic flyer that she explained was used by the local to announce meetings by filling in the date, time, and agenda, and then posting on the union's bulletin board at the mill. I told her she was welcome to use it, but that from now on we were going to communicate through leaflets, handed out at the plant gate on all shifts, ensuring that every worker received a personal copy.

I asked the committee to handle the initial distribution without me as I was scheduled to return home for several days. The timing of meeting announcements is essential. If you leaflet during the prior week, most people have forgotten before the date arrives. If you leaflet the day before, many don't have time to make arrangements for child care and other necessities. The perfect time to leaflet is forty-eight hours in advance.

In 1989, the advent of user friendly computers was still in the realm of science fiction, and leaflet preparation involved an entire day's work. I wrote copy on my portable typewriter the next morning, suffering through the inevitable delays caused by typos, whiteout, etc. I located a printer across town and presented him with layout instructions, including headlines to be typeset, then cut and pasted into the text.

The next afternoon I returned to pick up the several hundred copies I'd ordered, relieved that paragraphs remained in the proper sequence with the headlines correctly placed. I entrusted them to Percy and began the long drive east as daylight faded, stopping at a hotel in central Tennessee after midnight.

I turned south onto I-26 the next morning, planning to divide my personal time by first visiting Stacie in South Carolina and then my daughter in Chapel Hill. It was somewhat of a surprise that Stacie actually wanted to see me. During our last encounter she had pleaded with me to stay in Andrews and take a job at the factory so that we could be together.

"You knew this was coming from the very first day," I told her. "Wherever I end up, we can still stay in touch and see each other sometimes."

"And what the hell kind of future is that?" she demanded with a fury fueled by alcohol. "The only thing you care about is the damn union! You care more about the damn union than me and your daughter put together. You think you can buy her love with gifts now but one day she'll figure it out."

"That isn't true and you know it," I tried to reassure her. "But my whole life has led me to this job and it's something I believe in. I'm not going to just quit. Why don't you take a week's vacation and come back with me to North Carolina?"

"What's the point?" she responded, storming out of my apartment.

Stacie Summers greeted my return late on Thursday evening with hugs, kisses, and falling tears. She lived in a trailer on the same property as her parent's doublewide in Summersville, a rural community where three-quarters of the five hundred citizens were named Summers.

She climbed into bed wearing a black lace garter with stockings, and we began to make up for lost time. I didn't consider ours to be a relationship rooted in true love or profound communion. But there are instances when an intermingling of the innate sweetness and fire within two people eclipses the lack of genuine intimacy.

Apart from the obvious, I didn't get much sleep. Stacie was in the habit of rising every hour to smoke a cigarette before resuming her slumber. The click of her lighter always woke me. At 4:30 a.m. she began the sanctified ritual of perfecting her appearance for the coming workday.

I headed north on Saturday morning, feeling as though it might be possible to stay connected with Stacie while stationed in Jackson. I arrived at my isolated farmhouse that night, unpacked, and drove to pick up Colie.

Even during this interval of relaxation, my mind kept wandering back to Jackson. Distribution of the recently prepared leaflet was scheduled to begin on Monday morning, and I couldn't avoid second-guessing my decision to leave the responsibility with Percy (Fig. 1, Appendix).

CHAPTER 2

I've never been the *Better Homes and Gardens* type. I had nothing of the picket-fence lifestyle to offer my daughter. She was able to enjoy some of that stability with her mom. My gift to her was the adventure of life and the empowerment to deal with it. We spent much of our time walking around town and eating in restaurants. Our favorite recreation venue was the local arcade. We called it "games." I had been taking her there since she was one.

There was something enchanting and almost mystical about the experience. I would set her up at machines for which she was far too young to understand the rules and objectives. Colie would go into a sort of trance, instinctively working the levers and buttons, consistently racking up the highest of scores, while the golden tokens she'd won poured through the chute. Sometimes crowds would encircle us to watch. It reminded me of the pinball wizard in *Tommy*. I would later work the small mechanical crane and snare a couple of stuffed animals for her collection.

On Sunday night we left "games" at 10:00 p.m. and walked down the street to my car. Colie stopped and threw up her arms, beckoning me to carry her as she held on to the newly won prizes.

I flew to Knoxville the next morning, where I would receive one of the remaining perks in my compensation package as a union organizer—a staff car.

Unions traditionally provide field staff with a leased vehicle, because it's far more economical than reimbursing scores of people for use of their personal transportation. It involves getting to pick a new car from a menu every two or three years, with all expenses paid. Ernest had explained that I would have to assume the remainder of a retiree's lease before being offered a choice.

I briefly introduced myself at the Tennessee Joint Board office and was directed to the parking lot where a rust-colored Buick awaited me. The odometer read ninety thousand miles, but the car handled well as I continued west toward Jackson.

Upon my arrival, I was pleased to learn that the committee had dutifully handed out the leaflet to A and C shifts earlier in the day. B and D shifts would be serviced when they returned to work midweek.

I felt the correct balance had been struck with my first written communication to the workforce. The union had escalated its position by one notch regarding vacation pay—hopefully sufficient to arouse curiosity in the membership without generating undue surprise among management.

I had taken the very unorthodox approach of inviting nonmembers to the meetings. The only way to build a strong local in the South is to increase membership. The only potential source of new members is nonmembers. In this situation, many were former members who had become disillusioned and prospective members who hadn't chosen to join for similar reasons. The only way to convince these individuals that a new day had dawned was to invite them to see for themselves. Once I explained this logic to the committee, they withdrew their objections.

A few minutes after 6:00 p.m. on Wednesday, A shift began to arrive at the conclusion of their twelve-hour day. As expected for this first gathering, turnout was light. A dozen employees took their seats, several of them shop stewards, and one nonmember.

I climbed the steps to the large wooden stage that spanned the width of the union hall. There was a podium at the center, and chairs were arranged in the left corner for committee members. Reverend Vandiver opened the meeting with prayer, and Percy introduced me, saying, "This is an organizer who the International sent in to help us, so pay attention and listen to what this man has to say."

I presented an overview similar to what the committee had previously received, minus some tactical details. I was fully aware that with each spoken word, the entire workforce was being addressed through these individuals, both hourly and management.

My first organizing move was to initiate a petition regarding vacation pay. Petitions are the perfect first step when inserted into a distressed local. One has to accept that the majority of workers are in a state of fear and despair. The solution is neither to berate them for this, nor act like a cheerleader, but rather to engage them in a series of activities designed to build their nerve and confidence.

Petitions offer workers a venue through which to act in consort. Even the most timid perceive the risk as minimal, with their signatures buried among dozens of others in their department. The exercise engages everyone who signs as part of the solution. On the other side of the aisle, management correctly perceives the petition as a first show of strength and unity. While legally it has no collective bargaining value, it's the inception of a currency worth even more: leverage.

I kept the petition language short and to the point, so workers could glance at it and sign in thirty seconds. My objective was collecting mass signatures, not sharing a philosophical treatise.

TO: PAUL POSTON AND HUMAYUN SHAIKH

The undersigned employees of Tennessee Textiles hereby petition Paul Poston and Humayun Shaikh for the following:
1. Immediate payment of all vacation wages
2. An immediate meeting between Paul Poston and all employees

I gave each committee member and steward a copy to circulate with instructions to solicit signatures from nonmembers as well. Those gathered were pleased by the increase of union activity and comfortable with its pace.

Few endeavors drain the life out of an organizer more than shift meetings. Though your rhythm and sleep schedule are utterly disrupted, it is essential to remain dynamic and spontaneous throughout each session, despite the redundant presentations. The next meeting was at 6:00 a.m. on Thursday morning, when I greeted C shift. Turnout remained light, but all embraced the call to action.

At 5:00 p.m. I made my first appearance at the plant gate, joining several stewards handing out leaflets to B shift. The looming magnitude of the ancient textile mill dominated its neighborhood. Four-story brick buildings connected through causeways ran the length of several city blocks, all within a chain-link perimeter topped by barbed wire. There were two main employee entrances in front leading to different work areas. A faint aroma of cotton dust and chemicals permeated the air outside.

The plant gate was the priority tactical location for an organizer back in the days when textile locals sprawled across the South. During this era, most contracts only allowed plant access to the union rep for the purpose of "investigating grievances." Visits were limited to a specific department and accompanied by management. The only opportunity to interact with the entire workforce was being on location during shift change.

While engaged in this cycle of union hall meetings and plant gate visits, I was already working on the next leaflet. The committee wanted to maintain its tradition of conventional monthly meetings, held on Wednesday evenings and alternating between A/C and B/D shift workdays. It would provide continuity of a familiar practice and another opportunity to meet with workers.

I continued to spend a lot of time with Percy, building the relationship that is appropriate with a local president. He invited me to his house for dinner and introduced me to his wife and children, doing everything possible to make me feel welcome. I had no doubts about Percy's sincerity and loyalty. He wasn't inept and arrogant like the leaders I had first encountered at Oneida, but I was still assessing the extent to which alcohol compromised his effectiveness.

On Monday, I was back at the gate with the next meeting announcement. Frequent appearances at the worksite build an organizer's profile and establish the union's presence. It's not unusual for a mid-level member of management to appear unexpectedly in an effort to intimidate the union rep.

The law allows for the distribution of printed materials while standing on a public right of way (which includes the city streets surrounding a plant) and even permits an egress of fifteen feet onto private driveways if necessary to avoid obstructing traffic.

That afternoon, a burly man dressed in plaid shirt and jeans gruffly told me I was standing too close to the gate and needed to back up. I held my ground, looked him in the eye, politely introduced myself, and shook his hand, which I squeezed tightly and held onto a moment longer than is customary. I offered him a recitation of the governing legal statutes.

The man told me he was going to call the police. I said that was an excellent idea and presented my business card so he could be informed about the object of his complaint. I offered the parting suggestion that he might want to consult with the company's attorney before acting rashly. We resumed our distribution of leaflets without incident.

Between shifts I held another session with the committee to continue with training and preparation for what was yet to come. When the meeting concluded, Georgia Bond lingered as others left the hall. "I really need to talk with you, alone," she said. "Can you call me at home on Thursday afternoon when I'm off?"

We agreed on a time.

The union meeting began on Wednesday at 5:00 p.m. Around twenty workers showed up in addition to the committee, which was the largest simultaneous gathering at the hall since my arrival. I recognized several faces I'd encountered at the gate.

Formalities consumed the first half hour of the meeting. The financial report was read, followed by a motion to approve, which was duly seconded and then voted upon. The procedure was repeated with the reading of minutes from the previous monthly meeting. I observed heads nod and eyes glaze over.

Once done with protocol, Percy warmly introduced me to the membership. I paced the stage overlooking the seated workers, glancing at faces for reaction and making eye contact with everyone. As we were still in an introductory phase, I reemphasized points made during shift meetings and pushed the petition. When finished, I invited questions and comments by a show of hands.

I made a mental note that within a few weeks, I would suggest to the committee that they dispense with bureaucracy at the beginning of meetings and allow me to cut to the chase with the organizing program. Most union activists would consider this sacrilege, and labor attorneys might suggest that it violated Department of Labor requirements. I was neither an idealist nor a lawyer and was undaunted by these concerns. People don't come to the union hall to be bored. They come to be inspired.

Earlier that week I'd received a call from a terminated employee named Leo Boyland. He had been discharged in November 1988 and subsequently represented by the committee at their stage of the grievance process. The case was denied by the Weaving Department manager on December 15. It then became the responsibility of Representative Eddie Cox, who was pleased to honor the company's request to leave the matter in abeyance while the plant sale was being negotiated. I invited Leo to meet with me at my hotel room on Thursday.

The knock on my door came promptly at 1:00 p.m. Leo entered the room dressed in tattered, filthy clothes, reeking with the stench of a man who hadn't bathed for weeks. He said he had been living in his car for the past several months. I asked him to explain the circumstances of his termination.

The previous fall, Leo had learned that his immediate supervisor was having an affair with his live-in girlfriend. The supervisor became hostile when confronted, objecting to Leo's audacity in challenging his prerogatives. A few nights later when Leo reported to work, the supervisor claimed that he smelled alcohol on his breath and sent him home on suspension. Two days later he was fired by senior management.

I asked Leo if in fact he had been drinking.

"I'd had me a beer with lunch several hours before my shift, like I always do," he answered. "He might've smelled that on my breath but I wasn't drunk."

Union contracts require a burden of proof to support disciplinary action. Allegations of substance abuse at work must be substantiated by a laboratory, using Department of Motor Vehicles standards for alcohol consumption. The most conspicuous aspect of Leo's situation was that management failed to verify their suspicions in this manner.

I was appalled that this case had been on hold for several months and extended my apologies to Leo on behalf of the union. I offered him twenty dollars to get some food and assurances that I would schedule a grievance meeting with the plant manager as soon as possible.

Leo shook my hand and left just as the hour arrived for my phone appointment with Georgia. She wasted no time getting to the point: "Look, I believe you is sincere. We've needed someone like you sent here for a long time. But if you're serious about wanting to build up this local, there's something you need to know. The biggest reason people is getting out the union is Percy. The peoples got no respect for him anymore.

"Understand, I've known Percy a long time and I don't mean to bash him . . . but the man's got a serious drinking problem. He's always drunk when he's at the union hall and at union meetings. That's why the people have stopped coming by. Some of these folks will never trust you or get back in the union as long as you're standing next to Percy."

I soaked it in like a sponge, planning to sort through it later. I told Georgia that I understood what she was saying but, having just gotten to town, needed to take things one step at a time.

The next day, I drove to Atlanta for a regional staff meeting. Within an hour of arriving, those attending were subjected to an array of speakers from early morning through nine at night, with no letup during lunch and dinner. In addition to reports from Bruce Raynor, there were politicians, professors of labor studies, and guest officials from other unions.

Some of the lecturers would have been worth listening to on their own merits, but presented in merciless succession for three days, it all swirled together into an agonizing haze. After awhile, I felt as though every cell in my brain was screaming in a different key.

On Saturday evening, the staff was expected to fraternize in the hospitality room. The hotel suite was cramped and dense with cigarette smoke. There was a fully stocked bar and an array of snacks to be enjoyed while the television blared forth a basketball game. As I neither drank nor enjoyed televised sports, I didn't find this to be a recreational event. One of the business agents repeatedly leaped to his feet and charged toward the TV, screaming and waving his fist, as if by volume and intensity he could somehow influence a favorable outcome for the play in motion. Once my presence had been duly noted, I retired to my room hoping to rejuvenate for the final day's litany and return drive to Jackson.

My schedule was comparatively light through the next week. I had introduced a ration of unexpected ideas to the workforce, which they needed time to digest. One of an organizer's pitfalls is being perceived by the workers as a new taskmaster. Once the fire has been lit, the blaze must be nurtured according to its own unique attributes. It was not yet time to flip the switch that would make management escalate from yellow to red alert.

The interlude provided an opportunity to escape the purgatory of the Ramada and seek more hospitable lodgings in Jackson. I found a rental agency and began to review their listings. Part of each day was spent at the union hall with committee members, investigating grievances that had come to my attention.

Percy once again invited me to his home for dinner. With his salary as a skilled mechanic, he could afford a comfortable brick house in a quiet neighborhood. We relaxed in the living room after dessert while his wife cleared the table and I shared my experiences in Atlanta.

"I remembers a trip I made to Georgia a few years back," he cut in. "I was behind the wheel, riding alongside three of my buddies to visit some peoples we know down that way. It was the middle of the night and there wasn't another car in sight, so we be hittin' that bottle pretty hard, if you get my meaning. All of a sudden, out of nowhere, there comes the flashing lights behind us. 'Oh shit, we is fucked!' I said.

"'Maybe not,' says one of my friends from behind. He starts passing out these big ol' cigars. Well, we fire them up and by the time the state police knocks on my window, the air is so thick with smoke you could hardly see inside, let alone smell our breath. We just talked to that police nice and proper, answered all of his questions, and damned if he didn't send us on our way."

Percy slapped his thigh and guffawed at the cunning of his narrow escape, glancing into my eyes for approval.

There are spontaneous turning points of insight that remain forever embedded within one's memory . . . germinal moments from which ensue everything that is to unfold for decades.

I awoke one morning at the Ramada and was sitting in my room, still groggy from sleep but coming into focus as I drank a cup of coffee. Once more, that deepest voice within me arose and said: *You're probably going to be in Jackson for a year. You've made a commitment to this campaign and have to see it through. But after that, do whatever is necessary to get yourself back to North Carolina, or twelve years from now you'll be looking into the blue eyes of a sixteen-year-old stranger who used to be your daughter.*

I continued meeting with Byrnice, maintaining my posture as a conventional business agent and further positioning myself to interface with management. She was pleased to tell me that the overdue vacation wages would be paid on May 5. This marked an earlier than expected validation of the union's increased activity, and I immediately shared this with the committee. I then received a phone call from Byrnice, who explained the need for delay until May 12.

On Thursday evening, I began the long drive east for an off-weekend. I had made the decision that if I was getting paid to travel through beautiful places, I might as well take advantage of it. I headed south, just east of Knoxville, onto a semicircle of two-lane roads that winds through the Smoky Mountains and eventually curves north to reconnect with I-40 near Asheville. I pulled over periodically at viewing areas and got out of the car. The spring air was clean and fragrant as mountains stretched to the horizon. I felt my batteries recharge and some of the stress and exhaustion slip away.

CHAPTER 3

On returning to Jackson, I was successful in finding a field residence that exceeded my expectations. It was a furnished house on Riverside Drive, a curving residential road near the outskirts of town, just a few minutes from the union hall. It belonged to an old woman who was now in a rest home.

Byrnice called to inform me that the vacation pay would once again be postponed until the nineteenth. Instead of building my credibility, this situation now threatened it. Circumstance had presented the platform and timing for the next phase of escalation.

I mailed formal notice to Byrnice of the union's intent to proceed to arbitration regarding the vacation issue and reactivate the Leo Boyland grievance. Shift meetings were scheduled for the following week. Like a furious tennis match, the ball was about to begin ricocheting between opposing courts.

Ernest had an expression that impressed me: "The people will forgive you if you fight and lose. The only thing they won't forgive is if you don't fight."

I determined that it was time to begin dealing directly with Plant Manager Paul Poston and placed a call on May 9. My introduction by phone was cordial, but he lost no time telling me how distressed he was with the union's heightened activity and especially the leaflets.

Plant managers tend to despise leaflets above all else (with a couple of exceptions.) It is a phenomenon that unexpectedly descends upon their facility and over which they have no control. On distribution days, the flyers permeate every nook and cranny of the plant. They will at times become incensed over inferences not intended, like a mentally deranged person arguing against insults that were never proffered.

I told Poston that I was getting paid to do a job and he shouldn't take it personally, any more than he would expect me to be offended by the fact that he had a job to do. I assured him that if he worked with me in good faith, it would be reciprocated. This wasn't disingenuous. Most workers in union plants are simply looking for good representation that has a positive impact on their lives. It's of less concern whether this is the product of conflict or amicable negotiations. They'll rally behind results achieved through either means.

We briefly discussed the Leo Boyland discharge and scheduled a grievance hearing for the following week.

Poston informed me that an agreement had been reached for the plant's sale to a newly formed corporation named American Mills. He would remain as general manager but was unsure about the status of other positions. The new employer would be represented in discussions with the union by an attorney named Ted Yeiser. Poston provided his phone number and suggested I contact him. He asked that the news remain confidential until a public announcement and I agreed to honor what had been shared off the record.

I got off the phone and drafted a formal letter of introduction to Ted Yeiser that included the following position statement:

> Please be advised that if all 1988 vacation wages which remain in arrears have not been paid within seven business days of the Closing Date, we will initiate immediate legal action.

The shift meetings began on Wednesday afternoon. Attendance was double that of the previous set. The workers were becoming impressed, or at least intrigued, by the union's follow-through and tenacity on the vacation issue. For people who live paycheck to paycheck, infusing several weeks' pay into their budget can make a big difference.

I immediately focused my remarks on the matter at hand, telling the membership, "None of you are so naïve that you believe the laws and scales of justice in this country are tipped equally in favor of the wealthy and working people. You all know that for a working or poor person dealing with the system, the game is rigged.

"Sometimes what's right and what's legal in this country aren't the same thing. When that happens it hurts, but someone in my position has to be real, wrap his mind around it, and move on to issues he can win.

"But sometimes, what's right and what's legal are the same thing. And when that happens, you have a powerful combination. You hold a winning hand. This vacation pay issue is such a situation.

"I guarantee you that I will stop at nothing and that you will get paid. The only question is whether it will be sooner or later and that depends on you. The union has filed this case for arbitration. We will eventually win, but you all know that the arbitration process can take months before a decision. And I know that you want your money now!

"Workers everywhere are intimidated by management. That's because they are experts at divide and conquer. But fear is a sword that can cut both ways. Do you want to know the secret terror that haunts every small group of people that controls and exploits a large group? It is that the larger group will call their bluff and start sticking together. If we stand together now, I believe the company will cave in and pay us soon. It's a better alternative than having us in their face all the way to a losing arbitration."

I repeated this message throughout the two days of meetings. At the conclusion, we had petitions totaling 228 signatures, and I congratulated the leadership on their hard work.

In any conflict involving an insurgent force, an early victory is essential to coalescing support and building morale. I felt confident this was going to be such a battle. Once achieved, everyone would feel they had participated in the outcome. The ensuing pride and self-respect would outvalue the remuneration and could be channeled onto a broader front.

Textile operations were spread out and compartmentalized to an extent that various departments often had different cultures, issues, and degrees of union support. To build a viable union local, an organizer had to not only approach the workforce as a whole but initiate targeted efforts within each manufacturing area.

Based on relative union strength and number of open issues, the logical place to begin was Weaving. I presented several shop stewards with a "drop leaflet" to hand out within the department, announcing a schedule of shift meetings for the following week and containing the message:

Are you tired of being treated with less respect than
the machines you operate? Of working 12 hour shifts
without a decent lunch break? Of being pushed around
by supervisors who need a good attitude adjustment in
common courtesy?

IT'S TIME TO STRIKE BACK!!!

I spoke with the company's new attorney and scheduled a meeting
to include senior management and the committee. The lawyer explained
that we would have to convene in a hotel conference room, as he represented American Mills and technically the plant would still be under the
ownership of Tennessee Textiles.

At the conclusion of Thursday's meetings and calls, I packed and
headed into the night for another long trip home. I made it as far as
Crossville, Tennessee, checked into a hotel, slept until late morning, and
returned to the interstate. When I refer to this journey as a thirteen-hour
drive, it's in terms of time actually spent behind the wheel, factoring in
pit stops for meals and gas. But the unfolding of events does not hit the
pause button to accommodate travel schedules and all business trips are
punctuated by phone calls.

This has become a seamless process since the advent of cell phones,
but in 1989 the only means to maintain contact in transit was through
pay phones. This entailed frequent stops at rest areas and convenience
store parking lots. If the number was busy or the phone was broken, it
meant driving for another half hour and trying again. If one was driving
through bad weather and the time arrived for a previously scheduled
call, it meant getting wet. Every time I stopped for gas, food, or to stretch
my legs, I checked the answering machine at my Jackson residence, and
there were invariably calls to return.

I contacted Ernest at the Howard Johnson's in Greensboro where we
had first met to provide a status update. He told me that rather than talk
on the phone, I should stop by on the way home. He provided his room
number and told me to knock, regardless of the hour.

I showed up at his door at 11:00 p.m. and found it cracked open.
Ernest shouted, "Come in."

He resumed a phone call that lasted for twenty minutes. We were
just starting to greet each other when the phone rang again. He remained

sitting on the bed and talked until midnight, at which time our meeting began.

Ernest saw this as a perfect opportunity for in-depth review and strategic analysis. As our conversation progressed, the level of his exhaustion became increasingly apparent. For the last couple of hours, he talked lying on the bed with his face turned toward me. He appeared to be physically shrinking, until eventually he looked no more than two feet tall and like a light bulb about to flicker out.

We were finally done at 4:00 a.m. I told Ernest to stay where he was and offered to show myself out. Ernest shut his eyes and went deep within himself. For a brief moment, it was like he was no longer present.

Suddenly, he leaped to his feet, beaming and smiling, with an outstretched hand and a twinkle in his eyes. It was as if, within ten seconds, he had enjoyed eight hours' sleep and a good breakfast. He warmly shook my hand and wished me an enjoyable weekend at home.

CHAPTER 4

I spent most of my time off with Colie. We walked around downtown Chapel Hill until all hours of the night, made our routine pilgrimages to the arcade, ate in her favorite restaurants, and sneaked into a small playground that was closed. We also enjoyed a day at the zoo in Asheboro.

It was difficult on both of us that we could only see each other for whirlwind visits every other week. I would always ask if she was ready to come back with me to Tennessee for a couple of weeks, but she wasn't. Two weeks is a long time for a little girl to be away from her mom, and it was much farther from home than she had ever been. I never pushed her. I simply let her know that the invitation remained open.

On Tuesday, May 16, I met Paul Poston for the first time, to represent Leo Boyland at the final step of the in-house grievance process.

The language in the grievance article was comparable to most collective bargaining agreements. It was a dispute-resolution procedure regarding alleged contract violations and provided a framework of accountability.

The first step involved the aggrieved employee, shop steward, and immediate supervisor. The second step was heard by the plant superintendent and included the Shop Committee. At the third step, all of the above were joined by the union representative and plant manager. If the grievance remained unsettled, the matter was submitted to binding arbitration.

Employees unfamiliar with unions will often reproach an organizer by asking, "What does it matter if you have a contract? The company is still going to do whatever it wants!"

It is because of the grievance procedure (when competently enforced) that this isn't the case. If management attempts to ignore the terms of the agreement, they are ultimately obliged to reverse their position. The leverage is that unresolved violations result in arbitration.

The process costs an employer thousands of dollars in regard to shared expense of the hearing and its own legal fees. The amount of preparation time is formidable, and defeat means being discredited before the workforce. There is little point engaging in a pitched battle when the odds strongly favor your opponent.

Arbitration is a Damoclean sword seldom allowed to drop and persuades the parties to embrace reason during the end game. It cuts both ways. The union is compelled to withdraw cases, however sympathetic, when the body of evidence presented during the grievance procedure fails to endorse its position.

The two most important words in a union contract are "just cause." This simple phrase invokes a doctrine that has been interpreted and refined over the decades through enough case law to fill a library.

The Just Cause Doctrine incorporates seven tests, all of which the employer must meet to uphold discipline or discharge. The ones that most often win cases for the union are:

> —Can the company meet a burden of proof in regard
>   to the employee's guilt?
> —Does the punishment fit the crime?
> —Has the plant rule in question been enforced consis-
>   tently and in the same manner for all employees?

Union contracts bring due process marching through the plant gate and onto the shop floor. A union worker has the same rights in a discharge hearing as a defendant in criminal court.

Paul Poston was a short, unimposing man of slender build. His wrinkled face, graying hair, and stooped shoulders marked him as perhaps in his late fifties. An authoritarian, irascible demeanor made up for what he lacked in stature.

I had done my homework on Poston. He had spent much of his career with JP Stevens, had little love for the union, and even less comprehension. As was my practice, I shook his hand like a gentleman. Poston reciprocated, but his manner was stiff and cold.

Leo Boyland was present and respectably attired, having attended to his personal hygiene. Once everyone was seated around the plant conference table, I presented Poston with the vacation pay petition. He shoved it back at me, saying, "This has no legal merit. The contract makes no reference to petitions. I don't want it."

"I'm fully aware that it has no legal merit," I responded. "It's a statement from your employees about how strongly they feel concerning this issue. Are you telling me, and the committee, that you don't care about how your employees feel? If that's the case, we'll be sure to pass it on."

I slid the petition back across the table, and this time he accepted it.

I next engaged Poston in a discussion about plant operations and the textile industry in general. It was an attempt to build bridges that wouldn't compromise our position.

After we dispensed with preliminaries, the grievance hearing began. I offered Poston the courtesy of presenting his case first. I then expounded on the just cause violations that had riddled the discharge process, including management's failure to test for alcohol, compounded by the supervisor's indiscretion as motive to frame the grievant. I had prepped Leo for the meeting, and he acquitted himself well. As was customary, Poston told us he would review our evidence and respond in writing.

The Weaving Department shift meetings ran from Tuesday evening through Saturday morning, attracting moderate but spirited participation and resulting in the filing of a group grievance that stated:

> Weaving Department employees work twelve hour
> shifts without appropriate lunch periods and breaks.
> Employees are held accountable for efficiency and qual-
> ity problems which are beyond their control. Supervi-
> sors routinely address employees in a rude and abusive
> manner.

I prepared a separate grievance form for each of the shifts and requested that stewards obtain signatures from all their coworkers. This once again gave me a chance to engage the workforce, allowing everyone to become part of the process and solution, while simultaneously demonstrating organization and strength to the employer.

Filing a grievance in this manner also provides contractual foundation to compel management to meet with an entire department while it is being represented by the union. (For example, this contract stated that management would meet with the aggrieved "employee or employees.") A group grievance meeting is a dramatic display of power and influence that management despises and fears (even more than leaflets) and which workers remember for the rest of their lives. Being right, legal, and organized is the ultimate formula for victory.

The weaving department in a textile mill is located towards the end of the manufacturing process, where previously spun yarn is woven into long rolls of cloth.

It would be difficult for anyone unfamiliar with industrial settings to imagine the environment of a weave room. A chamber the size of a football field is lined with rows of enormous mechanized looms. Each weaver maintains several of these, serviced by a support crew which keeps them supplied. The noise level is equivalent to a dozen subway trains, and the air is thick with the scent of cotton dust. Loom shuttles move with the force of artillery, and serious injuries are not uncommon.

Weavers are among the most highly skilled production workers, earning wages through a complex piece-rate system. An experienced operator can usually beat the base rate by 20 to 30 percent and be paid accordingly. When running conditions fall below normal, union contracts require that weavers receive their average pay and aren't penalized for circumstances beyond their control.

Every piece rate contains a "personal and fatigue allowance" to accommodate reasonable rest periods. Management claimed that this only referred to the occasional bathroom or cigarette break and cited the need to maintain continuous loom operation. Most textile mills employed "relief weavers" to travel between loom sets, providing break and meal times for the operators. In 1987, Tennessee Textiles had eliminated these positions to reduce costs.

Weavers were at the end their rope after two years of remaining on their feet for twelve hours straight without nourishment. Adding insult to injury, they were seldom compensated for "off-standard" operating conditions and lost income when efficiency declined because of mechanical or product issues.

By mid-week, I received an express-mail package from the AFL-CIO Research Department containing detailed background materials on Ted Yeiser.

The majority of company labor attorneys are not truly adversarial if one knows how to engage them. They speak a common language with union negotiators and, even when instructed to "tough-bargain," aren't driven by underlying dogma. Another type, encountered less frequently, can best be described as union busters. They work for virulently anti-union firms ranging from small partnerships to large conglomerates. It is never a random choice when an employer retains counsel.

Ted Yeiser was the author of several books including *How to Decertify a Union* and proudly claimed to have coined the phrase "union free." He was cofounder of Tactical Advisory Group (TAG), which frequently gave seminars nationwide with names such as "Defending Union Free Status." Yeiser boasted that he specialized in running decertification campaigns.

In 1979, an AFL-CIO field representative had infiltrated a TAG workshop facilitated by Yeiser. His detailed notes said that Yeiser, "Admires the behavior modification techniques used in training German officers during WWII."

There are two variations on how a plant is sold. In the more common scenario, a new owner acquires an existing business and continues to run it under the same name. The National Labor Relations Board requires that the new owner recognize an existing union and be bound by the contract (much as continuity is maintained in all other contractual relationships).

When a company is seriously distressed, the resulting sale sometimes takes the form of an "asset buyout." The new owner purchases the business's assets (buildings, equipment, inventories, etc.) but not the business itself. What follows can then be either a liquidation or a reopening of the facility under a different name. In these instances, federal law mandates that the new company recognize and bargain with an existing union, but not necessarily accept the contract.

Yeiser had informed me during our phone call that the sale of Tennessee Textiles was going to be an asset buyout. He told me that the employer would be exerting its right to enter into negotiations regarding a new collective bargaining agreement and that he planned to present the union with a list of management's more significant proposals.

At 11:00 a.m. on Friday, May 19, I gathered with committee members at the union hall to prepare for the meeting with Yeiser. I told them we were going to listen to the company's proposals, no matter how offensive, without offering any comment.

"They're going to be providing us with a lot of information about themselves. Let's not return the favor. Let's keep them guessing."

I knew the proposals would be concessionary and cut deep. Yeiser would be braced for the stereotypical outbursts of indignation from the union. If we could remain calm and unresponsive, it would throw him off balance, contradicting what he had prepped management to expect.

At 1:00 p.m. we entered a conference room at the Hampton Inn. Ted Yeiser, Paul Poston, and three department managers were seated at a table on the far end, backs to the wall and facing the door. Yeiser was smartly dressed in an expensive suit sporting a gold diamond-studded tie clasp. He appeared to be in his early forties.

Instead of our chairs being set on the opposite side of the table, they were arranged in rows theater-style, separated from management by several yards. It was evident Yeiser wished to address us, rather than enter into a discussion. This coincided with my own intentions so I raised no objection.

I strode to the table, shook Yeiser's hand firmly, and stared into his eyes. "I'm very pleased to meet you," I told him and then shook hands with management.

I returned to where the committee was seated, and they each rose to offer a brief introduction. I then asked Yeiser to update us regarding the plant sale.

He began by extending his arm, palm upwards, and stating in a soft, ceremonious tone, "On behalf of the new owners, I would like at this time to extend recognition to the union."

He looked about the room with a slight smile on his face. I caught his eye and nodded. As previously noted, he was legally obliged to make this overture. It was like standing before the cashier at a convenience store and with flourishing gesture declaring, "I have chosen to pay for the gasoline."

Yeiser explained that the new company was incorporated as American Mills and closing of the sale would occur in six days. The principal owner was a Hong Kong businessman named Dominic Poon with minority interests held by several parties, including Paul Poston. The attorney stated that while formal recognition had been extended to the union, management would exercise its legal right to renegotiate the contract.

"In an effort to expedite the reaching of a new accord between the parties, I would like at this time to verbally present you with the company's opening proposals. I've prepared an outline of these proposals for you to take with you and consider."

He began to elaborate as a member of management handed out the two-page document. The company's proposal included substantial reductions in vacation and holiday benefits, wage concessions, and increased employee contributions for medical insurance. The summary concluded with a request that the union withdraw all outstanding grievances "and to instead begin the current relationship with a clean slate."

You've to be kidding, I thought to myself but continued to stare in polite silence at Yeiser, as one sits through a waiter's recitation of the day's specials.

Yeiser asked if we had any questions or comments that we'd like to share. I was in the midst of responding, "We'll review your proposals and continue the discussion at our first bargaining session," when Percy forcibly interjected.

The first wage cut on the company's list involved the loom fixers. Percy regaled management about how hard his group worked and their skill sets, noting that they were always willing to come in while off-shift to help with an emergency. His remarks were on point but, unfortunately, not his timing.

I did my best to bring the meeting to a cordial end and remained behind with the committee in the conference room. I acknowledged the difficult position we were in but explained that federal law protected us on two fronts.

While the new company wasn't obligated to accept the contract, it did inherit all outstanding grievances and arbitrations. "If I were to honor their request to drop all grievances, you should take me out to a field and shoot me," I told them.

Most important, while a new contract was being negotiated, management remained bound by the "status quo" of the old contract. This meant that all existing terms would remain in effect until either a new agreement was signed or the company could successfully claim that "impasse" had been reached.

"Nobody is going to get their pay cut or lose anything else, unless this new company wants the feds crawling all over the place. You need to take these proposals back to the plant. Explain to people that this is what they would be getting paid; this is what their benefits would be, starting next week, if they didn't have a union."

I shared what I had learned about Ted Yeiser's background. "This guy's a professional union buster. There's only one reason a company hires someone like him. We've started a program to rebuild this union, but now it has to go into overdrive. If we don't get people to stand together now, this new company is going to run over us like a freight train."

I drove to the post office to check the union's mailbox and found Poston's response to the Leo Boyland case. Not surprisingly, he had denied the grievance and upheld the termination. He failed to acknowledge or respond to any of my well-prepared legal arguments, simply reiterating the company's earlier position that intoxication would not be tolerated at work and that the supervisor had smelled alcohol on Leo's breath.

I arose early on Saturday morning to meet with weave room employees at 6:00 a.m. The meeting ended at 7:30, and I was left with an entire day on my hands to be exhausted and bored—a suffocating combination. The extent of my isolation in Jackson was getting to me. I was six hours by car from the nearest ACTWU union local or office, and thirteen hours from my daughter, friends, and personal support network. I recalled a Sean Connery movie, *Outland,* in which, as a law enforcement agent in the future, he is assigned to a remote moon of Jupiter to maintain order in a rough mining colony. Thereafter, in the privacy of my thoughts, Jackson became "Jupiter's Moon."

On Monday morning, I called Paul Poston to arrange for the arbitration of Leo Boyland's discharge. In the normal process of arbitrator selection, the charging party requests a panel from an agency specified in the contract. The opposing representatives alternately strike names from the list, and the last arbitrator remaining is assigned the case.

The Tennessee Textiles contract contained an intermediate step requiring that the parties meet in an "attempt to agree on an impartial arbitrator to hear the dispute." Mark Pitt had recently mailed a thick packet containing names of labor arbitrators based in Tennessee, along with their résumés. I told Poston that these materials were available for our mutual convenience.

"I've got a million things on my mind right now, what with the plant sale closing this week, but things are only going to get busier," he said. "We might as well get this over with."

He told me to come by his office the next morning.

Formal notice of the plant sale had been posted throughout the mill. The transition would provide fertile ground for scheduling shift meetings with the Spinning Department. Uncertainty and curiosity aroused by the pending change would fuel the union's momentum and generate turnout. I hastily prepared a drop leaflet similar to the one previously issued in Weaving, then sped across town to the printer with a rush job, arriving out of breath and protein deprived.

"I'll stay late and call you this evening when it's ready," said the printer to his new best customer. "Man, you're going to give yourself a heart attack if you keep running like this."

On Tuesday morning, I politely greeted Poston in his office. Every horizontal surface above floor level was covered with information sheets about the various arbitrators. We paced about the room reviewing them, placing the few that either of us considered a promising candidate in a central location. We eventually agreed on Gordon W. Ludolf, a professor at East Tennessee State University.

I told Poston that I would contact Ludolf to inquire about available dates, which I would then run by him and Ted Yeiser. I packed up my materials, wished him luck with the change of ownership, shook his hand, and prepared to leave.

"Never in my life have I been so insulted!" Poston exclaimed.

"What are you talking about?" I asked.

"I sat with you, listened to your arguments, and then rendered my decision. Now, you want to bring in a third party to challenge my judgment."

From my perspective, this reaction was the mark of an amateur, but there is nothing more futile than berating someone already flush with indignation. Instead, I tried to suggest he not take this personally and that we were all getting paid to fulfill certain responsibilities, reminding him that his signature was on a contract providing for dispute resolution through arbitration. I once again bid Poston good day and shook his hand.

"Never, never have I been so insulted," he muttered under his breath.

The committee member in the Spinning Department was Betty Trice, a short, slightly overweight woman in her late twenties with a pleasant face and eyes that twinkled when she smiled. Though lacking the forceful personality of her counterparts, she was conscientious and eager to learn. Betty had worked with other shop stewards in her department to generate respectable attendance at their shift meetings, which consumed much of the next three days.

Spinning is an intermediate phase of textile production. The intake of raw cotton in bales occurs in the opening room. The cotton begins its transformational journey to fiber in the Carding Department, where it is extruded into a fluffy, rope-like product called roving, which is then manufactured into yarn within the Spinning Department. Yarn is further processed by the smaller adjoining areas of Twisting & Winding, and Yarn Prep. At the conclusion of this cycle, the thread is wound onto large spools several feet long (called warps), which are used to supply the looms that weave it into cloth. (There are certain variations between facilities, depending on machine vintage and products manufactured.)

Spinners patrol long frames that refine whirling bobbins of roving, located towards the top, into yarn, which is wound around bobbins near the bottom. It is their responsibility to insure that the machines run as seamlessly as possible, intervening with haste when a strand breaks or a channel becomes clogged. Like weavers, they are serviced by a support crew.

One of the more interesting jobs is that of the doffer (pronounced *dolfer*). A doffer's task consists of bobbin interchange, harvesting completed bobbins of yarn and replacing them with empties. He pushes an enormous cart, several feet long and chest high about his work area. An experienced doffer moves with the grace of a ballerina and the speed of a kung fu master. All one can see is a circular swirl of bobbins between the spinning frame and cart that rivals the juggling act in any circus.

There were numerous complaints from each shift regarding inadequate meal breaks. The situation wasn't comparable to Weaving because most days still included a scheduled lunch period. However, these were often cut short when a supervisor burst into the canteen, shouting at employees to return to the work area immediately because of production issues. One had no choice but to shove half a sandwich into their mouth, toss the other half in the trash, and return to their frames still chewing.

The primary concern was the department's filthy and unsanitary environment. Cotton waste is an inevitable byproduct of every phase in textile manufacturing. In a spinning room, large mechanical vacuums circle the frames from overhead, inhaling the clumps and particles of cotton fiber. Within this facility, the vacuums were in poor operating condition and hadn't been serviced, let alone overhauled or replaced, in years. The wheels of the huge buggies were so clogged with lint that they posed an ergonomic hazard. Every employee in the department was required to transport materials via cart on a daily basis, and the incidence of back and shoulder injuries was increasing. It was a classic example of management prioritizing cost savings over employee safety.

On Saturday evening, I was again invited to dinner at Percy's house. A genuine bond of affection had grown between us. The president attended all meetings and was the person I could most count on to join me at the plant gate for leafleting. He didn't throw his weight around and was comfortable rendering assistance without being in control.

It was also increasingly clear that most of his coworkers had little respect for him and regarded him more as a drunk than a leader. My close association with him hampered my own credibility (even though it was the workers who had elected him).

Percy told me he'd recently had his driver's license revoked after being convicted of a third DUI. There would be times when I might need to shuttle him to and from union events. Starting in mid-June, his sentence required that he spend several weekends in jail. He profusely apologized that he would be unable to assist with leafleting on weekends during this period but assured me he would remain available until then.

I consoled Percy on his misfortune and then asked if he had ever been to an Alcoholics Anonymous meeting. As a teenager I had managed to survive the streets of a big city without using drugs or drinking excessively, but there was a time when most of the people I loved were heavy users. I accompanied friends to AA meetings and was impressed with their impact on those I cared for.

"I'm not speaking to you right now as your union rep," I told Percy. "I'm talking to you as a friend. You've got a really serious problem and you know it. You're good people and a good union president, but we're headed into a war and you've got to soldier up and get your head straight. If you don't do it for yourself, do it for the people."

I committed to finding the time and location of a meeting the following week and promised I would go with him.

Later in the evening, when Percy excused himself to use the bathroom, his wife pulled me aside in the living room. "Phil, I pray to Jesus that you can find some way to help this man. I'm at my wits' end. You don't know how bad it really is. He'll go on down to the liquor store, buy a pint of whiskey, stand there in the parking lot and drink it down, then go back in and buy another."

On Sunday evening, Percy joined me at the gate to begin leafleting the various shifts about a union meeting on Wednesday that would focus on the upcoming contract struggle.

When drafting a union leaflet, one must remain mindful of two audiences. The primary focus is naturally the workers. In a cultural environment such as this, nearly a quarter were functionally illiterate, with the majority at third- to sixth-grade reading levels. Complex business situations must be distilled to a bare essence that is accessible and user-friendly. Dim lighting conditions within the plant and little time to read are also considerations.

The secondary audience, which should never be overlooked, is management. Company representatives bring leaflets into their well-lit offices and scrutinize every word, holding meetings and phone conferences to analyze in depth. A savvy union representative plays to this process as well.

In this announcement, I took a strong stand on behalf of the membership while apprising the new owners that we remained open to diplomacy and reason:

> We welcome Dominic Poon and the new owners and
> wish them luck. We'd like to work with them to make
> this plant successful. But they have to realize one thing:
> WE ARE THE COMPANY! THE PLANT WON'T RUN WITHOUT
> US! THEY CAN'T REACH THEIR GOALS WITHOUT US!
>
> They won't gain our good will by trying to squeeze
> blood from a stone! They won't gain our cooperation by
> imposing new hardships on us and our families!!

My priority during the first half of the new week was organizing attendance for the union meeting. We had reached an abrupt turning point in the campaign. The retention of Ted Yeiser and the concessionary proposals had unmistakably declared the new company's intentions and thrown down the gauntlet. The period of reconnaissance and gradual insertion was to be replaced by open conflict. The local union would either coalesce more quickly than anticipated or be crushed.

Within a couple of weeks after my arrival, the stream of requests to withdraw from the union had dwindled to a trickle and then ceased. At the plant gate and within the departments, we'd signed thirty-four union cards. I considered this a favorable rate of progress before the new owners unveiled their tactics. We would now have to initiate a membership drive with vengeance.

I had spent two weekends on the road and was due extended time-off at week's end. It seemed like an opportunity to swing through Andrews, visit Stacie, and then head north to see my daughter. I called Stacie on Monday night, expecting her to be as excited by the prospect as I was.

Stacie was surprisingly cold and distant. "I don't think that would be a good idea."

"What's the problem?" I asked." Are you upset that I've been gone for so long?"

"I don't think you want to know."

After a bit more coaxing, Stacie blurted out that she had become involved with Reggie—a committee member I'd mentored who became one of my closest friends at the Oneida local. He had a family but also a reputation for playing around. Once past the admission, I could sense an undercurrent of satisfaction as she shared more details of the liaison than I needed to know. There was clearly an element of hurt and payback in her remarks. I was deeply shaken by the news but did my best not to show it.

I understood Stacie's reasons. She had never fully comprehended what the union meant for me as both a cause and career. She felt jilted and knew that my lifestyle would never allow for anything more than an intermittent affair.

Reggie's motives, on the other hand, I really didn't get. My confusion smoldered into quiet rage. The two of us had become like brothers, and I'd infused a sense of purpose into his otherwise dreary life at the factory. I wondered if, in some subliminal way, this was his effort to hold on to

me . . . or if in an equally subconscious manner, he'd secretly resented my
authority and this was a macho gesture of supremacy, as one lion might
exert over another. Perhaps it was just curiosity, to sample a previously
un-tasted flavor.

All of this flashed through my mind in less than ten seconds as I remained calm and politely concluded my last conversation with Stacie. I
wished her well and told her she had meant a lot to me.

On Tuesday evening, I met with Local 281 sergeant at arms Rick Hardin.
(Within this and many other textile locals, the position was referred to
as "sergeant of arms," which always evoked Krishna-like images in my
mind.)

The sergeant at arms is essentially the local's bouncer at union meetings but within ACTWU, it was primarily a figurehead position. He sat
in a special chair positioned between the door and the seated membership, but in reality, it was up to the speaker at the podium to maintain
order.

Rick had requested the meeting, and I was happy to oblige. He was
a friendly and charismatic young man in his late twenties, with one foot
in the thug world and the other holding down a job. I instantly liked him.
He knew the streets, understood the system, and we had things to share.
He said he had been impressed with the union's new response to management and wanted to know how he could become more involved.

Afterward I drove from the hall to Percy's house and accompanied him
to his first AA meeting. It was a well-run group, and he seemed to hang
on to every word. On the way home he promised to continue attending a
couple of times per week. I told him to call me any time he needed a ride.

I got together with the committee at 4:00 p.m. on Wednesday, prior
to the union meeting. I asked them to dispense with opening formalities
and turn the session directly over to me.

"But what about the bylaws?" Betty asked. "The bylaws say that we
have to begin every meeting with a reading of the minutes and financial
reports and let the members vote on them."

"To hell with the bylaws," I said. "We're at war. The only thing I care
about right now is what works. What's going to work is making this
campaign the greatest show to ever hit Jackson, with the union hall offer-

ing ringside seats. Every moment has to be exciting, not boring. Are you with me?"

Everyone's head nodded. Georgia smiled and said, "As always, Phil, I'm with you."

There is never a convenient manner to gather employees who work at a continuous operation, and every option is awkward in its own way. Local 281 union meetings began at 5:00 p.m. for the benefit of workers on their way into night shift. They would exit at 5:50 and day shift workers would begin arriving at 6:10. Off-shift and eight-hour employees straggled in throughout the two-hour session. It meant giving my full presentation twice, with omissions for some and redundancies for others.

By 5:15 I saw more seats filled than ever before at the Jackson union hall. It was gratifying to note the presence of many individuals who weren't working that day. People were angry, scared, and confused. Everything they had labored for was threatened.

Following Reverend Vandiver's prayer, Percy welcomed the membership and introduced me. I shared information about the new owners and Ted Yeiser, then ran through their proposals.

"I'm not interested in any givebacks!" I said. "Are you?"

They all shouted "NO!"

"Now that I know how you feel, I need to know what you're willing to do about it. Not only am I not here to negotiate concessions, I think, now that the company has money again, that everyone is overdue for a raise! I think everyone is long overdue to get their damn vacation money!"

"You know that's right!" a man yelled, and everyone leaped to their feet, applauding with shouts of approval.

"I am your soldier. As long as this fight lasts, I will live for you and if necessary die for you. But I'm only one man. I am not the union. The committee is not the union. YOU are the union! That's more than just words. There's a lot of work to be done and you're going to have to be the ones to do it.

"I appreciate all of you taking the time to show up today. But there are still more members absent than present. And there are still more non-members than members. As long as the company sees us as weak, they will treat us as weak. Every one of you needs to become an organizer.

You need to take what you've heard here today back into the plant. We're going to be handing each of you a few union cards to take back to your department. It won't matter how good a presentation I make to the company if I don't have a show of force to back it up."

When finished, I opened the floor to questions and comments. A burly, middle-aged man near the back raised his hand, and I pointed to him.

"Say, we've always had a practice of not telling people what gets said at union meetings., When peoples ask, what went on at the union meeting, we tells them, 'You should have been there! Be there next time and you'll know.'"

"Look brother, I share your frustration," I responded, "but shutting people out is not the way to get them involved. Has it ever worked before? If people are curious, that's a first step. Tell them something they like hearing and maybe next time they'll satisfy their curiosity in person."

A slender white woman, wearing a work apron and shower cap (to keep cotton dust out of her hair) spoke next. "I've been a member of this union for twenty-two years. I've seen some things that are good and others that have been . . . well forget it. I've read the company's proposals you put on the leaflet. I want to say first that I appreciate your being honest with us. There's lots that would have just kept this under the table, at least for now.

"I don't like these proposals. I'm a single mother with four young'uns and I have a tough enough time paying the bills now. But the truth is, I don't think there's anything the union's going to be able to do about it. You're going to meet once or twice and then the company is going to do whatever it wants to, just like always."

There were murmurs of agreement with heads nodding up and down. Percy arose from his seat. "We are not going to let the company get away with this, because . . ."

As politely as possible, I cut him off. "Please, let me respond to this."

I explained the company's legal obligation to bargain a new contract and the prohibition against unilateral changes during this process. "The law is on our side," I told them. "That gives us protection and will take us so far. But the real power comes from all of you. Let me tell you about a large group of people that is intimidated by a few. They're like someone that has a gun in their house but has forgotten where to find it. One night there's a home invasion and they can't defend themselves. The fact is, they had a loaded gun all along, but it was tucked away in back of a closet and of no use to them.

"You're all like that person. You've always had a loaded gun but it's become lost. You have superiority of numbers, the legal right to organize, and the fear that strikes into the hearts of the few who to run a large factory such as this. If we start sticking together and flexing our muscles, I guarantee you the company will back off its proposals and start listening to ours."

A man wearing a faded plaid shirt, jeans, and suspenders leapt to his feet without being called on. His slurred speech betrayed a level of intoxication. "My name is Benjamin Royston and I want to know what happened to my grievance from two years ago!! I filed a grievance about harassment from my supervisor and a write-up that was truly and clearly unjust and I gave it to my shop stewardess and I haven't heard anything since! That's why I got out the union."

"Look, I can't possibly know about things that happened two years before I got here. If your steward dropped the ball on a grievance, that shouldn't have happened. The good news is, you didn't get enough write-ups to get fired, and under the contract, after a year, write-ups expire and can't be used against you. If you're still having problems with your supervisor, stick around after the meeting and talk to me. I'll straighten him out personally."

"Well, that's OK. I have a different supervisor now and we sometimes go fishing together. Don't worry, I plans to get back in the union, or I wouldn't have showed up this evening."

These exchanges continued until it was time to repeat my opening presentation. It was a healthy interaction and part of the local's healing process. For the most part, people waited their turn, and there were few interruptions. It was the type of group dynamic that allows anxiety to evolve into resolution.

Contract negotiations were scheduled to begin the following week on June 8. I wrote a letter to Ted Yeiser requesting updated employee information, OSHA 200 (accident and injury) logs, and "Material Safety Data Sheets for each hazardous material and chemical used in the plant." I also sought to quantify the impact of the company's wage proposal:

> Monthly earnings reports for all Tennessee Textile
> incentive employees during the past twelve months,
> broken down by individual employee, job, department
> and shift, indicating the percentage of earnings for each
> category derived from standard incentive and the per-
> centage of earnings derived from various bonuses.

Federal law requires an employer to provide the union with all information that might be relevant to contract negotiation or administration.
The union is thereby afforded due diligence and can bargain from an
informed position. A barrage of lengthy information requests can also
serve as a firewall against impasse, forcing management to waste inor-
dinate time and resources while responding. In any venue the law tends
to be complex and arbitrary; the trick is knowing how to make it work
in your favor.

Ernest had scheduled an early-morning meeting with Mark Pitt at his
office the next day. Typewriter-generated correspondence always took
longer than expected, and it was after six by the time I hit the interstate.

During the past three days, I had pushed the farewell conversation
with Stacie to the back of my mind so I could focus on the problems of
others. This is both an occupational necessity and hazard for anyone in a
stressful leadership position. In the short term, it eases the pain more effectively than inebriation. One can sometimes be amazed by their own ability
to remain a pillar of strength. But there's a price to be paid at the back end.
During the first pause in the action, when the pressure is suddenly off,
compartmentalized emotions burst through their dam like a tidal wave.

As I drove through the night, I was overwhelmed by feelings of hurt
and betrayal, and the new magnitude of personal isolation I now faced
in Jackson. This wasn't the aftermath I'd envisioned to what had been a
historic campaign in Andrews.

Part of my mind was able to keep things in perspective, while another part, stoked by unwinding stress and exhaustion, spun out of control like a tornado, dense with the debris of rage and self-doubt. I was
still haunted by my breakup with Colie's mom and needed these feelings
stirred up like a hole in the head.

I arrived at the outskirts of Knoxville shortly before midnight. At
this stage of my career, experience hadn't yet schooled me in the wisdom

of always booking a hotel room in advance. I was about to get my first lesson.

I pulled off I-40 to a Comfort Inn and was surprised to find that this unassuming establishment was full. Unconcerned, I continued into Knoxville.

I made my way toward downtown, stopping at a dozen hotels along the route, all with the same result. Apparently, some event that weekend had assimilated all hotel rooms within a twenty-mile radius.

I was starting to get desperate. It was now 4:00 a.m. I was fast losing my ability to drive safely, and didn't want to present myself at an important meeting utterly sleep deprived.

A towering luxury hotel loomed to my right. I pulled into the semi-circular driveway. There was a vacancy. The room price was $143, which was expensive at a time when a business-class hotel room averaged $40 per night. But I was past giving a damn about how the union would view this. I entered my suite, set the alarm for seven, and crashed on the bed. I was out the front door and waiting for the valet to retrieve my car by 7:30.

"Did you have an enjoyable stay with us?" the bellman asked.

"I was here for three hours. There wasn't much to enjoy," I replied while handing him two dollars.

The meeting with Ernest and Mark began at 8:00 a.m. I arrived on time, exhausted and disheveled. We discussed the upcoming contract negotiations and underlying campaign. Both seemed pleased with my analysis of the situation and progress. It was agreed that Ernest would join me at the table for the first bargaining session, and I would handle it from there.

I did my best to hold up my end of the meeting, but it was difficult to conceal that I was preoccupied and not in top form. I was irritable and short in some of my responses. When we were done, Ernest said, "Let's take a walk."

We strode a couple of blocks in silence until he asked, "What's going on? I can tell something's bothering you. Did Mark or I say something that pissed you off?"

I hadn't planned to share what was happening in my personal life, but Ernest's overture was sincere, and he needed to be assured that my present mood was unrelated to work.

When I'd finished telling Ernest about the recent call, he said, "You know, none of us were ever really sure what was going on with you and Stacie, if she was just a piece of ass or if you were in love."

"Neither one," I answered. "There's a lot of middle ground in between. I never saw the relationship as lasting forever but I did feel for her. What really upsets me is the way it ended."

Ernest thought for a moment and offered, "I'm sure Reggie's thing with her is only temporary, and once it's over and he's had time to think about it, he'll be sorry for what he did to you."

"Big fucking deal," I replied. "Do you know what the tombstone should read for 90 percent of the people on this planet? 'I'm sorry.'"

He put his hand on my shoulder. "Look, whatever else happened, you ran a nearly perfect rebuild at Oneida. You took a totally fucked-up unit and turned it into one of the best locals in the Southern Region. Nobody can ever take that away from you."

We turned around and walked back to the office. I got in my car and headed home.

CHAPTER 5

I had three days to unwind in North Carolina and catch up on being a daddy. When the weather was warm, Colie and I would visit a park that had a stream flowing through the far end, spanned by a wooden foot-bridge leading to nature trails. At this site, we'd reenact one of the many strange fairy tales that all parents are obliged to read to their children hundreds of times during their formative years—Billy Goat Gruff, the delightful saga of a goat pursued by a hungry troll.

Colie would be Billy Goat Gruff and walk across the bridge. I'd hide underneath as the troll. Alerted by her approaching footsteps, I'd emerge with a roar while hurling myself over the railing. I'd declare myself to be a troll with a taste for goat and then chase her all over the park for ten minutes amid her shrieks and laughter. Eventually I would catch up and carry her to the "cooking area."

Once the dinner ritual was over, Colie would inevitably make one of the most frequent declarations of her childhood, "Let's do it again!"

And we would.

On Monday evening our bags were packed. I was preparing to drop Colie at her mom's and then head west. Colie was dragging her little suitcase along the hallway floor as she headed towards the door.

Suddenly she stopped, looked up at me, and said, "Wait. The high-way calls my name. I want to see Tennessee."

"Are you sure?" I said, kneeling in front of Colie. "It's a long, long drive, and you won't be able to see your mommy for two weeks. It's too far away for anyone to come and get you if you become homesick."

"I know. I want to see Tennessee," she answered.

I loaded her in my car and we headed down the road. About an hour into the drive, I stopped at a pay phone to notify her mom. Her name was Hollie, and we had met while driving buses. Things were still difficult between us, but she appreciated my devotion to our daughter. She understood the life I led and realized that Colie and I shared something special in the midst of it.

Colie fell asleep within half an hour of the call. I put a country music station on low volume, drove for a few hours, and found a hotel.

The most mundane and redundant of life's necessities become magical when shared with a child and viewed through their eyes. We had a breakfast of eggs and giggles at the Waffle House down the road, finishing with our customary ritual of making soupy mixtures out of leftovers and condiments. I'm proud to say I taught my daughter the fine art of how to play with your food.

We now faced seven hours of boring travel down I-40, difficult enough for me but an eternal vacuum for a child. To pass the time, I invented a game for us to play.

When the tractor section of an eighteen-wheeler is traveling between destinations without a trailer, it is referred to as "dead heading." Our new game was called "Dead Head." If one spied what looked like a truck without a trailer on either side of the highway and was the first to scream, "Dead Head!" the player received a point. However, a measure of restraint was advisable because, if it turned out that a trailer was in fact attached (perhaps a flat bed not readily apparent), then a point was lost. A correctly identified dead head with a double smokestack was worth two points. Conversely, an error involving a vehicle with twin smokestacks cost two points.

We arrived at my house in Jackson on the afternoon of Tuesday, June 6. I was grateful for having found quarters suitable to share with my daughter. There were only a couple of hours to spare before I had to be at the plant gate, where Colie would receive a hasty introduction to the local.

The scheduled activity couldn't have been more perfectly suited for a child's participation, while at the same time it involved the number one union activity most despised by management—stickers.

The National Labor Relations Act guarantees workers the right to demonstrate union support at their facility without reprisals, so long as production isn't compromised. This is deemed "protected activity." One of the ways unions apply this during periods of dispute is to distribute stickers for employees to wear at work, brandishing a brief, cut-to-the-chase slogan.

It is a logical next step up the ladder of escalation. Having survived the petition process unscathed, most workers feel comfortable wearing a sticker if surrounded by coworkers who are doing the same. For forty-eight hours, brightly colored stickers dominate the shop floor. Management cannot look at a group of employees without their eyes being assaulted. For the workers, it's fun. Everyone has an inner child susceptible to being tickled. The discomfort and frustration on management faces makes it even more amusing. The inner child within members of management is engaged in a different way.

The message on this sticker simply read, "NO MORE CONCESSIONS!!" It was sufficiently universal to appeal to nonmembers and even those who were antiunion. What industrial worker secretly aspires to lower wages and reduced benefits?

Colie arrived at the main gate of American Mills, laughing and excited, having plastered six stickers across her clothing. What child would not relish a sticker party aimed at upsetting those in authority?

We had a few minutes before the arrival of D shift, and I enjoyed introducing my daughter to Percy and the other stewards. I was already viewed as being full of surprises, but no one could have expected this. Colie was an instant sensation as people competed to fawn over her.

Stewards fanned out to cover the entrances as workers began to straggle in. Colie wasn't at all shy about approaching people and reaching up with a sticker in hand. Even the most strident nonmembers smiled back at her and took one.

The truth is that Colie was politically worth her weight in gold wherever we traveled. Her presence communicated my humanity and values more eloquently than anything else I could have said or done. Poor working women appreciate a man who is devoted to his children. This wasn't the reason I took Colie with me. It was simply a collateral benefit.

Following shift change, I drove Percy home, where he invited Colie and me to stay for dinner. His wife offered to babysit whenever necessary.

The next afternoon, I had a second step grievance meeting. A union representative doesn't normally make an appearance until the third step, but I was looking to accelerate results. Byrnice informed me she would be joining department managers arguing the company's side. She had no objection to Colie's a presence "so long as she won't be a distraction."

Colie had been attending meetings since she was eight months old and knew how to conduct herself. I explained the three cases to her in simplified terms as we drove to the plant. "The people who run the mill have done some things to make the workers unhappy and I'm going to meet with them to try and make things better."

"Is Percy unhappy?" she asked.

"He's unhappy because some of the things that got done hurt his friends."

The most significant grievance involved a Yarn Prep employee named Deirdre White, who was terminated for allegedly directing profane remarks at management. On a night when operating conditions were poor and tensions high, a frustrated Deirdre exclaimed, "Damn it!" during a stressful encounter with her supervisor. She was ordered to immediately punch her time card.

The Yarn Prep manager didn't contest this account. I thus elaborated on the obvious distinction between directing profanity at another person and simply cussing out loud. I referred to the record and noted, "The grievant did not say 'damn you.' She said 'damn it.'"

It's difficult for many educated, middle-class Americans to comprehend the calloused indifference with which the livelihoods of industrial workers are routinely treated by management. Within a union facility, there's at least the benefit of contractual due process and representation. Deirdre's discharge was a blatant violation of the Just Cause Doctrine in that the punishment did not fit the crime.

As we drove back home, Colie asked, "Is that lady going to get her job back, Daddy?"

"I don't know," I said. "I have to wait a few days for the company to give me its answer. If they say no, I'll have another meeting. If they still say no, I'll bring them before a judge. It's very sad that she has to wait and be afraid while all this is happening. I hope she and her children have enough to eat."

By the time we returned to our house, it was nearly six, so I put some chicken in the oven for dinner. Before my evening meal I always worked out. I'd practiced karate since my early twenties. I wasn't an expert, but it had been a foundational discipline in my life. Martial arts clear the mind and strengthen the body like nothing else.

I began teaching Colie when she was two, on the premise that since my routine wasn't going to be suspended on nights we were together, she might as well be included. We made a game of it. She followed me through the warm-up stretches and into the exercises until she became bored or tired, at which point she'd sit and watch.

Sometimes I would get down on my knees, so that our shoulders were level and say, "It's time for kumarti" (ritual sparring). I would block, and Colie would try as hard as she could to hit me. When her guard became sloppy, I would pull her ear or tweak her nose as she squealed with laughter.

After our workout, we both showered, and I prepared a salad to go with the chicken. We watched TV for a couple of hours; then it was time to put my yawning little girl to bed.

"Will you read to me, dada?" she asked, looking up at me with huge blue eyes that I could never resist.

I got out Mother Goose and she recited along with me as I read. As I put aside the volume, Colie snuggled under the covers, clutching a stuffed animal we had won at "games" and asked me to sing her to sleep. I tuned my guitar, playing old country songs and lullabies I had written for her until she was breathing softly with eyes tightly shut.

The opening round of contract negotiations had been scheduled for 1:00 p.m., and my morning was tense and busy in preparation. I made eggs for breakfast and told Colie to brush her teeth and get dressed as I prepared my materials. I dropped her off with Percy's wife and headed to the union hall where Ernest was supposed to meet me at 11:30.

Ernest turned into the front yard of the hall right on schedule, making a larger-than-life entry as he emerged from a high-end rental vehicle, designed so the entire side of the car swung upward to allow exit.

We reviewed the documents I had brought and discussed our bargaining strategy as we awaited the committee's arrival at noon. Part of ACTWU's culture at the time was that everybody asked everyone else what they thought about various people in the organization.

"What do you think about Mark?" Ernest inserted into the discussion.

"He's smart and committed but his approach is kind of dry and without passion," I replied. "Where you and I are fire, he's ice."

"That's all true," said Ernest, "but you should know that he's probably the best joint board manager in the region. He has an enormous territory to cover, and he's stretched way too thin. Mark is an institutionalizer. He's about building and maintaining the organization. You're a campaigner."

We discussed our proposals with the committee once they arrived and agreed on the protocols of presentation. Percy rode the several blocks to the mill with me.

"How have things been going with AA?" I asked.

"Well you know, things have been so hectic and crazy lately, that I thought it maybe best to put if off until after these first negotiations. But I'm planning to attend me a meeting next week."

I inhaled the faint aroma of morning whiskey on his breath.

The parties assembled in the plant conference room. Ted Yeiser was impeccably dressed in a well-tailored pinstripe suit, sporting his signature gold tie clasp. Ernest and I wore sport jackets without ties. For all his fiery rhetoric and militant views, Ernest was calm and professional during a business encounter. He and Yeiser politely shook hands and exchanged business cards.

The first bargaining session is usually a short meeting during which opening proposals are reviewed but not contested. The true tone of the engagement generally doesn't reveal itself until the second meeting. An experienced union negotiator always sets the stage by requesting a detailed report of business conditions. It's important to understand a company's requirements and limitations in order to craft proposals that not only satisfy workers' needs but are economically feasible. Ernest asked about the new owners, and Ted Yeiser accepted the invitation.

Dominic Poon's father was the founder of a prominent textile corporation in China. The son had wanted to expand the family's interests by buying a plant in the United States, eventually deciding on Tennessee Textiles. He believed the business had potential for stabilization and growth if properly managed.

Loans amounting to $6.7 million were secured from three sources for the acquisition and initial operation of the mill. An additional promissory note of $2 million was signed with a liquidator named Gibbs Machinery for the purchase of fifty-four Sulzer looms, considered high-end weaving technology at the time and representing an opportunity to capture new markets. Substantial allocations were also made for structural repairs and rebuilding equipment throughout the plant.

Yeiser explained that Paul Poston wasn't at the table because he was in France inspecting the used looms and finalizing the sale. Gibbs Machinery was in the business of purchasing and reselling equipment from closed factories.

He informed us that American Mills would soon be adding 100 to 125 new jobs. I could envision the thought balloon over Ernest's head: *A bigger local with more members!* I was thinking, *That will take our percentage back down to where we started, and it'll be my job to sign everyone up.*

Ernest thanked him for the information and then asked me to address our list of preliminary concerns prior to the exchange of proposals. I reminded the company that more than ten days had passed since the closing, and 1988 vacation money had yet to be paid. We estimated that the total amount due was $322,000, not including vacation benefits accruing during the present year. I asked Yeiser if he wanted to set a date to select an arbitrator.

He held up his hand and said, "I don't think that will be necessary. I appreciate your patience, but if I can ask your indulgence for just a bit longer, I think we can straighten this out."

He made the commitment that 1989 vacation would be scheduled and paid according to the existing contract. While there had been numerous false hopes raised by management over the past six months, none of them had come from Yeiser. He would have one opportunity to make good on his word.

Yeiser handed me a manila envelope containing OSHA 200 logs and employee data as an initial response to the union's information request. I asked him to commit to a deadline regarding the remaining items, and he agreed, "No later than the end of the month."

The attorney then redistributed the outline presented at our introductory meeting and discussed the wage and benefit concessions. He characterized the existing pay system as "inefficient," proposing to eliminate incentive earnings in exchange for minimal increases to hourly rates, plus reducing the night-shift differential from twenty to five cents per hour.

The new employer also sought the right to subcontract janitorial positions as these could be filled less expensively through an outside agency.

The nine employees impacted would be able to exercise seniority and move into other jobs.

Ernest briefly addressed Yeiser and then suggested that I distribute our presentation. As the ranking union official, he was technically first chair, but Ernest didn't want to portray me as a subordinate, implying that he should be contacted whenever management disagreed with me.

The union's proposal called for a 4 percent wage increase, adding Martin Luther King Day to existing holiday and vacation benefits, scheduled breaks in Weaving, and procedural changes to expedite grievances involving discharge.

I began my remarks with a comparison of the wage proposals. "It's going to be obvious to your employees that you're spending millions of dollars on equipment, while at the same time you're taking money out of their pockets. We appreciate that Dominic Poon wants to invest in the plant and add jobs. But at the same time, he needs to invest in the employees who are going to run those jobs.

"The union already made concessions to Tennessee Textiles when it was operating at a loss, and we felt it necessary to protect jobs. Don't confuse this with a willingness to accept even deeper cuts from a new owner who has come to town with money to spend. I've got to assume that Dominic Poon is an experienced businessman and can't be so naïve as to think he can begin a new venture in the middle of a labor dispute."

Yeiser started to interject, but I raised my hand and spoke forcefully. "I haven't finished my presentation. I sat politely through your remarks without interruption and now I expect the same courtesy from you."

I reviewed our remaining proposals and concluded by stating that we were unwilling to agree with subcontracting janitorial jobs at this time but would be open to further discussion within the context of a global settlement.

Yeiser politely said he would take our position under advisement. We adjourned shortly thereafter and scheduled our next session on June 21. Ernest shook my hand, saying, "Stay in touch," and sped off to the Nashville airport to catch a late flight to some other location where crisis was brewing.

I drove Percy to his house, where he invited Colie and me to stay for dinner. Afterward, we stepped outside to take in the night air while our children played and his wife watched television.

He lit a cigarette and handed me the second-step response to the Weaving Department grievance, signed by Manager Derald Gilmer. (The committee had handled this in the traditional manner, as I wanted to reserve my presence for the meeting with Paul Poston.) It stated in part, that "we are addressing the question of lunch periods and breaks," adding that a "smash hand" would be hired on all shifts, which would allow those employed in one of the support positions "to have one 20 minute lunch break/shift."

The answer further noted, "Supervisors do not address employees in loud or abusive manners. The Supervisor works to lead the employee as all employees must strive for better and acceptable quality and efficiency."

I called Poston the next morning to arrange a third step meeting. I suggested that, for the sake of our mutual convenience and time management, we schedule one meeting to which all the grievants were invited.

Poston was aghast at this proposal. "How will we be able to have an orderly discussion, with everyone speaking at once?" he asked, requesting that I choose several representatives from the department to appear for the rest.

I informed him that a high level of professional decorum was maintained at all my meetings and that each person who signed the grievance had a contractual right to be present. I offered him a choice. We could have a hundred separate meetings, in which the same arguments were made by both parties for the benefit of the grievant in attendance, or we could consolidate into one efficient and well-run meeting. It was an offer he couldn't refuse and arrangements were made for Thursday afternoon of the following week.

I then told him we would need to schedule an inspection of the Weaving Department in preparation for the hearing. The contract permitted the union representative to visit a specific work area, accompanied by management, for the purpose of investigating grievances. Poston said he would be available for a tour on Monday.

I next called Byrnice to follow up on smaller issues and was surprised to hear a male voice answer, introducing himself as Bob Knuckles, the new personnel director. I asked under what circumstances Byrnice had departed and was told that he didn't know. We agreed to meet while I was at the facility for the inspection.

A prolific little artist, Colie lay on the floor drawing pictures with her crayons and pastels while I moved through my sequence of phone calls.

Sometimes she needed attention but always waited until I was between discussions. This wasn't the product of enforced behavior. She understood that what I was doing required focus but that she would never be ignored for long.

I prepared an announcement regarding the group grievance meeting for the Weaving Department. The intent was to promote awareness among the workers and generate participation, while simultaneously reinforcing the message to management that effective representation and good labor relations were not mutually exclusive. The drop leaflet portrayed the hearing from this perspective:

> After much discussion, the Company has agreed with the Union to sit down in good faith with Weaving Department employees to try and resolve long standing problems.

> If you feel strongly about any of the above issues:

> BE THERE

> A grievance is only a piece of paper unless it's backed up by people!

I typed another leaflet that contained as much information about our first bargaining session as could fit on an 8½ x 14 sheet of colored paper. Colie and I hopped in the car that evening and careened through the streets of Jackson so we could make it to the printer before closing. I then took her to the Ramada for dinner.

Saturday provided some leisure time until we had to pick up leaflets and return to the gate. An interesting benefit of being with a young child is that one can satisfy secret urges to engage in corny activities that would otherwise feel embarrassing if done alone or with another adult. I'd grabbed a couple of tourist brochures at the Ramada the previous evening and learned that one of the few attractions offered was the house of Casey Jones, the railroad engineer immortalized in song. Colie liked the idea, so off we went.

I was amazed by how small the house was. The several rooms could all easily fit within my bedroom. I browsed the literature. Casey Jones was actually scab labor who kept the railroad running during a nineteenth-century strike. The song commemorated the long hours he remained at the throttle without sleep in his dedication to management. The irony amused me. The domicile was sufficiently strange and antique for Colie to be entertained as well.

We ate fish sandwiches at McDonald's and headed across town to the printer. I would be bringing the first of many contract updates to the mill that evening; having done my best to provide an accurate summary that both reflected the sentiments of workers and acknowledged any positive responses from management. It was a stick-and-carrot approach. A negotiator who shows up at the table with a stick in both hands is destined to fail. The astute player possesses an instinct to maneuver his opponent toward a tipping point in his risk/benefit assessment. To achieve this, the other party must come to understand not only the consequences of opposition, but also the rewards of cooperation (Fig. 2).

We swung by Percy's house and headed to the plant. I was disappointed on arrival by the lack of participation from other officers and stewards who were off-shift. Perhaps they didn't want to interrupt their weekend of family or partying. In any event, we were on our own. I remained with Colie at the primary gate while Percy walked down the street to cover another entrance as the first D shift employees made their appearance.

At around 5:30 I spotted a worker who had been to one of the meetings and to whom I had previously handed a union card at the gate. His response at the time had been, "I'll think about it." This is the most annoying phrase that a union organizer in the South repeatedly hears during the course of his career. The epitaph for most nonmembers who worked in a union shop should read, "I was thinking about it."

I asked Colie to take charge of the leaflets for a few minutes and approached the young gentleman, who had worked in the card room for the past three years. "What's going on man? Have you signed that union card yet?"

"Not yet," he said. "I'm still thinking about it."

I wasn't prepared to let him off that easy. "Hey bro, you've got a few minutes before you have to punch in. Check out the difference between the union's proposals and the company's. Tell me which one you prefer. As you're reading them, understand that if it wasn't for the union, you would already be living under what the company wants."

He wasn't hostile and seemed genuinely curious about the leaflet.

"If you can honestly tell me that you prefer the company's proposals, then I'll respect your point of view and I'll never ask you about the union again," I told him.

"It's not that," he replied. "But aren't I going to end up getting the same thing as everyone else whether or not I'm in the union and paying dues?"

"That's exactly the way the company wants you to think. It's true. You'll get the same as everyone else. But everyone, including you, will be getting less if you and others don't stand together now and join the union.

"Tell me something. Do you like the fact that the new owners can't just come in and slash your wages and benefits? Do you like that there are people trying to get you more instead of less?"

"Well yeah, I do guess I think that's a good thing," he admitted.

"Look," I concluded, "this whole society is out to screw the working guy. Politicians, big business, the cops—who the hell gives a damn about us? I'm going to give you the number one reason to join the union . . . something even more important than money in your pocket . . . and that is because it's the right thing to do. You're fortunate enough to work at a place where there are people, a movement, that's standing up for your rights. You've told me that you're glad it's there. If you agree with something, the right thing to do is join it and make it stronger, not hang back and make it weaker."

I handed him a fresh card.

"Can I take this in the plant with me and think about it a little bit longer?" he asked.

"No," I said, looking him in the eye. "I need you to sign it now. It'll just take a second."

He borrowed a stack of leaflets to use as backing and filled out the card. I shook his hand. "Welcome to Local 281. If you ever get jammed up with the company, I want you to let me know immediately."

"Maybe I'll see you at the next meeting," he said, then turned and walked through the gate.

At five minutes before six, Percy returned to our station. I told him that as the plant would be standing on Sunday, we should do our best to catch the flood of B shift employees who would be pouring out of the mill within a few minutes. We agreed to remain together and cover the most heavily trafficked area.

The street emptied by 6:10. I was staring off across the road at the employee parking lot when the ground shook with a loud thud, as if someone had thrown a sack of potatoes off the mill roof. I spun around; with one eye saw Colie standing safely and with the other a lack of noticeable debris. I did not see Percy, however.

"Colie, did you see where Percy went?"

"No, dada, I didn't. Where is he?"

I spent five minutes looking about. There was no reason for him to have gone into the plant, and he didn't have a vehicle.

I suddenly came upon him, lying in the gutter between a parked car and the curb. He had collapsed and was out cold. I was able to rouse him and, with Colie's help, got him into the backseat of my car. Percy was dazed but conscious. I told him we should drive to the emergency room. He protested that he just wanted to go home, but I insisted.

Once Percy was admitted, Colie and I remained to see if he was going to spend the night or need a ride. An entire evening at the emergency room in Jackson thus unfolded. I wasn't a stranger to this setting. I had often accompanied residents of the cheap hotel I managed to the hospital and assisted the infirm while driving gypsy cabs.

The waiting area was crowded and noisy, and it was difficult to find two chairs together. We were the only white people present. Colie quickly found a boy her age, and they began playing in the middle of the floor. After about half an hour, Colie returned to touch base with me and then looked back at her new playmate.

"Hey Blackie," she called. "Hey Blackie, do you still want to play?"

It was one of those moments when you visualize yourself just sinking through the floor and dematerializing. I said to Colie, "Let's go down to the cafeteria and get some ice cream."

Once we were seated with our bowls in front of us, I said, "I know you didn't mean anything wrong, but there are some people in the waiting room who were probably upset that you called your friend Blackie."

"Why?" she asked, looking up at me with huge, serious eyes. "I didn't know his name, and he's black, so I called him Blackie."

This was to be the unexpected discussion with my daughter about racism in America. I had made an early decision that this was one slice of reality I would allow her to remain innocent about for as long as possible. When distinguishing among or identifying individuals, I had never used race as part of the description.

If Colie were to ask, "I forgot who Mary is," I might respond, "She's the tall skinny woman with wavy dark hair and two small boys." I would refrain from indicating her race. I'd discussed this with Hollie, and she had agreed to support me. In regard to this facet of existence, Colie had remained blissfully unaware until June 10, 1989, in Jackson, Tennessee. It was time for her to emerge.

"There's a very sad thing about the country we live in that I have to share with you," I said. "We both know that people come in different colors, just like dogs or kittens, but underneath they're all the same and deserve to be treated nice. But not everyone understands this.

"There are some groups of white people that hate all black people and want to hurt them. And because they've been hurt, there are some black people that hate all white people. Most people aren't like this and we're not like this. But we have to understand that this is part of the world we live in and try to be sensitive to people's feelings. There might have been people in the waiting room that weren't sure if you were trying to be friends with that boy or trying to tease him. It's not because you meant anything wrong. It's because of what other people have done. It's really sad that we live in a world where we have to worry about things like this."

Colie appeared stunned by this revelation but soaked it in as she did all new information. "Should we go back upstairs so I can say I'm sorry?"

"No," I said. "Let's just finish our ice cream and then go see how Percy's doing."

We walked back upstairs to the admissions desk but there was still no word, so we returned to the waiting room. I was relieved to find that the mother and child, along with some of the witnesses to the innocent indiscretion, had left. Colie drew pictures while I sat in utter boredom for another two hours. An attendant finally entered the room and called my name.

We were led through the treatment area to a room where Percy was lying on a gurney and told he would be spending the night for further observation. Percy warmly grabbed my arm and shook my hand, thanking me for bringing him to the hospital.

It was 10:00 p.m. by the time Colie and I got home. I carried her from the car as she slept and put her to bed. She'd certainly had an interesting first week in Jackson.

On Monday afternoon, I had my first meeting with the new personnel director. Bob Knuckles was a fairly tall man, portly to the point of obesity, with a graying blond beard and mustache. He held out a thick strong hand to shake mine. A casting director looking to portray a small-town southern sheriff could not have done better than him.

We sat and spoke for an hour. Within fifteen minutes, I liked him. He was a man who had needed a job and found one. He was tough but didn't appear to have any axes to grind and had previous experience working with unions. It was obviously his job to be the company's man, but at least we could understand each other.

My inspection of the Weaving Department was scheduled between 5:00 and 7:00 p.m. so that it would run through shift change. Poston hadn't cared for this arrangement, but I told him it was essential to my investigation that I receive input and observe operating conditions on both crews. In truth, I was unlikely to learn anything beyond what had already been explained at the union hall. This was an opportunity to demonstrate union presence within the plant and organize turnout for the group grievance.

I met Poston in the reception area. He handed me a set of industrial ear plugs and we walked through the maze of heavy metal doors and corridors into the weave room. The assault on one's senses, walking through the final set of doors, was instantaneous and overwhelming. The existing looms were old to the point of being antiques, with intensified levels of noise and dust.

I took control of the visit by stepping out in front of Poston and leading the way, approaching weavers and support personnel as I encountered them. I often had to bend and speak directly into someone's ear to be heard, and in turn offer my own to listen. During one of my initial discussions, I found Poston standing directly behind me. I motioned for us to step away from the machinery.

"You have the right to observe," I told him, "but I have the right to talk to my members in privacy. I'm hoping that the new company will be sincere in its efforts to work with me in resolving longstanding problems. I can't offer meaningful input and separate the wheat from the chaff without conducting a thorough investigation. Don't take this personally, but we both know that workers aren't likely to open up and speak their mind when management is listening."

We returned to the work area with Poston maintaining a respectful distance.

A few minutes before six, I migrated to the time clock where I could briefly speak with clusters of employees on their way in or out. It was like holding mini–union meetings on the shop floor. For the moment, Poston had grown weary of challenging me.

As I made my rounds through C shift, I came upon a young weaver operating a loom set. She glanced over her shoulder as I approached and flashed a smile, her teeth shining pearly white through milk-chocolate complexion. Her dirty work apron and hair bandana couldn't disguise that underneath stood a beautiful woman. I recognized her instantly— a wild child after my own heart, sweetness and trouble, damaged and defiant, hiding behind instinctive charm and deep, sexy eyes.

"I'm Phil Cohen, your new union rep," I said in the same professional tone with which I addressed everyone, but making slightly more eye contact.

I stretched out my hand, which she grasped softly and said, "I know who you is. Hollis Wade, on the committee . . . I'm his daughter."

I spoke with her about the grievance and moved on.

Several stewards joined me at the gate the next day as we distributed the bargaining update to the remaining shifts, capitalizing on increased interest by continuing to sign new members. That evening, Reverend Vandiver sauntered up to me. He was a tall, broad-shouldered man with an agreeable face that readily broke into a wide smile but could just as easily register intensity. The Rev handed me four union cards.

"I'm doing my best to get the word out in the card room," he said. "The people like the changes they've been seeing, but some are still skeptical that it's going to last. They've all seen organizers come and stir things up for a few months, then leave and things go back to how they were."

"That's not what's going to happen this time," I assured him. "I've been sent here by the highest levels of the union with instructions to stay until the job is finished."

"Well, I'm glad to hear that. Look, how about we get together sometime, just you and me, so we can talk man to man? Is it OK if I call you at that phone number you gave us?"

"Please do," I told him as we shook hands. His initiative and forth-rightness hadn't escaped my attention. I asked him to pass the word that I was in the process of scheduling meetings for the Carding Department.

Between shift changes, I joined the committee in presenting five grievances at the second step and was introduced to another new member of management, Plant Superintendent Bill Cooper, serving as the company's lead spokesman. He was of average height, slightly stocky in build, courteous in a somewhat haughty and self-congratulatory manner. I asked if he had any prior experience working with a union.

He took delight in informing me that not only had he worked at several union facilities, but the most recent had been an ACTWU mill in Roanoke Rapids, North Carolina. He smugly dropped the name of Joint Board Manager Kyle Barrow, as if to instill in me a sense that his connections at a higher level of the union could make me accountable.

Kyle was part of the old guard and held in low esteem by reformers within the Southern Region. He was already in Ernest's gun sights. I understood perfectly why management would have found him "reasonable" to work with.

Cooper seemed surprised and taken aback by my lack of response. "Kyle Barrow . . . ehhhhh . . . Kyle Barrow," he gurgled out the side of his mouth.

Bob Knuckles was seated to his right with pen and notepad at the ready. They were flanked by two supervisors and Weaving Manager Derald Gilmer, a gruff, heavyset man who had risen to his position through experience rather than formal education. The caseload involved pay discrepancies and matters of discipline.

I opened the hearing on behalf of a weaver named Arthur Fuller, who had received a two-day suspension. Management alleged that he had abandoned his job to take a lunch break in the canteen while his looms were low on supplies and in danger of cutting off. (When looms stop running, restart protocols are time consuming and result in production losses.) He had been located by his supervisor and ordered back to the department with a reminder about plant policy. Several hours later, Arthur was once again discovered away from his assignment.

I then presented Arthur's version. He claimed that his workload was caught up and the looms sufficiently supplied to tolerate a short break.

Having missed breakfast, he was feeling light headed and planned to take only five minutes to eat a sandwich. His supervisor stormed into the canteen, loudly ordering him to leave. On the second occasion, he had simply accessed a pressurized air hose to blow dust off his clothing because of allergies.

I asked Arthur when he had been informed of the disciplinary action. He responded that nothing more was said about the incidents for three weeks. One morning, he was summoned to the department manager's office, handed paperwork, and sent home on suspension for job abandonment and insubordination.

While Arthur's story appeared credible, I pointed out that debating events was unnecessary in this case. The Just Cause Doctrine implies that discipline must be administered in a timely manner. Management's failure to do so invalidates corrective action on its face, regardless of merit. While there is no explicit definition of "timely," three weeks is considered excessive by any criteria.

Cooper and Knuckles remained poker-faced but Derald Gilmer was livid at what he found to be the most absurd reasoning he had ever encountered. "My supervisors and I have a department to run!" he thundered. "Sometimes we get behind handling situations like this."

"Let's not waste time arguing," I said, turning to Knuckles. "You have a new lawyer. I suggest you consult with him before making a decision."

As the meeting ended, Bill Cooper shuffled his papers, thanked us for our input, and said, "We'll look into all of this."

"Bill, want to know what the union considers the most offensive words coming from the mouth of management?" I asked, and then paused momentarily. "'We'll look into it.' It's a gentleman's way of saying kiss my ass. It means give me a week, and I'll provide a polite explanation as to why we're denying your grievances."

Cooper blanched but remained silent, so I continued. "Having a good relationship is about more than amicable meetings and cordial correspondence. This is a business relationship and that means it's about results. I came to the table prepared and presented viable matters of contract. I don't know or care what you're accustomed to from Roanoke Rapids. The only thing that interests me is results."

As I walked down the corridor from the conference room to the lobby entrance, I encountered Paul Poston and a young Asian man moving toward me. I greeted Poston and shook his hand.

"Let me take this opportunity to introduce you to Dominic Poon, the mill's new owner," he said.

Poon was of slender build and less than average height with an unassuming demeanor, dressed in a long-sleeved business shirt and khakis. Our brief interaction was pleasant but unsubstantial, punctuated by mutual assurances that we looked forward to working together.

I left the facility with sufficient time to visit Percy in the hospital before returning to the gate. He told me that he was being kept for observation but expected to be released shortly.

The Weaving Department grievance hearing convened in the plant conference room at 2:00 p.m. on June 15. Participation was less dramatic than I had hoped, though it probably exceeded Paul Poston's worst nightmare. Every seat around the long table was filled, and we were surrounded by an equal number of workers who remained standing.

Poston began the meeting by asking if I'd received a copy of Derald Gilmer's answer. When I said yes, he responded, "Then I don't see why this meeting is really necessary. We have given you our commitment that we are evaluating this situation and plan to make the necessary adjustments when feasible. Derald has conducted his investigation regarding supervisor misconduct and found that here hasn't been any."

"The current level of response is insufficient," I replied. "The union requires a remedy with specific details and timeframes for implementation. There is also testimony from some of your employees which I believe you need to hear in person and will find compelling."

I began my presentation with the issue of break schedules. It's a total waste of time to chastise an employer on humanitarian grounds; an approach guaranteed to alienate management and portray the advocate as a bleeding heart with no business sense. It's preferable to engage company representatives within the arena of their self-interest.

In his first employee memorandums on behalf of American Mills, Poston had stressed health and safety. His June 2 notice listed "things you will see happening," which included:

> Reinforce safety programs and hopefully have one of
> the safest plants around. This can save the company
> money and reduce the hurt to the employees. The past
> record at TenTex was so bad that they were put in

> assigned risk for insurance and had to pay exorbitant
> insurance rates. Let's not let that happen to us.

I decided to base our arguments on his own pronouncements. The company's OSHA 200 logs indicated an alarming injury rate within the Weaving Department. Some had involved horrific encounters between flesh, bone, and moving machine parts, while others were ergonomic in nature.

I pointed out the correlation between exhaustion and these types of injuries. "Working on one's feet for twelve hours straight without eating is bound to reduce alertness and reaction time. It's hard to imagine that whatever payroll savings and production gains you've realized from these policies have justified the increased cost in workers' comp premiums."

I also noted that long-term exposure to these working conditions would inevitably reduce the overall health of the workforce, resulting in an increased rate of absence and need to fill jobs with off-shift employees being paid overtime.

The floor was then opened for union members to recount how they had been personally affected. The process remained orderly and systematic, offering no fodder for Poston's stereotype of an unruly mob. He looked at each employee as their turn arrived and remained expressionless.

When it was time for me to resume, I turned to Derald Gilmer. "Your investigation into supervisor misconduct was superficial and self-serving. I haven't heard any complaints about you acting disrespectfully to employees. But let's use a bit of common sense. Your supervisors aren't going to act unprofessionally in your presence, and they're certainly not going to confess when you ask them about it.

"I'm a firm believer in the principle 'where there's smoke, there's fire.' Reports of this nature have been ongoing and widespread, some of them coming from your best employees and people who haven't filed a grievance in years. Let me offer some examples."

Once again, the workers shared in turn what they had personally endured or witnessed. While use of profanity was grounds for employee discharge, it was commonplace among supervisors, especially on the night crews.

I fixed my gaze on Poston. "Your message over the last few weeks has been that American Mills represents the dawning of a new day for both the company and employees. The union joins you in that sentiment and is open to working with you to make it a reality. But you can't bring about meaningful changes by ignoring the input of 90 percent of the people who work in this building.

"We're not on a witch hunt and don't need to document who said what, or the rights and wrongs of each incident. I'm not requesting that you take action against any of your supervisors or share with me what gets said to them. All I care about is that going forward, people are treated with respect."

We addressed the remaining issues, including management accountability for poor operating conditions and violations of job-posting procedure.

Paul Poston was walking a tight rope. On one hand, it was his agenda to tough-bargain with the union and limit its influence. On the other, he could ill-afford to initiate a new business venture during an escalating labor crisis. Demands of paramount importance to the workers had been put on the table that represented little expense (and perhaps cost savings) to the company.

I let go of the reins and allowed some spontaneous dialogue between management and employees. When this ebbed, Poston was ready to call it a day, but I pressed him for closure. We remained for another hour and a half until arriving at a settlement.

All Weaving Department employees would be provided with a twenty-minute paid lunch period and two ten-minute breaks. Supervisors would be retrained in employee relations and a joint study conducted to identify nonstandard working conditions not factored into piece rates.

I expressed my appreciation to the workers for remaining throughout the long meeting (especially those on their feet) and to Poston and his staff for participating in a productive process that would benefit all concerned.

"I think the only reason you come to these meetings, Phil, is to show off to everyone how smart you are," Poston responded.

He got up and left the room without shaking my hand. The Weaving employees lingered about, waiting to embrace me before departing. It made me feel a bit shy and awkward, as if this reception of gratitude was better deserved by something greater, for which I had only been the vehicle.

I exited the plant and drove toward the hospital to pick up Percy. He was rolled out in a wheelchair but walked to the car. There was no doubt in my mind that excessive drinking was taking a toll on his body. His lawyer had called with the court's final disposition. Percy would spend the next several weekends in jail with furloughs to work scheduled shifts.

We arrived at his house, where Colie and fried chicken were waiting. After dinner, my daughter and I returned home to retrieve our luggage, which was already packed. We headed toward Nashville, and as was usual on night drives, Colie fell asleep when it became too dark to see out the window.

We arrived at a Holiday Inn on the outskirts of town at 10:30. Colie perked up with a child's enthusiasm to check out the new environment. We entered the room, and she began jumping on her bed as I situated our belongings. I joined her and we jumped together for fifteen minutes and then had a pillow fight. I hoped the walls were thick enough to muffle our laughter.

We had breakfast in a nearby diner and headed off to the amusement park at Opryland. I enjoyed the old-timey atmosphere punctuated with country music, while Colie thrilled to the various rides. We spent an hour in the arcade and won a pink stuffed elephant.

Colie and I approached an attraction that had both fascinated and terrified her at other theme parks. It is essentially a long, vertical shaft with a compartment on each end. The device spins in a full circle at speeds that blur the bystander's vision, rendering the occupants upside down atop its circumference.

Colie held my hand and starred at the attraction, transfixed for fifteen minutes. "Let's do it!" she said.

We waited in line for forty-five minutes. As we were finally being strapped in, I couldn't resist making up a story about how we were being abducted by aliens who were going to experiment on us.

"Stop it, Daddy!" Colie said, slapping me on the thigh.

The machine began to spin, and for the next few minutes, all I could hear were shrieks of delight and laughter. As we were being unstrapped, Colie proclaimed the inevitable, "Let's dooit again!"

I was nauseous and my head was spinning. "Maybe later."

Our next destination was Knoxville, where I had to pick up records from prior contract negotiations to serve as context for the present round.

We arrived at dusk and found a room. In the morning, we made a brief appearance at the Joint Board office and continued driving.

"Do you want to take the fastest way home, or do you want to drive through the mountains and stop at other fun places?" I asked.

Colie thought for a few minutes and chose the latter. We turned south onto the winding two-lane roads through the Smoky Mountains, one of the most scenic routes I've ever taken. No stretch is longer than twenty yards where the road remains straight, and there are numerous viewing areas to gaze out across the mountain range.

We stopped for lunch in Gatlinburg. This is the sort of tacky tourist destination I would normally consider a blight on the natural landscape and avoid at all costs, but with a child it's a vision of utopia.

We went on a helicopter ride and drove a wooden stock car around a twisting track. My most vivid memories of being with Colie in amusement areas always involve being inundated by peals of never ending laughter. She enjoyed the rush that comes from feeling scared but in control. She was her daddy's girl.

CHAPTER 6

I began my return trip on Monday after thirty-six hours at home. Colie was making up for lost time with her mom, and events were unfolding quickly in Jackson. I arrived the next day in time for meetings with A and C shifts of the Carding Department. A drop leaflet had been distributed in my absence:

> American Mills may be a new company, but Carding Department employees still put up with the same old working conditions and problems. If you're tired of just sitting around and waiting for things to get better
>
> BE THERE!!
> THE TIME FOR CHANGE IS NOW!!

The issues within Carding didn't appear to be as serious as some of the other areas, but I wanted to get up close and personal with every department. There were concerns over production rates, job transfers, and safety that warranted investigation. I had arranged for Donald Vandiver to be off work for all the meetings and encouraged him to co-facilitate. He had the natural ability to lead in an easygoing way, and his years on the pulpit made him comfortable with public speaking. I sensed that he belonged in the foreground and followed my instincts.

The next morning, we were back in contract negotiations. I greeted members of management in the conference room and we all took our seats.

"We recently had a productive meeting with Weaving Department employees which resulted in mutually beneficial solutions," I began.

"This is the sort of win-win bargaining that I hope can characterize our relationship going forward. It sets the stage for improved employee morale and lends credibility to promises of change more effectively than anything either of us can put in our handouts."

Yeiser nodded his head politely while Poston continued to stare straight ahead. Bob Knuckles scribbled furiously on his notepad, trying to take down every word in preparation for the company minutes, which his secretary would later type for lengthy analysis at strategy meetings.

I further noted that the Spinning Department grievance had been presented at the first step and rejected on all shifts, suggesting that for the sake of efficiency, Poston and I both appear at the second-step hearing.

"Are you wanting to stampede a whole department into my conference room again?" Poston asked with obvious irritation.

Following the anticipated banter with Yeiser, we scheduled a meeting for the following Wednesday.

It was the employer's turn to make and respond to proposals so I relinquished the floor. Yeiser rejected all the union's proposals while holding fast to his own—with one notable exception. He withdrew the demand to eliminate the third and fourth weeks of vacation.

I expressed appreciation for his "flexibility" as protocol required and said, "That takes care of things going forward. What about 1988?"

"I'm glad you brought that up," he replied. "Mr. Poston has prepared a bulletin board notice which will go up this evening, announcing that all vacation monies in arrears will be paid to employees via separate check."

I restrained from any show of enthusiasm and without turning my head, glanced out the corners of my eyes to make sure the committee was doing the same.

"That is a positive development," I said.

I knew that I would have to prepare a hasty leaflet and be at the gates the next day, to steal the company's thunder and have the union credited for its intervention. I found a pretext to end the meeting in time to accomplish this.

We were at the gate in force by 2:00 p.m. on Thursday to cover the eight-hour shifts.

The short 8½ x 5 leaflet was printed on green paper, speckled with dollar signs and an image of folded bills. Many of the workers had yet to see the company's notice, and they were in a state of elation and disbelief. Restoring faith to the disheartened is perhaps an organizer's most profound calling (Fig. 3).

Paul Poston walked up behind me and took a leaflet. "I feel like I've just been kicked in the nuts," he proclaimed, shaking his head and looking me in the eye. My admonitions to not take things so personally fell on the usual deaf ears. Poston retreated back into the mill.

Between shifts, I pulled together a hasty gathering of Spinning Department stewards to prepare for next week's grievance meeting. My ongoing investigation had broadened the list of hazardous and unpleasant working conditions. The prevailing complaint remained the daily need to push and pull on heavily laden carts with damaged wheels, and the resulting injuries. Anticipating the inevitable denial at the first step, I had ordered some materials.

I've mentioned that above all things in creation, plant managers despise union stickers. I had prepared what was to become the most despised sticker of my career. Against a bright orange rectangular background was a black line drawing of a buggy with an obviously broken wheel and the caption, "BACK BREAKER!"

I told stewards to pass them out within the department for everyone to wear and for trusted union members to plaster covertly all over the offending transports. This technically crossed the line of our legal right to engage in union activity as it involved the "defacement of company property," but I really didn't care. The dilapidated condition of the carts represented a far greater defacement, not only to equipment but to the bodies of employees. I just wanted to ensure that nobody got caught and I emphasized discretion.

This tactic would provide an ongoing source of humiliation for the company (which was periodically inspected by customers, loan officers, etc.) and amusement for the frustrated workers.

There is a stereotype of contract negotiations being held behind closed doors by the representatives of both parties, with workers only being informed of the final outcome during ratification. This is in fact standard procedure for some unions. Workers hate being kept in the dark as much as management hates stickers. I scheduled union meetings for Tuesday and Thursday of the following week and provided a detailed update within the announcement.

I endured another isolated weekend on "Jupiter's Moon," punctuated by leaflet distribution on the various shifts. I was seeing new faces on every visit to the gate, and it was obvious that American Mills had begun its hiring process.

The only means to maintain and build membership under these circumstances involved a relentless regimen of individual house calls to supplement activity within the plant. I spent much of the weekend engrossed in what I considered the most monotonous task of a union representative. In this pre-computer age, one had to periodically merge the company-provided list of bargaining-unit employees (organized by department and shift) with the list of dues-paying members (arranged alphabetically). This was accomplished by manually highlighting the names of union members on the master printout. Stewards then received a breakdown for their departments and shifts, and house-calling itineraries were prepared.

Even when in the field, I looked forward to the reduced workload of weekends and the opportunity to renew my energy levels in preparation for what was to follow. My efforts in this regard were undone by restless sleep on Sunday night.

Ever since leaving New York, I had been plagued with recurring nightmares of driving taxis. The dreams always began with a logical and well-constructed pretext for why I found myself once again behind the wheel of a taxi, driving through the streets of New York. In this instance, there had been an unexpected layoff of union staff and because of my relatively low seniority, I'd been affected. Driving downtown on Lexington Avenue, I was suddenly overwhelmed with the sensation, *Oh God, I can't believe I've ended up back here!*

I bolted off the pillow in a cold sweat with my heart racing and lay awake for hours.

I spent Monday in transit between the union hall and the gate. It rained that afternoon but the leaflets went out on schedule. When workers see that extremes of weather cannot deter an organizer, it strikes a chord deeper than the written word.

As I sat at my desk drying off, Sergeant at Arms Rick Hardin sauntered into the hall. While he didn't contribute much to the campaign, I enjoyed his company. He was someone I could talk with unabashedly about the sordid details of real life.

"Who's that really pretty weaver on C shift?" I asked.

He thought for a moment and then broke into a grin. "Are you talking about Hollis Wade's daughter?"

I nodded my head.

"Oh, that's Tina. She and I go way back. Listen, if you're looking for a ho in Jackson, I can hook you up."

"I'd be down for that," I said.

"OK," Rick offered. "I'll give her your phone number and tell her you want to talk to her. She'll call you."

I let it go at that. I tended to be very cautious about initiating romantic involvements within my locals. I didn't believe in becoming intimate with a leader and always waited for an overture from anyone else. An ill-perceived advance or liaison gone bad can compromise one's standing within a community. I never lost sight of the fact that I was in town to do a job.

That evening, I conducted my inspection of the Spinning Department accompanied by Bob Knuckles. Workers were spread thin as they patrolled the long frames, and we sometimes walked for five minutes before encountering anyone to speak with. The sound of whirling bobbins made communication difficult, but did not compare to the thundering assault of a weave room. Spinners pointed out holes in the floor, puddles of grease, and places where the roof leaked, pushing me into the aisle on several occasions as the large vacuum hoses orbiting the frame crossed our path. Some of these mechanisms did little more than rearrange the clumps of cotton fiber littering the work station. I zigzagged through the department at random, like a cat running about the house, making it difficult for the personnel director to shadow me.

At the end of the tour, Knuckles invited me back to his office, where he presented two documents. The first was his response to the grievance concerning the untimely suspension of Arthur Fuller. He was awarded full back pay. I also received earnings information about job classifications for which pay reductions had been proposed.

Paul Poston requested a private meeting the next day so I could give him a list of specific issues to be raised during the Spinning Department grievance. I had no problem with this. If he arrived at the meeting prepared, he would be in a better position to discuss resolution. I explained that the majority of complaints involved dilapidated mill conditions and the impact on health and safety.

"Some of these repairs are going to be costly," said Poston. "Mr. Poon is already investing millions of dollars to revitalize this business, and I'm not certain how much is going to remain in our budget. I'm not saying that some repairs aren't needed or that we plan to overlook our responsibilities, but I'm not sure this is the best time to push some of these issues."

"That's exactly my point." I replied. "If Poon is investing millions of dollars on new equipment he can afford another hundred thousand to make the mill a safe place to work. Besides, it will pay for itself over time in reduced workers' comp premiums.

"Paul, I hope we get to the point where you and I can do business as gentlemen without the need for coercion by either party. But with tomorrow's meeting, there are two options. We can develop an action plan and timeframe for implementing the necessary repairs. I'll be responsive in regard to cost options and scheduling concerns. I know you have a lot on your plate right now.

"The alternative is that I file a complaint with OSHA and hold a press conference. I don't think that's the kind of exposure Dominic Poon or American Mills is looking for at this time. That's not what I want to do. If it was, we wouldn't be discussing it privately. You'd have found out about it on the six o'clock news. I know you have phone calls to make regarding budget allocation. I appreciate that we've had this opportunity to talk and set things in motion."

The union meetings for A and C shifts began that evening. Three months earlier a handful of bored and skeptical individuals had been scattered among rows of empty chairs, but now most of the seats were filled.

I began with a review of recent accomplishments, raising my voice and speaking slowly. "The company has made a commitment that everyone will receive a separate check for their full 1988 vacation money this week, along with their regular paycheck!"

"That's what I'm talking about!" exclaimed Reverend Vandiver, rising to his feet and applauding on the stage behind me. The membership took his cue and joined him.

A woman near the rear of the assembly remained standing after the others were seated. "What I want to know," she said, "is if we're going to have to pay taxes on this money?"

"Look, I don't negotiate with the IRS," I replied. "People would go to jail if the money was paid and the government didn't get its cut. But the reason you'll be receiving separate checks is so the tax bracket will be lower and the deductions less for each check."

"I think we waited long enough we shouldn't have to pay no taxes," she grumbled while taking her seat.

I ran through the group grievance settlement in Weaving and the initial progress made in contract negotiations. "How many weeks of vacation do you think you'd be getting this year if it wasn't for the union?" I asked.

It was Percy's turn to leap to his feet behind me. "We'd be getting only two and nothing more!"

"What would your paychecks look like right now? How many holidays would you be getting this year?" I continued.

"Whatever the company has in those proposals, that's what we'd be getting right now. I know 'cause I done been sat across the table with them," Percy slurred with passion.

"Do you know why the company's backed down so quickly on so many important issues?" I asked. "Do you think it's because I'm the God-father and left a horse's head on Paul Poston's bed post?

"The reason is because all of you have had the guts to step up and stand together! It doesn't matter how good a job the committee and I do at the bar-gaining table if the company knows that we're standing alone. For years you've all been scared of management. Now, they're scared of you!"

I asked for impressions of the new hires filtering into various departments.

"Most of them are white," said Georgia. "The talk is that there was a textile mill that shut down, nonunion, in Huntsville Alabama, and that the company put out a job offer to all its employees. I can tell you this. They ain't got no love for the union . . . least not the ones I've spoken to."

I solicited feedback from those who had already been to introductory meetings with Dominic Poon.

"He seemed like a pretty nice guy," a gentleman responded. "He was polite, soft spoken, and said he wants to make the mill a better place for all of us."

"He ain't nothing but a snake in the grass, waiting to strike," exclaimed Georgia.

When the exchange of commentary had run its course, I said, "The union stands willing and open to take Poon up on his word and work with him to make the mill a better place. But this little rich boy from China has got to understand that our definition of 'better' doesn't include having less money to feed our families.

"Action speaks louder than words. Poon hired Ted Yeiser, the union-busting attorney, to represent him. That's a decision, not an accident. He tells you that he considers you his new family, while his lawyer is telling me that he wants to cut your wages and benefits."

The next afternoon, Spinning Department employees began filing into the conference area. Within fifteen minutes, the room was completely packed, with far more people standing than sitting.

Poston glared at me solemnly and held up one of the "Back Breaker" stickers. "I would like you to tell me which employees are responsible for placing these on company property."

I met his gaze. "On what company property did you find them?"

"These are stuck all over half of the buggies in the Spinning Department. There are several inside the restroom stalls."

"My instructions were for people to wear them on their personal clothing, as is their right," I rejoined. "I never told anyone to place them on company property. I have no more way of knowing who is responsible than you do. That said, even if I did know, I couldn't tell you. It would be a conflict of interest. I legally represent all of your employees."

"Well, when this meeting is over, I expect you and your committee to go upstairs with cleaning materials and remove these union stickers from our buggies. This is a disgrace," exclaimed Poston.

"I'm not available to perform manual labor at the plant," I answered, "and you have no legal right to place this demand on the committee. The real disgrace is the condition of your buggies. I've studied the OSHA 200 logs and the number of back and shoulder injuries is shocking. Routine servicing of the cart wheels would have been a low-cost item that Tennessee Textiles could've easily afforded, even with its cash flow problems. It didn't happen because it wasn't a priority. You might want to reconsider your definition of disgrace.

"I suggest you refer this task to your janitors and that we define measures and a timeframe to correct the problem. It would be incomprehensible if by now, you weren't as eager as everyone else in the room to accomplish this."

There was a spontaneous round of applause from the workers and Poston's face turned crimson. Bob Knuckles maintained his composure, like a man who understands what's going on and isn't perturbed.

It was agreed that the repairs would begin immediately. I acknowledged Poston's point that requisitions would have to be filed for the purchase of new wheels, and this would delay work by several weeks on those carts which required them. The deadline for concluding the project was September 1.

Within the next hour numerous safety and sanitation matters were discussed, including missing guard rails and a broken air conditioner in the cafeteria. The repair deadlines ranged between two weeks and two months. Those impacted by off-standard working conditions would receive their average hourly wage.

The private meeting of the previous day had been to good effect. Aside from his initial burst of indignation, Poston had come to the table prepared to do business. He wanted to be in and out of the conference room as quickly as possible. He preferred running the mill to being on the wrong side of a theatrical performance.

I was glad to be done earlier than expected and returned home by 4:30. A few minutes later, the phone rang.

"Hello," I said. There was silence on the other end. "Who is it?"

"It's me," said a soft, somewhat throaty voice.

"Tina?" I asked.

"Yeah. Rick says you want to talk to me."

"I do. I'm glad you called."

"Well, here I am."

After a few minutes, I invited her to have dinner with me but told her the timing was a bit awkward. The plant was scheduled for vacation shutdown during the week of July 4, and I would therefore be headed back home. I said I didn't mean to rush things but if we wanted to get together beforehand, it would have to be the following evening.

"You going home to see your wife?" she asked.

I told her that I wasn't married.

"What about a girlfriend? You got a girlfriend waiting for you back home?"

"I don't have anybody, except for a daughter. She's only four and I make a point of being her daddy. I haven't seen her in two weeks."

We agreed that she would come to the union meeting and we would go out afterward.

On Thursday, I presented a third step grievance involving an employee named Johnnie McBride who was terminated for absence without notice. Bill Cooper appeared as Paul Poston's designee. Johnnie had been jailed the night before his shift for driving while intoxicated and was unable to contact the mill. In its earlier grievance response, the company cited "information received that Mr. McBride has had a history of Drug/Alcohol related problems."

I argued that a discharge based on one no-show was inconsistent with company policy and failed to meet the Just Cause standard of punishment fitting the crime. I pointed out that the company's "information" regarding a history of substance abuse was unsubstantiated hearsay and that an employee's recreational activities while off-shift were outside management's jurisdiction.

I later met with various shop stewards regarding issues in their department until it was time for the B and D shift union meetings. Despite the fact that B/D was overall a weaker crew than its counterpart, turnout was nearly as good, and the response remained positive.

There was a lull between when night shift departed for the mill and day shift arrived. A few off-shift workers stayed to discuss individual concerns. It was during this interlude that Tina made her way into the room, quietly taking a seat toward the rear. We caught each other's eye, and my heart skipped a beat, but the rhythm of my dialogue remained steady.

Once B shift was seated, I launched into my presentation for the fourth time that week. I sensed that Tina had far less interest in the message than in watching me perform and noting how people responded. As the crowd thinned, she remained behind until the hall was empty.

I sat down next to her. It was the first time I had seen her hair uncovered—raven curls that fell between her ears and shoulders. She was dressed simply in a short tank top which revealed her flat abdomen and tight fitting jeans.

"How you?" I asked.

"It all be good," she said, flashing a brief smile.

"Where do you like to have dinner?"

"If you want to eat, I can come with you, but I already had mine."

"That's OK. You don't have to sit around and watch while I eat," I replied. "Where would you like to go?"

"Wherever you want to take me."

I locked up the union hall; we got in my car and headed to my house.

"I like your ride," she said, patting the seat.

A few minutes later, we were standing in my kitchen, facing each other from two feet apart, both of us momentarily awkward and staring into each other's eyes.

"Why me?" she asked. "You could have any woman in the plant you wanted. Why you want to talk to me?"

"Because there's something special about you. You're not just beautiful outside. There's something beautiful inside. I look in your eyes and see someone who's sensitive and more alive than most people."

"You think? No one's ever said that kind of shit to me before."

I kissed her. Her lips yielded instantly, opening wide with a sweet, soft tongue, like a woman who has given herself freely to many men . . . the sort that drives me crazy.

I led Tina to the bedroom and watched as she stripped off her clothes and lay waiting on top of the covers. She was even more alluring than I'd envisioned. We kissed, and my lips wandered to explore her mysteries . . . Afterward, I cradled her head on my chest. Ever since my teens, I had always trembled like a leaf following my first sexual encounter with a girl I felt connected to.

"Is you cold?" Tina asked. "Should we get under the blankets?"

"No, it's OK. It just means that I like you."

"No one ever did that to me before," she murmured.

"Do you mean have sex with you?"

"No," she said, poking me in the ribs. "I mean what you did with your mouth . . . down there."

I expected her to stay the night but around ten she sat up and started getting dressed. When I asked why, she said, "You need to be getting ready for your trip home and besides, I didn't bring my toothbrush or nothing."

"Why? You weren't planning to come home with me?"

"Silly boy, I didn't know what I was planning," she said with her big grin, slapping me on the butt.

The next day, after a few phone calls, I was packed and driving to North Carolina. Those were the days when mainstream country music, at least some of it, was still written from the heart and contained a message. I always drove with the radio on or listening to a tape, preferring the likes of Tom T. Hall, Lacy J. Dalton, and Waylon Jennings.

I stopped for lunch at a restaurant near Nashville that had a gift shop. There was a large stuffed caricature of a tomato with dangling arms and legs, and a funny face. I bought it for Colie. Three hours later I found a room on the far side of Knoxville.

After having breakfast at a local diner the next morning, I continued toward home. The music soothed my nerves. My back was to Jackson as I prepared for a week in Chapel Hill, and my thoughts wandered back to my bus-driving days.

During the final years, I had used my seniority to become a relief driver, briefly assuming various routes while the regular drivers were on break. I traveled between pick-up locations in a Transportation Department vehicle. It was far less monotonous and allowed me to interact with members of the local union.

On nights when I had Colie, I was responsible for picking her up at daycare. The problem was that the center closed at 5:30, and my shift ended an hour later. Following my final relief assignment, I had to return to the garage and take out a bus for the "high school tripper." This involved driving to the parking lot of a nearby high school to be available for any students who had missed the school bus. On most occasions, it was an empty run.

I would retrieve Colie from daycare in a town car and return to the garage. I detoured into the employee parking lot, briefly placed Colie in my personal vehicle, and then reported to the dispatcher for bus assignment. Following a hasty inspection, I fired up the bus, pulled it off the line, stopped alongside the employee lot, and hustled Colie on board.

The reason for the subterfuge was that it violated regulations to bring a child onto the bus without another adult to supervise and I didn't have that luxury. Besides, it was a thrill for Colie to ride her daddy's bus.

One evening, we arrived at the school parking lot and as usual, found it deserted. I sat Colie on my lap, driving the big city bus in tight circles as she screamed with laughter. What better sport could there be for a working guy and his two-year-old daughter?

I returned to the garage, put Colie back in my car, parked the bus in its designated space, and signed out with the dispatcher. As I exited the front door, a supervisor named John Farrish motioned me over to a transit vehicle where he was sitting behind the wheel.

"I just want to give you a heads-up," he said. "The dispatcher called me to the window shortly after you pulled out and said that you had been spotted bringing a child onto the bus, and that Lois [the garage superintendent] wanted me to follow you and investigate. I told her to tell Lois that if she wanted you followed, she could take a car and do it herself. I just wanted you to know because you may be asked about this."

John had a reputation for being rigid and overzealous about enforcing the rules. He'd worked in a factory before being hired as a bus driver and eventually promoted to supervisor; and was eager to do whatever necessary to please senior management. His blatant insubordination in this instance was one of the most out-of-character gestures I'd ever witnessed.

The dispatcher who had relayed the message was a good friend of mine, so the next day I asked her what had happened.

Lois was openly having an affair with the assistant director of the Transportation Department. Her lover had taken a day's vacation and while out jogging, had detoured onto the premises to see if she was in her office. He'd passed by the employee lot just as I was slipping Colie on the bus and dutifully notified the superintendent.

If John had followed instructions and found me whirling around the high school parking lot in a city bus with my daughter on my lap, that would have been it. I'd have been called in for a termination meeting the next day. While the transit administration had a come to accept my role as local union leader, being provided with such ironclad grounds for my discharge would have been cause for celebration.

I would not now be driving toward home in a union staff car in the middle of an organizing assignment. Local union leaders sometimes get hired by an international union. Someone who held a position two years ago, but wasn't currently even a union member, does not. Like all things in life, the dots have to connect.

In retrospect, this had been one of the truly pivotal moments in my history. There was no telling how or where I might have ended up if events had unfolded normally. The entire trajectory of my existence would have been different.

CHAPTER 7

It felt unnatural to suddenly be back at my farm house, surrounded by the beauty and stillness of ancient trees, each day flowing into the next without an onslaught of meetings, phone calls, and multiple deadlines. Adrenalin is a rush but it comes with a heavy price on the back end. I drifted through the week feeling dazed and unfocused.

Colie was dropped at my front door on Sunday evening. Once she was situated and sitting on her bed, I presented the stuffed tomato being I'd purchased for her on the trip home. Her face immediately contorted in fright as she burst into tears.

"Make it go away!" she screamed.

This wasn't the reaction I anticipated, but I honored her feelings.

The next night as I was tucking her in, she asked to see her present again. She studied the gift for a few minutes and then fell asleep with it wrapped in her arms. She later named him "Mr. Tomato" and slept embracing him every night she was with me throughout her childhood.

It was difficult to stop thinking about Tina and our intense first night together, followed by the immediate need to leave town. Women who are fundamentally insecure do not like to be ignored but they are equally uncomfortable when bombarded with attention. I decided to pace myself.

Colie was with her mom on Wednesday night, and I called Tina around eleven. She was genuinely surprised to hear from me. "Is your girlfriend out by herself?" she asked in her soft voice. "What's she going to say if she walks in?"

"I told you. I don't have a girlfriend . . . except maybe you. The reason I'm calling tonight is because my daughter is back with her mom."

After that she relaxed. We talked and flirted until it was time to fall asleep.

With the campaign sufficiently underway, it was time to develop a distinctive newsletter for the local. It would serve as an overview of recent activity and acknowledge the efforts of committee members and stewards. I spent part of my vacation finishing articles and neatly typing them in the format of two-column pages. Having solicited contributions from the leadership, I tried to strike a balance between editing rough, handwritten submissions and preserving individual style. I left for Jackson on Monday, stopping at a printer to drop off the newsletter materials with layout and shipping instructions.

There was a committee meeting scheduled for the next afternoon. Shortly after it began, an irate Percy informed me that the company had "made fools of us all" by unilaterally implementing its proposal to subcontract janitorial jobs.

The National Labor Relations Board draws a distinct line between bargaining-unit positions represented by the union, and non-unit positions such as management and clerical staff. An employer is prohibited from filling bargaining-unit jobs from external sources without the union's consent. I was surprised that a sophisticated player like Ted Yeiser had allowed this indiscretion to transpire.

I assured the committee that I would inform our legal department about this violation of the status quo and that charges would be filed with the NLRB. We turned our attention to preparations for the next bargaining session, scheduled for July 21.

"You think the company is really going to back off these pay cuts?" asked Hollis Wade. "You say they will if we all stick together, but some of these peoples is weak. I mean weak! You can't teach an old dog new tricks."

I looked in his eyes and could tell he had no knowledge about Tina. I had no idea how he would have reacted if he did know.

"I never said this would be easy," I told him. "It's up to you to do your best to get through to some of them. It's their money at stake, not just yours."

Cartons arrived the next morning, filled with the first edition of the *281 Thunderbolt*. Beneath a masthead dramatically crafted by an artist friend, it began with the headline *"WORKERS SEEK RELIEF. PLANT WIDE GRIEVANCES."*

The process and results of the group grievances in Weaving and Spinning were reviewed, recognizing participants and ensuring that those who hadn't been involved knew whom to thank. A column titled "The Grievance Board" provided details of other cases.

Several workers had received back-pay awards ranging from twenty-six to ninety-three dollars after being bypassed for overtime or paid the wrong rate when transferred to another job—meaningful sums to those living on tight budgets. What was most significant, however, is that these people found the courage to come forward when shortchanged by the system and were rewarded for their efforts. That is a lesson and life experience which is never forgotten.

I knew that Tina would be awake by mid-afternoon, so I gave her a call. This was the final day in her shift rotation, and I was hoping we could get together the next evening.

"I can't do tomorrow," she said. "I'm working. I volunteered to come in and work overtime."

We agreed that I would stop by her apartment on Friday night.

"But look, if you wanna see me tomorrow night, I have my dinner break at eleven. If you come by the weaver's gate, I'll meet you there."

At 5:00 p.m. we were on the gates with the newsletter. Stewards whose articles had been published or who had been instrumental in the most grievances became shop-floor celebrities for the next week.

From my perspective, the campaign was going well. Management had clearly come to its senses in recognizing the value of labor peace during the launch of a new company. The grievances of the past two months could easily have dragged on into the next year. Legal argument would have ultimately prevailed, but not this quickly. Membership among the former Tennessee Textile employees had surpassed 50 percent. I was most concerned about the new hires and made them a priority.

I joined the committee in presenting third step grievances the next day, with Bill Cooper once again presiding for management. One of the cases involved an employee who had been on medical leave for the first half of the year due to a work-related injury. The company wouldn't allow him to return until his workers' comp claim was dropped. This illegal practice was commonplace and went unchallenged in nonunion facilities. Following a review of the "fit for duty" recommendation by the grievant's doctor, he was told to report to his previous assignment on Monday.

Afterward, I held a private follow-up meeting with Cooper and Knuckles regarding two of the recent terminations. We reached a settlement in both cases. Deidre White (profanity incident) would be reinstated with full seniority. She wouldn't receive back pay but the discipline would be reduced to a written warning. Johnnie McBride, (no-show incident) would also be reinstated with seniority but no pay if he successfully passed drug and alcohol tests.

Both resolutions involved compromise and remained tentative pending acceptance by the grievant. Only politically correct intellectuals and emotionally unbalanced workers believe the process to be a quest for perfect justice. The objective is to secure a person's quick return to work rather than subject them to the same ordeal as Leo Boyland.

Deidre was stunned and delighted when I called her that evening. She had been receiving foreclosure threats from the bank and was in no position to await arbitration for the sake of several weeks' pay and a write-up. She sobbed and thanked me profusely.

Johnnie had a lawyer to pay because of his DUI and no time to waste. He assured me that he could restrain his activities to pass substance-abuse tests.

I drove to the mill that night, arriving at the weave room gate at eleven. I spotted Tina standing a few feet back on the lawn.

The factory resembled a penitentiary during working hours. It was surrounded by a chain-link fence topped with barbed wire. Entrances were locked thirty minutes into a shift. The company wanted to prevent workers on break from leaving the facility and returning late, thereby disrupting production.

Tina stepped up to the fence. "I brought you some dinner," I said, tossing a paper bag containing fried chicken and French fries over the wire. She reached out instinctively, caught the package and began to unwrap the food. "You didn't have to do this," she told me.

"I don't have to do nothing. I felt like it."

I could tell she wasn't accustomed to being the recipient of thoughtful gestures.

"This sweet of you," she said. "I'll eat it when I go back inside."

Tina wound her fingers around the chain link and stared at me. I reached through and lightly stroked her breasts. We placed our faces against one of the openings and kissed passionately, remaining in this embrace for nearly two minutes. I opened my eyes for a moment to glance around. I could see two female weavers standing near the door watching, but didn't sense any negativity. I closed my eyes and surrendered to the moment. Our intimacy, separated by the metal fence, was unimaginably erotic. She pulled her head back a few inches and looked at me. I stared down at her hips and envisioned everything that was covered by her jeans. She was mine but I couldn't have her now. We kissed again.

"Tomorrow night," she said, stepping away. "I need to go back inside while I still have time to eat that nice dinner you brought for me."

"Are you going to bring your toothbrush tomorrow?"

"What you think?" she said, walking toward the brick building, glancing over her shoulder with a momentary smile.

I spent the next day at the union hall, prepping witnesses for the Leo Boyland arbitration and assembling evidence for the newly filed Labor Board charges. I arrived at Tina's apartment a few minutes before seven, and she invited me inside for a brief tour. The most prominent features in her bedroom were two large posters of professional wrestlers. Tina proudly identified them by name, pointing out a masked tag team in particular.

"These are my favorite," she said. "I wish I could see them in person but there's no wrestling here in Jackson, so I have to settle for the TV."

I did my best to display interest and then suggested we go to dinner.

"You really got your mind set on taking me out to eat, don't you?" she replied.

"I've been working all day and I'm hungry. I bet you are too."

I felt the need to establish that there could be more to our relationship than my wanting to take her clothes off. I had never been any good at using people. Actually, I was proficient at using people when it came to business, but not romantically. In that area, I always felt compelled to give as much as I received. I secretly envied guys who could be more cavalier and selfish, moving through encounters without effort or encumbrance. It simply wasn't in my nature.

"Where do you like to eat?" I asked.

"Don't matter. Wherever you go is fine with me."

We hopped in my car and headed to a buffet I had become fond of. Tina switched on the radio and found a rap station. I enjoyed rap music about as much as root canals but pretended to appreciate her selection.

"This place has a large salad bar and also a hot bar. I hope that's OK with you. I like to eat a salad every day because it's healthy," I shared.

"Oh, I loves salads!" she exclaimed. "I like to fill my plate all up with lettuce and just cover it with lots of ham and cheese!"

We sat facing each other at a corner table, looking over our salads.

"Are your folks from North Carolina?" she asked.

"I don't really have any folks. I grew up in New York City and left home when I was sixteen. I was on the streets for years. I fought my way up from there. The only family I got is my little girl. Tell me about you."

"There really ain't much to tell. When I was growing up, all my folks wanted to do is beat me. I couldn't wait until I was old enough to get out of there. I left when I was eighteen."

I thought about militant and outspoken committee member Hollis Wade. He believed in dignity and justice for working people but apparently not his own daughter. Unfortunately, this phenomenon is not uncommon. I willed myself not to judge him, as he was one of my leaders in the field.

"What do the people you work with think about what's been going on with the union?" I asked.

"I'm not going to lie to you. Most of them on C shift where I work appreciate what you trying to do . . . especially getting our breaks back. But the talk is that you're here today and gone tomorrow, and what they're going to be left with is Percy, without you there to keep him in line.

"You got no idea some of the things gone on at that union hall. People would come over there to discuss a problem and find Percy drunk with a few of his buddies shooting craps. They figure once you're gone, the company just gonna have its way again, and they ain't about to sign no card as long as Percy's the man gonna be left in charge."

I looked Tina in the eyes and thanked her for being straight with me.

We finished dinner and returned to Riverside Drive, the car reverberating to the beat of rap music. I asked if she would like to watch some TV.

"That's OK," she smiled. "I'm ready for bed if you are."

"I might be persuaded," I said, shrugging my shoulders.

"You keep being smart with me, I might have to whoop your white ass." She sauntered towards the bedroom.

I couldn't take my eyes off the gyration of her perfect butt in tight dungaree shorts. She stripped off her clothes quickly, so I followed suit, and we slid under the blankets.

When I awoke the next morning, the bed was empty, but I found Tina at the kitchen table wearing one my union T-shirts. I joined her and lightly stroked a bump near her right shoulder that I'd seen the night before. "What happened there, sweetie?"

"A couple of years ago I tripped and fell into one of the looms. I broke my collar bone," she replied nonchalantly.

"That must have really hurt."

"Worst pain I ever felt. But it ain't no thing. Peoples get hurt up in there all the time. Last year, a man got his hand all caught up in some moving parts on one of the looms. It took the fixers a half hour to get him free, and he lost three fingers. A few years back, this woman got her eye put out."

She changed the subject. "Do you only take girls out to dinner, or do you take them out to breakfast too?"

"When they're sweet to me like you, they get both."

We threw on our street clothes and walked to the car. As we pulled out of the driveway, I decided it was my turn to take control of the radio and returned the dial to my favorite country station.

On Sunday afternoon I received a call from Percy, requesting that I pick him up at the county jail that evening.

A few hours later, I found him standing on the street outside the prison, looking about with hands in pockets. He climbed into the passenger seat, and we sped off down a winding road. Percy was talkative and boisterous, seeming none the worse for his incarceration. This had been the final weekend of his sentence.

Percy shared a tendency with other inveterate alcoholics I had known. He would offer commentary on a mundane subject and then burst into fits of forced laughter at his own remarks. He periodically slapped his thigh exclaiming, "Ha! Ha! Ha!" leaving me in the somewhat awkward position of wondering whether I should also feign laughter even though I found no grounds for amusement.

I asked how he had fared in jail.

"It ain't so bad," he said. All we do is sit around and talk and play cards. The only thing is, by the time I gets out, I'm hungry! You know what they serves us for lunch? Bologna sandwiches . . . two pieces of bread with one thin slice of bologna in between. I mean, no mustard or ketchup or nothin'.

"By the way, I been meaning to give you this. It's a grievance I wrote for one of the loom fixers who was written up by Derald Gilmer last week."

He withdrew a neatly folded sheet of paper from his shirt pocket and handed it to me. I propped it on the steering wheel and read as we hit a straight stretch of road.

A properly written grievance briefly notes the allegation, relevant contract articles, and remedy sought. Argument supported by evidence is reserved for the meetings. Percy had used every available line on the grievance form to editorialize the incident in his scrawled handwriting; concluding the presentation by stating, "and the company still sees fit to treat people like dawgs!"

"You certainly let them know where you stand," I said.

"I always do," he replied.

I accepted an invitation to join his family for a dinner of meatloaf and mashed potatoes. His wife whispered to me in a moment of privacy, "I'm so grateful you were there to pick him up this time. Usually he just walks from the prison a couple of miles down the road to where there's a liquor store and buys him a bottle. When he's good and ready, he calls one of his buddies for a ride and by the time he gets home, he just stumbles to the bed."

Her eyes momentarily watered, but she blinked back the tears with the grace of someone who has learned to endure hardship with dignity.

I had dinner with Mark Pitt at the Ramada the next evening. He had driven from Knoxville to serve as first chair in the Leo Boyland arbitration. This was to be my first appearance before an arbitrator, so it made sense for Mark to handle it.

I had come to appreciate Mark's level of competence and dedication, but he had the lack of sensitivity and narrowness of vision consistent with a man whose entire life revolves around work. He focused primarily on the organization, not the people who comprised it. Yet, despite our differences, I grew over time to like him and enjoy his company.

"How you been?" I asked.

"Right now, pretty wasted," he replied. "Bruce called me at midnight and we stayed on the phone until 2:00 a.m., talking about every damn thing going on in the Joint Board. Then I had to get up at six to take care of a few things at the office and drive here. Have you got Leo and all the witnesses lined up?"

I told him yes, but that we had a logistical problem. Leo was staying with friends out of town and would need a hotel room prior to the hearing.

"I've never heard of that one," he responded. "Our budget doesn't normally include hotel rooms for grievants."

"If we don't give him a place to stay, he's not going to be there, and the whole thing will be a waste of time. I've got a suggestion."

There was an enormous skid row hotel in the middle of downtown Jackson. The red brick building was the sole structure within a triangular configuration of city streets. I imagined that if aliens had been looking down on Jackson, they might have considered it the geographic heart of the city. Its inexpensive rooms were home to welfare recipients and drug addicts. I was certain that Leo could handle himself there for one night. I had slept at establishments which were far worse.

Mark and I met in the front-office lobby of American Mills at 8:30 a.m. on July 19, and the receptionist ushered us in. Following the customary polite introductions, Ted Yeiser requested a sidebar in one of the smaller offices. He offered a heads-up that the hearing would begin with a motion to deny arbitrability of the grievance on grounds that it had been filed against Tennessee Textiles, which was no longer the employer.

Mark launched into a tirade. "You tell your fucking client that if he refuses to arbitrate this case, then I'm going to shut this fucking place down!"

I knew for certain that we lacked the strength to stage a wildcat strike, but management's level of assessment probably wasn't as clear.

Yeiser shuffled his papers, calmly stating, "Let me go speak with my client," and left the room. He returned shortly and said he was prepared to proceed without making the motion.

Leo and the other witnesses showed up a few minutes before nine. Leo was smartly dressed, well groomed, and appeared to have his wits about him. We entered the conference room and introduced ourselves to Arbitrator Gordon Ludolf.

Labor arbitration is similar in formal procedure to a courtroom trial but takes place in a more casual setting. Tables are arranged in horse-shoe formation with opposing parties facing each other. The arbitrator occupies the connecting table and a chair for witnesses is placed in the center space. Testimony is given under oath and then subject to cross-examination. Rebuttal witnesses are allowed to take the stand before adjournment.

The issue before the arbitrator was whether the grievant had been terminated for just cause. After opening arguments, company witnesses were sworn-in to present their evidence.

Leo Boyland had been employed as a weaver for twelve years. At the beginning of the night in question, several of his looms needed repair. Following procedure, Leo wrote their numbers on the fixer's board, but two of the entries were noted incorrectly. A fixer named Marvin Jones responded to the breakdowns and subsequently informed Supervisor James Grey (known as Chop) that Leo "smelled like a brewery." Marvin wasn't a union member, and under cross-examination, admitted that he and the supervisor were close friends.

Chop testified that under the circumstances, he felt it appropriate to have a conversation with Leo, during which he also smelled alcohol. He informed Department Manager Derald Gilmore, who supported his supervisor by stating that he too had smelled alcohol on Leo's breath, but under cross admitted that he hadn't observed conduct consistent with impairment. He made the decision to send Leo home on suspension and two days later, after consulting with superiors, handed Leo his discharge papers.

Leo remained surprisingly calm and articulate while on the stand, presenting a sequence of events that addressed several points omitted by his former employer:

Chop had been on vacation the week prior to the incident that led to termination. Leo became ill at work one evening and clocked out. On re-turning home, he encountered his supervisor.

"What are you doing at my house?" he inquired.

"Well, me and your woman's friends," was the answer.

In response to Leo's indignation, Chop replied, "You work for me and you won't get away with this."

Leo had heard rumors that Chop was often seen near his home and was involved with his common-law wife. Two days later, he knocked on Chop's door to further discuss the matter and was punched in the face. Chop had been arrested for assault, convicted, and given a suspended sentence. This was supported by court documents.

At the beginning of the shift marking Chop's return from vacation, the odor of alcohol was "detected" on Leo's breath, setting in motion the process which resulted in discharge.

Leo testified that he had drunk a glass of beer with lunch several hours before the shift began but wasn't intoxicated. During the incident he had the presence of mind to request either a breath or blood alcohol test but was refused. The employer failed to contest this during rebuttal.

The parties were given a month to file briefs, and the arbitrator committed to rendering his decision thirty days later.

Leo pulled me aside in the parking lot. "Listen man, I really appreciate what y'all done for me in there, and I hate to ask this, but could you lend me twenty dollars for gas and to buy some food?"

I slipped him a twenty and told him to keep the faith.

Committee members met with me at the union hall the following afternoon to prepare for contract negotiations. Percy called to excuse himself because he wasn't feeling well but promised he would join us at the table. Following a review of our proposals, I turned the discussion to membership and the department/shift employee lists that had been provided. I received eleven cards and was surprised to learn that three of them were new hires.

I recognized the committee's efforts and asked about obstacles they were still encountering. The room was silent for nearly a minute—perhaps the longest I'd ever heard this group remain still.

Finally, Georgia spoke up. "Phil . . . I don't mean to talk trash behind no one's back. I'm not about that. But I think by now you know what our biggest problem is as much as we do."

She went on to describe, as tactfully as possible, the same scenarios about Percy that Tina had mentioned over dinner.

Hollis rose to his feet, as he was accustomed to doing when addressing even a small group. "I don't know what we're going to do about this

man. Me and him go way back, I means way back. I sat in more negotiations with him than I can remember. But I'm tired of trying to hand
people a card and having them talk shit about our president, telling how
they filed this grievance and that grievance and never heard nothing
back . . . until finally they just got out the union."

He thought for a moment and then took his seat, slowly shaking his
head from side to side.

It was Reverend Vandiver's practice to listen carefully before joining
a discussion. "I remember Percy from back in the day also. I think we
need to be fair to the man. There was a time when he really stood up for
the people when no one else would. No man in this room can fault Percy
for being a coward. He really cared about the people and the union and
I believe that deep in his heart, he still does. He's not a bad man and no
one ever accused him of being crooked. But he's got a problem . . . a bad
problem . . . and we all know what it is.

"Being a good man is one thing and being fit to hold office is another. I don't know what the answer is. The ones complaining the loudest
chose the easy way by getting out of the union, instead of staying in the
union and electing someone else. The one thing I do know is that some
of these people, right or wrong, would sign up for me if we didn't have
this problem."

My role was to listen without comment, and the committee respected
the delicate position I was in.

I joined the committee in the conference room shortly before ten the
next morning. I felt a twinge of guilt as I greeted Percy, knowing that I
had sat through the denunciations without rising to his defense.

The management team, with Yeiser in the lead, entered a few minutes later. I studied their expressions as they shook hands with each
committee member. They averted their gaze and looked toward the floor
while taking Percy's hand. It was obvious they had little respect for him.
Georgia made them a bit uncomfortable, and they were caught off-guard
by her cheerful greetings. Everyone met the Reverend's eyes and offered
him a manly handshake. The remaining encounters were cordial but
indifferent.

The session began with the customary business report. Yeiser relinquished the floor to Paul Poston, who said the new company was off to
a good start, while stressing the magnitude of its overhaul and related
costs.

I then presented a written analysis of the earnings information provided by management. The elimination of incentive bonuses, offset by the small increase to base rates offered as compensation, resulted in net wage reductions ranging between thirty-one and seventy-two cents per hour. The union's across-the-board rejection of the company's position was reiterated

Yeiser politely thanked me for the report while Paul Poston glowered over his copy, nervously crumpling its edges while he read. Bob Knuckles scribbled furiously, and Bill Cooper had a look on his face that I interpreted as, *I wish I were playing golf.* Both understood their spectator role in these proceedings.

"It doesn't appear as though we're going to make any progress regarding economics at this time," said the attorney. "Why don't we try to get through some of the language instead?"

Collective bargaining agreements embody numerous and sometimes lengthy articles that define the rights of both parties and rules of engagement. Yeiser slid booklets of the company's language proposals across the table. I agreed with his suggestion and presented the union's packet.

Both parties flipped through their proposals, offering a brief overview of intent regarding each article. When we concluded, the lawyer glanced at his gold watch and suggested we adjourn for lunch.

I took my group to the buffet. Being treated to lunch is a customary perk for bargaining committee members. It is a meaningful form of recognition for people who can rarely afford to eat in a decent restaurant, and breaking bread is perhaps the most primordial of bonding rituals.

We were left with a few minutes to relax after eating. One of the women on the committee said with admiration, "You have such a sweet and obedient child. You must be very strict with the discipline to teach her to behave in public the way she does."

I looked at her calmly. "I've never laid a hand on my little girl. If anybody else ever did, they'd wake up in intensive care. That's a natural fact."

Most of the committee members stared back at me nonplussed. Georgia, who was sitting next to me, squeezed my arm gently for a moment. Her eyes were moist, and there was the hint of a smile on her lips.

Negotiating contract language is an intricate, time-consuming affair requiring attention to detail. Eventually, a final version of each article must be drafted that both parties are willing to sign. Every paragraph ends up as a finely woven matrix of compromises. An individual section of an important article can be pages long, with the underlying meaning and balance of power pivoting on two words. The results are imperfect but create circumstances far more preferable than when an employer has sole discretion to legislate and selectively enforce its own rules.

Most Americans consider due process of law to be an inalienable right that was contemplated by the founding fathers. But in a nonunion industrial environment, workers are stripped of these basic entitlements each time they pass through the plant gate. Most factories are managed with the ethics and compassion of a third-world dictatorship.

"We're trying to run a business" is the usual justification. A well-written union contract demonstrates that remaining competitive and treating employees equitably aren't mutually exclusive principles.

We returned to the table and found management already seated. I had thoroughly reviewed Yeiser's materials and found nothing onerous. It was the sort of opening-language proposal one expects to see from a company that anticipates reaching an accommodation with the union.

The attorney's demeanor was, in fact, more relaxed and good-natured than I had expected based on the research file. Either he had mellowed over the years or simply had the good sense to recognize that it was in his client's best interests to negotiate and settle.

We discussed several of the shorter articles, identifying common ground and debating our differences. The parties arrived at their first TA (tentative agreement) over language that defined the company's recognition of the union and its local representatives. We reached a natural stopping point and scheduled our next meeting for the following Wednesday.

I decided to remain in Jackson through a second weekend and arranged to spend both days making house visits to nonmembers and signing union cards in the difficult, old-fashioned way.

I was joined on Saturday morning by a heavyset shop steward from the card room named Harvey Thaxton, who navigated while I drove.

One never knows what to expect from a day of house calls. An hour might be spent knocking on doors in a housing project, and then you find yourself out in the county, winding down a dirt road toward a dilapidated trailer. You have to be prepared to deal with everything from dogs snapping at your heels to a shotgun pointed in your face. But most of the time, if you know how to present yourself, folks will at least sit down and talk.

I explained the union's benefits and need for solidarity in dealing with management, reinforced by Harvey's personal experiences. We primarily focused on former Tennessee Textile employees but included a few of the new hires when proximity presented an opportunity.

Most organizers find house calling to be the most tedious and strenuous part of their job. You can drive for hours, knock on twenty doors, and find no one at home; until finally spending an hour and a half with a cantankerous individual who asks repeated questions, only to come away empty-handed. But in the long run, the personal touch pays off, and a persistent organizer will change minds and sign cards.

Harvey and I had a decent day. We found seven people at home and signed three new members. I took him to dinner at seven, and we agreed to continue our efforts the next day, after he attended church.

I had called Percy the previous evening, asking to stop by his house when I finished work on Saturday because there was something important we needed to discuss. It was nearly ten when I knocked on his door, but he didn't seem to mind. Percy led me into the dining room and we sat at the table.

"What's going on?" he asked. "The company up to some new underhanded shit? I wouldn't doubt it. That Yeiser, he's a snake in the grass! You called that right from jump street."

"No, it's something else," I said. "This isn't going to be easy, so I'm going to just get right to it. I love you like a brother. You're as strong a union man as I've ever met. But you've got a problem. We both know what it is."

"I know, I knows. I drinks too much. There's just been so much going on, what with the new company, and negotiations, having to be in jail. I know you right about them meetings. I'm gonna get back with them as soon as things calm down a bit . . ."

I cut him off as gently as I could. "It's past that point. A lot of people have been talking to me in recent weeks. Folks in the mill have lost their trust in you. It's not because they think you're crooked or won't stand up. Everyone knows better than that. It's because they've come down to the hall or looked to you for help and found you drunk one time too many. There's some that are ready to sign a card, but they won't because of you.

"I'm sorry. I know that hurts with all you've put into this local. But I'm just telling you what I've been hearing and seeing."

Percy looked me in the eyes. "You telling me that you want me to step down?"

I was relieved that he had spared me from having to say it. "Yes. I'm sorry. I still want you on the committee and to stay involved. But your reputation has gotten too jammed up behind this problem. There's only so far I can take this local as long as you're president. There it is."

Percy's eye contact didn't waiver. "Phil, I trust you. You've been nothing but straight up since you came to town. If you tell me that it's best for the local and best for the people that I step aside, then I resign."

Tears began running down his cheeks. He sat at his dining room table and wept like a baby. There is nothing more tragic than seeing a strong man broken. Percy was a man. He didn't argue or try to defend himself. He put the union local and the welfare of the people ahead of his own pride.

Percy asked who would take his place. I told him that according to union bylaws, the vice president gets to fill the vacancy.

"Well, Georgia, she'll be a good one. Does she know yet?"

"No one knows yet," I told him. "I owed you the respect of coming to you first and hearing what you had to say. I didn't come here to force you out. I don't even have that authority. But under the circumstances, I believe you did the right thing.

"I'll get with Georgia early next week. After that, if she's willing to assume the position, you know I'll have to put out a leaflet. I'll tell people that you resigned for reasons of health and praise your contributions to the union over the years."

"I've got just one condition, if I'm gonna do this," said Percy. "Next year, I want to go to the International Convention in Miami one more time. I don't have to go as a delegate. I'd just like to attend."

I promised to make it happen.

I drove away feeling hollow and despondent. This man and his family had opened their home and embraced both me and my daughter from the moment of our arrival. But I had done what was necessary. It was one of the saddest encounters of my career.

I picked up Harvey Thaxton at his house on Sunday afternoon to continue our regimen of house visits. A couple of hours into our itinerary, I remarked, "Driving around on a Sunday afternoon, knocking on people's doors, I feel like a Jehovah's Witness."

Harvey turned and looked at me. "I am a Jehovah's Witness."

I glanced at his face and could tell he wasn't pulling my leg. I continued driving for a moment in silence, unsure how to respond.

"I'm sorry. I didn't mean to offend you. It was just a joke . . . an offhand remark."

"Don't worry about it," said Harvey.

It was more difficult to find people at home than the previous day. We signed one new member and called it quits.

I approached the weave room gate at eleven that night with a bag of fish and chips in hand. I asked one of the weavers standing outside to please go in and find Tina. She emerged a few minutes later.

"I didn't expect to see you," she smiled.

"Well, here I am."

She glanced at the bag I was carrying. "What you brought for me this time?"

"You'll have to open it up and find out."

"What I got to do to get you to toss it over?"

"Come over here and I'll show you."

Tina pressed herself against the gate and we kissed. I threw her dinner over the barbed wire. This time she opened it immediately and began to eat.

"I've got a few days off coming," I said. "I leave for home on Thursday. Want to come with me? You could meet my daughter and some of my friends."

She stopped eating with food still in her mouth, thought for a moment, then hastily finished chewing and swallowed. "You want to take me back to where you really live . . . to meet your daughter?"

"Yeah, why not? We'll drive through the mountains, and I'll show you some beautiful places."

"That's really sweet of you to ask. I mean it. But I'm scheduled to be working most of those days, and I'd rather do it when I don't have to burn any vacation or attendance days. Maybe next time, after my crew rotates."

I invited Georgia to meet me at the union hall on Tuesday evening after work and informed her of Percy's resignation.

"Thank the Lord Jesus," she exclaimed. "Maybe now we can get some of these people to come around. When are you planning to schedule the elections?"

"I'm not," I responded. "Under the bylaws, the vice president moves up."

She stared at me for a moment. "No. I think the people need to make their choice. Besides, I'm good with where I am. I don't know if I'm ready to take on the responsibility of being president. I don't want to do something wrong and screw things up."

"Here's the deal," I said. "Elections are coming up anyway, in December. You can be acting president until then. Holding elections now would be a really bad idea. Anything could happen. People sometimes make hasty and irrational choices when there's an unexpected power vacuum to fill. Some loose cannon could get himself elected and turn everything we've worked so hard to build upside down on its head.

"There's a difference between being outspoken and knowing what it is you're speaking about. We're at a major turning point. We can't risk the local falling into the hands of someone who doesn't know the difference. Try it on for size. Give the people a chance to see that you do know the difference."

"Well, I don't know," she said. "I'll have to think on it."

"I'm starving. Let's go to dinner," I suggested.

Two types of people end up filling positions of local union leadership. Some find it the perfect vehicle for their rage, ego, and control issues. They're hungry for the position and will use slander and exorbitant promises to get it. Others are genuinely motivated by altruism and the desire to be of service. They're often reluctant warriors at first, believing that there must be someone out there who could do it better. It was this sort of humility, coupled with an inherent competence and instinct, which I sought in a local president.

I sat with my dinner in front of me while Georgia ate. "What I like about you is that you're not afraid to speak your mind but at the same time, you're not a know-it-all. Show me a person who knows what they know, and knows what they don't know, and I'll show you a person of infinite potential. I believe that's you. I believe you're hungry to learn. If you keep your mind and your heart open, I'll teach you more about the union in the next couple of months than you've learned in your whole life before."

"But what if I screw up and do something that hurts people?" she asked.

"The fact that you even ask that question means you care enough to do your best not to, and to learn enough to limit the chances. Look, what if I screw up and do something that hurts people? I'm not perfect. We're all human. To be a leader means being tough enough to take chances and strong enough to live with your mistakes.

"You're the golden one. The hand of fate rests on your shoulder, and the angels smile down. I need you to take those risks. The people need you."

I picked up the check for myself and the new acting president of Local 281.

The next morning, I gathered with the committee in the conference room before negotiations, telling the company that we needed half an hour. Percy was understandably absent. I explained to the group that Percy had resigned his position for reasons of health and that Georgia would serve as acting president until the regularly scheduled elections. Georgia graciously accepted a warm round of applause.

I'd arrived with a leaflet in anticipation of a favorable response. We agreed on gate assignments and paper bags stuffed with copies were passed out. I felt that it would be best to not personally participate in this distribution.

Once the company was seated, I informed them of the change in leadership. Ted Yeiser politely congratulated Georgia and told us to wish Percy a speedy recovery. He then asked why the union had filed a ULP (Unfair Labor Practice Charge) charge with the National Labor Relations Board.

"You already know why," I told him. "The company made a unilateral decision to subcontract janitorial work. This was an open subject of bargaining. Nine employees who had exercised their seniority to bid into these positions were displaced. They were forced to bump less senior employees on other jobs, who in turn did the same. People have ended up on jobs and shifts that weren't their preference and in some cases conflict with child care. The union had a responsibility to take the appropriate action and wouldn't have much credibility if it didn't."

"I'm not certain you're right about employee sentiment," said Yeiser. "The in-house janitorial staff had a history of doing sloppy work. The state of the restrooms was deplorable at times. It's my understanding that these conditions were raised during your group grievance meetings. Take a look next time you're doing an inspection. I believe that if we were to dismiss our new janitorial service and return to the old system, you'd have far more employee outcry than you're now receiving from a few displaced individuals."

"I'll inquire about employee reaction with the committee," I responded. "I think you've raised some legitimate points of discussion . . . but a discussion we should have been having before implementation. There's nothing that would have prevented our working something out before finishing the contract."

"I note your position," said Yeiser. "In the interests of showing good faith, we would like you to drop the ULP."

"In the interests of good faith, your client should have come to me first. At this point, I'm not inclined to drop the charge."

Paul Poston leaned over to whisper in the attorney's ear, after which Yeiser requested a brief recess. Management left the room, and I was given an opportunity to poll the committee.

"The restrooms have been a whole lot cleaner since the new crew began," said Betty Trice. "Some of the people in my department have been talking about it."

"That about sums it up for the weave room too," said Georgia. "The company's got us between a rock and a hard place. If we make them return to the old system and the restrooms get nasty again, the people will blame us. If we back off and drop the charges, we'll look weak."

Yeiser stuck his head in the door. "Are you guys ready for us?"

"Sure, why not?"

Once his team was seated, Yeiser said, "Mr. Poston has a somewhat unusual suggestion he'd like me to propose to you. We recognize that there are strong feelings on both sides of this issue. In exchange for the union dropping the ULP, the company would agree to allow the question of janitors to be decided by an employee vote."

"I assume that we're talking about a vote by union members," I replied. "This is, after all, a subject of bargaining."

"No. What Mr. Poston is requesting here is that this be a jointly facilitated vote for all employees."

"I'll consider your position and get back with you," I responded. "In order to assist the union with its deliberations, I'm requesting to be provided with a list of all employees who were displaced as a result of this process, indicating former and current job and shift. For the time being, the charge stands."

The lawyer nodded his head in acknowledgment. We reviewed our notes from the previous session, and then new business commenced with a comparison of our respective proposals regarding compensation for jury duty.

"We'll need about fifteen minutes to discuss your position," said Yeiser. "You can remain here. We'll be in one of the smaller offices."

After an hour I went looking for them, and Yeiser suggested we break for lunch.

We took seats around what was becoming our customary table at the restaurant.

"You're not seriously thinking about dropping those charges, are you Phil?" asked Georgia. "It will just give all them naysayers cause to complain once again that the company just does whatever it wants to."

"You were right back in the conference room when you said we're between a rock and a hard place," I told her. "I was straight up with the company when I said we needed more information . . . but I don't think they understand exactly why.

"I want to see precisely who was displaced and how badly it affected them. If most of the people who got inconvenienced were scabs . . . then pardon my language, but fuck 'em. If some were new hires that don't really know the difference yet and are just glad to have a job, that also tells us something. I need more input about what most of our members are saying.

"You know the old expression, 'You can please most of the people most of the time but you can't please all of the people all of the time.' This may be one of those situations. Sometimes we have to accept that the best we can do is satisfy the majority. But until I know more, we go forward with the charge. At the very least, the company will sweat before we drop it."

There were a number of important contract articles addressed in the union's proposal that weren't included in the company's packet. I focused on these when we returned to the table, beginning with Leaves of Absence.

Our proposal was similar to the old agreement. Before enactment of the Family and Medical Leave Act in 1993, when entitlement to twelve weeks of unpaid medical leave became law, employees covered by union contracts already received a full year of documented absence. During this era, pregnant or seriously ill workers in nonunion plants were frequently given the choice of returning to work prematurely or being terminated. I told the company there would be no contract if the existing rights weren't carried forward.

Paul Poston interjected and expressed concern about employees extending their leaves by presenting falsified medical documents. "There are some doctors in these parts . . . I don't know how to better say it . . . they're just quacks. They'll sign their names to anything for a buck."

I replied that while this was true, such abuses were probably rare since most employees who were medically fit for duty couldn't afford to stay at home. We then discussed the formation of a joint safety committee and the union's right to plant access.

The cornerstone of union contract language is seniority. It's often a lengthy and complicated treatise, addressing the application of seniority to job vacancies, shift preference, temporary transfers, layoff and recall. We proposed keeping the existing article with minor changes.

"We're not ready to discuss seniority at this time," responded Yeiser.

The parties adjourned, having had a productive conversation but making no additional progress. There was a lot to digest, but I also suspected that management considered the ball to be in our court regarding janitors and board charges. From their perspective, the numerous concessions of the past two months had been one-sided and they were now expecting something in return.

Committee members left for the plant gates in time to present D shift with a leaflet announcing the change in leadership (Fig. 4).

I returned home for a shower and drove to Tina's apartment. This evening, she directed me to a small family-owned restaurant in her neighborhood. As we were waiting to be served, she asked, "So when you gonna take me out drinking? I could show you some good places if you want."

"I hope this doesn't disappoint you," I told her, "but I don't drink anymore."

"Why not?" she asked, clearly astounded by my revelation.

"It gets in the way. It compromises my edge. I can't afford that with what I do."

A glint of recognition showed in her eyes and she smiled. "You must prefer some of that good reefer. You gonna roll me a couple of joints? You get me like that and I'll drive you crazy all night."

"I don't judge what anyone else does, but I don't do that either. Same reason."

She leaned back a few inches and broke eye contact. "Then what you do for your head?"

"I work out, play guitar. I like being outdoors in nature. There's a lot of ways to unwind and get your head straight. What about you?"

"Oh, you knows, I hit the pipe every now and then," she answered, flicking her fingers in front of her mouth against an imaginary stem.

Years ago in New York, some of my friends had been heroin addicts and meth fiends. But I'd never known anyone who used crack. My days on the street had preceded its arrival. Just when you think that you've seen it all, the unexpected comes knocking at your door.

That night, as she lay in my arms before sleeping, Tina asked, "Do you think I'm a bad person, that I'm trash, because of what I told you in the restaurant?"

"No," I answered, stroking her hair. "I told you. I ain't about judging people. Just be careful. I've seen a lot of bad things happen to people I loved behind what they were into."

I had received authorization to fly home on alternate visits. I dropped Tina at her apartment the next morning and headed to the Nashville airport.

CHAPTER 8

I picked Colie up from day care on Friday evening in my rental car, and we went to dinner at one of her favorite restaurants. As we ate, I remembered an evening three years before when we sat at the same table. She was one and a half at the time. I had looked up from my plate and noticed that her seat was empty.

As every parent would have done, I leapt from the table with my heart racing and began to search the restaurant, calling her name. She was nowhere to be found. As I approached the cashier, I turned to my right and looked into the adjacent lounge.

Colie was sitting on a bar stool with the body language and demeanor of a grown woman, surrounded by three utterly charmed young men. Her elbow was on the bar, with her chin resting on the palm of her hand, an engaging little smile on her lips. I remained in the background to watch in amazement as the admirers vied for her attention. Suddenly Colie looked up and, returning to her present age, burst into tears. "Where's my daddy? I want my daddy!"

I rushed over to scoop her up in my arms and walked back to our table.

The next day we visited friends, and then I took her to South Square Mall in Durham to buy clothes. The shopping center was slowly deteriorating, as were the surrounding neighborhoods. However, it had an arcade to rival the one in Chapel Hill.

During our shopping spree we passed by a jewelry store. I realized that within the protocols of a high profile guy dating a poor working girl, I was overdue to buy Tina a gift. We entered the establishment, and Colie enjoyed looking at all the "sparkly" items as I made my selection. I wanted something that wasn't ostentatious but showed some class. I decided on a simple gold necklace about 3/8 of an inch wide.

Dusk was falling as I carried Colie back to the elevated parking area. I initiated one of our instructional games. "Three hundred sixty degrees," I said. "Tell me everything that's going on around us. No turning your head."

She thought for a moment. "There's an old lady pushing a shopping cart . . . and there's two teenagers walking behind us . . . but I don't think they have bad vibes. How did I do, Daddy?"

"You did perfect. Good job!"

In a relaxed and casual manner, I schooled my daughter throughout her childhood not only in self-defense but also understanding the street. I wanted her to feel safe in the world, not because she had been sheltered, but because she was strong and knew how to handle herself.

I drove Colie to daycare on Monday morning and headed to Raleigh for my flight.

I returned to Jackson in time to join committee members at the gate with a union meeting announcement for Wednesday evening, which would include swearing in Georgia as president.

An unexpected group issue had arisen during my absence. The Spinning Department consisted of both twelve and eight hour crews. A spike in production had required the eight-hour shifts to work seven days during the previous week. Under the contract, these employees were entitled to double time on Sunday. On receiving their checks, however, they found they'd been paid only the standard overtime rate of time and a half. When Betty Trice presented what she imagined to be an oversight to Bob Knuckles, he told her that this was intentional and represented an ongoing policy.

It was incomprehensible that, having cleared the slate on so many contractual issues, the company would now make such a blatant violation. I told Betty I would have a grievance prepared for her the next day.

On the evening of August 2, workers began to filter through the union hall doors a few minutes before five. As seats filled up, I could tell this was going to be our largest turnout thus far, including a number of nonmembers.

Reverend Vandiver opened with prayer and turned the meeting over to me. I gave a condensed review of negotiations and successful group grievances. I had learned there was no threshold for repeating good news to the membership. A third of the people were insufficiently literate to read leaflets and another third had limited retention. This observation is not intended to disparage these individuals, but rather the culture that failed to nurture them.

I introduced Georgia Bond and administered the oath of office, thus officially beginning her presidency. The crowd rose and demonstrated its approval. After the ovation ran its course, I invited Georgia to address the membership. Her remarks were brief, but articulate and on point. The crowd again applauded as she left the podium.

As the first of the meetings adjourned, several nonmembers approached Georgia uninvited and handed her their union cards. By the time both shifts had departed, I was left sitting at my desk sorting through twenty-seven new cards, including those presented earlier by the committee.

Tina had offered an unexpected invitation during our last conversation: "You say you like nature and being outdoors and stuff. There's a park on the outskirts of town with all sorts of big trees and a pond with paddleboats. I be willing to go on a walk with you, if you want."

I finished my phone calls the next morning, hit the pause button on my work assignment, and drove to her apartment.

The park was spacious and aesthetically pleasing. We strolled side by side down the winding paths, enjoying the pleasant weather with little conversation. The truth was that we had almost nothing in common and yet, on an unspoken level, we had everything in common.

We rested on a bench, and I said, "I've got something for you," handing her a gift-wrapped box from the jewelers.

She seemed genuinely surprised and gingerly opened it as if it might contain a scorpion. Her eyes grew wide, and she exhaled slowly as she viewed the contents, which sparkled as it caught the sunlight.

"Why you give me this?" she asked softly.

"'Cause I dig you. 'Cause I think a beautiful girl should have something beautiful to wear. Try it on."

Tina slipped it over her neck, and I fastened the clasp from behind. I knew that she felt awkward because she wasn't used to being pampered. I hoped I hadn't overplayed my hand.

"Thank you," she said at last. "I'll look at this in the mirror when I get home."

We walked to the pond and went for a paddleboat ride.

A good field organizer can't overlook practical matters while immersed in dramatic events. Workers had been complaining about temperature at the union hall. The sputtering, ancient air conditioner was insufficient to relieve the summer heat.

Betty Trice was off work on Friday to assist with visits to nonmembers in her department. I made a detour to an appliance store, and we picked out a new unit. I had previously seen to it that the union hall was no longer a place of boredom. Now it would be comfortable as well.

That evening, I relaxed alone watching a movie on television, with a spread of exotic cheeses and crackers laid out on the coffee table. An ad caught my attention. The following Wednesday, the Jackson Coliseum would host a professional wrestling event. Some of Tina's heroes would be among the contenders.

I'd always considered the pretense and overstatement of this sport to represent the depth of poor taste. However, I knew that treating Tina to ringside seats would be a huge thrill for her. For me, it would be a foray into the bizarre I wouldn't otherwise have experienced.

Tina was expected at my house around seven on Saturday evening, but she didn't show up until after ten. There were streaks of red in her eyes, and her hair was more tousled than usual. She seemed out of sorts and unresponsive until I brought up the wrestling match.

"No shit!!" she exclaimed. "I never thought wrestling would come to a place like Jackson! You gonna take me . . . and front row seats? I'm scheduled to work but I'll take me an excused absence. I got a doctor who'll write me whatever I tell him."

She moved close, nudged me with her elbow, and gave me a wink. I clasped her buttocks with both hands and pressed my lips to hers as they slowly parted . . .

The bargaining committee and I gathered in the conference room at eleven on Tuesday morning. As had become practice, the management team met in one of the smaller offices while we got ready. I was pleased to see Percy in the room. He walked up to Georgia, shaking her hand.

"My congratulations to you, Madam President," he stated with equanimity.

The gesture showed dignity and class, while his haggard face and hollow eyes betrayed that he had been drinking heavily during recent days.

Ted Yeiser opened the session with a business update. He said that while Dominic Poon remained optimistic about prospects for American Mills, initial operating costs were exceeding budget and the board of directors had authorized borrowing an additional $1 million.

I began the union's preliminary remarks by raising the matter of double time on Sunday, admonishing Yeiser, "I don't understand how your client can be so eager to resolve the current unfair labor practice charge and at the same time commit a far more serious violation of the status quo."

Bob Knuckles interjected, "Could I discuss this with you in a sidebar during one of the caucuses?"

I glanced at Georgia and she nodded her head.

Yeiser asked if the union had reconsidered its position regarding the vote on janitorial options in exchange for dropping the ULP.

It was obvious that the majority of employees were pleased with the new standard of hygiene provided by the contracted service. I also knew that management required a gesture of responsiveness from our side before further progress in negotiations would be possible. This represented the perfect opportunity to offer a concession. It would cost the union and its members nothing to agree. On the other hand, the benefits to management would be meaningful in terms of cost savings and withdrawal of a legally valid board charge.

We informed the employer of our agreement, conditional upon all procedures and methods of communication being worked out in advance. I scanned management's side of the table and sensed a bit of surprise accompanied by relaxation of body language. Yeiser requested a brief recess. He poked his head through the door after half an hour, and we beckoned his team back into the room.

"Bob Knuckles will be willing to meet at your convenience to sort through the details of the vote," said the attorney. "We appreciate the union's flexibility regarding this matter. I want to resume by addressing some of the articles we discussed at our previous session."

The company accepted the basic terms of our jury duty proposal. Twelve-hour employees who missed a full shift would no longer have compensation limited to eight hours. Workers on night crews would be excused and paid if due in court the next morning. We went back and forth on the exact wording until reaching agreement.

It was nearly 1:30 by this point and we broke for lunch. On our return, Bob Knuckles motioned for me to join him in a side office.

He cleared his throat. "I've prepared a response regarding the grievance about double-time pay on Sundays. In the interests of avoiding conflict among the committee members, I thought it might be best to broach this with you privately. Apparently there had been an agreement between Percy Long and the management of Tennessee Textiles that double time would no longer be paid to eight-hour employees working their seventh consecutive day. It's the company's position that as we're both bound by the status quo during these negotiations, that should include all existing side agreements, in addition to the printed contract."

"I assume that you're now going to show me a signed memorandum of agreement," I said.

Knuckles exhaled and thought for a moment. "To the best of my knowledge, there is no signed agreement. This rests on the word of Paul Poston and Derald Gilmore."

"You've got to be kidding," I told him. "You expect me to ignore employee rights under the contract based on hearsay? Even if there was a written agreement, you know as well as I do that a local officer doesn't have authority to change the terms of a collective bargaining agreement negotiated by the international and ratified by the members."

"Don't shoot me, I'm only the messenger," said Knuckles, handing me the grievance response. "I wasn't even there when any of this supposedly happened. I have no idea who said what to who." He shook his head and looked me in the eyes. "I deliberately left the date off of this to give you some wiggle room in terms of when you show it to the committee."

I thanked him for his candor and discretion, and rejoined the committee at our side of the bargaining table.

Yeiser proceeded to address plant rules. He accepted our counterproposal requiring the company to notify and meet with the union prior to implementing new policies, as well as the union's right to immediate dispute of reasonableness. We concluded the afternoon by agreeing on language regarding union bulletin boards. It had been a productive day. A potential gridlock was broken and progress had ensued.

I called Percy at home that night to ask privately if he had ever entered into an agreement with management to eliminate double-time pay for eight-hour crews on Sunday. He said that a couple years earlier Paul Poston had approached him during a period when cash flow was critical and employees were working a lot of overtime to meet customer deadlines. He had agreed to a temporary suspension of this benefit until the orders in question were filled but not to a permanent change in contract language. I believed him, as such a change by definition would have existed in the form of a signed memorandum.

The next afternoon, card room employees gathered in the conference room for their group grievance. The greatest concern was a dilapidated climate-control system that made the summer environment stifling and winters frigid. There were also overloaded jobs and piece rate concerns. Bill Cooper and Bob Knuckles presided for management. I offered a brief overview and allowed Reverend Vandiver to present the details. An action plan leading to remedy was quickly agreed upon.

That evening, I picked Tina up at her apartment. We had dinner at the buffet and drove to the coliseum. I asked if she had ever attended a wrestling match before.

"Yes, a couple of times, in Memphis. But I sat way up in the back where I could barely see. I've never been anywhere close to the ring before."

I could tell she was genuinely excited. It appeared as though many others in Jackson shared her sentiments because the parking lot was overflowing. It took fifteen minutes to find a space.

We made our way down a long aisle to our seats in the ringside area, several rows back from the ropes. As I sat, I remembered how TV cameras pan out from the ring in fighting sports, taking in the nearby fans. I thought how mortifying it would be if a channel-surfing acquaintance saw me at a wrestling match.

The first event began with deafening roars of approval from the crowd. The contrivance of professional wrestling is even more transparent in person than on television. It's like a poorly scripted and unrehearsed high school play. This didn't concern the spectators. They cheered (or booed) the various outcomes as if they had the significance of a presidential election.

I was surrounded by a transfixed multitude, immersed in blood lust, screaming at the top of their lungs for the various champions to

dismember opponents in accord with their own morbid fantasies. Proc-
lamations of "Gouge his eyes out!" and "Break his leg!" permeated the
night. Nobody was more consumed with frenzy than Tina. She sat atop
the back of her chair with shoes on the seat, flailing her arms wildly and
invoking carnage.

I must have been the only stationary and silent person in the coliseum. The poorly choreographed dramas within the arena were of no
interest to me, so I studied the audience. We were surrounded by white
males in the throes of predatory exultation. Tina and I appeared to be
the only mixed couple on premises.

I realized with a shudder that there might in fact be an unscripted
confrontation that evening—one that would involve me having to fight
my way through the parking lot back to my car. I looked at the twisted,
screaming faces around me and wished that Tina could be just a bit less
high profile. She had grown up in these parts and understood the realities. But she was lost in a comic-book reverie, close enough to smell the
sweat on the heroes who covered her bedroom walls.

My considerations instinctively became tactical, as I envisioned responses to varying levels of hostility within this crowded environment.

It was suddenly time for intermission and the unexpected silence interrupted my thoughts. The people sitting in proximity began turning
toward us and talking. "Hello. How are you? We haven't seen you at a
match before. Are you enjoying yourselves?"

They seemed to understand the awkwardness of our position and
were actually going out of their way to make us feel welcome. Two of
the fans brought out their programs and indicated with relish what they
expected to be the most exciting events of the second half. With their
craving for gratuitous violence temporarily satisfied, all that remained
was their underlying humanity.

The grand finale of the evening was a last-man-standing event involving the full roster of contestants. By comparison, all that came before had been the Olympics. The wrestlers crowded into the ring and
fell on each other like a saloon brawl in a grade-B western. Within sixty
seconds, half were either "knocked out" or thrown beyond the ropes.

One of these was a young man of fit but normal build, having neither
the weight-lifter physique nor several-hundred-pound girth of the others. He'd been introduced as the hometown favorite and local champion.

A tattooed giant crashed into him with his protruding abdomen, causing him to fly back, hit his head against a corner pole, and be rendered unconscious.

The melee continued until only one of the grotesque participants remained upright. This bald-headed fellow was shorter than many of the others but had enormous body mass and hairy arms protruding from a sleeveless T-shirt. He'd been presented earlier as a mentally deranged individual who'd escaped from the asylum to participate. Just as the referees were about to declare him victorious, the young man from Jackson staggered to his feet.

The enormous contender roared with indignation and charged, lost his balance, and fell through the ropes onto the floor. The local hero, as the only individual remaining awake in the ring, was proclaimed triumphant.

Thousands of spectators leapt to their feet in frenzied exultation. The liberation of Paris would have paled by comparison.

A few minutes later, in a reverent ceremony, the young wrestler received the prize money—a check for $25,000. The audience again thundered its approval. I presumed that he was either the high school or amateur champion of Jackson and probably the only participant who normally engaged in wrestling as a legitimate sport. I wondered how much he was actually getting paid.

Tina and I shared an uneventful walk through the parking lot. I inquired about her work schedule and asked if she could join me when I left for North Carolina the following evening. She took my arm, smiling, and told me to pick her up at six.

Bob Knuckles and I met the next afternoon to discuss procedures for the "janitor vote." Afterward, I stopped by Paul Poston's office to offer a gentleman's opportunity to reconsider his position regarding double time on Sunday but found him irritable and defensive.

"You once again choose to insult me by not taking me at my word," he complained. "I have managed eight different plants during the course of my career and never have I been so disrespected. I told you what was agreed to and even have Derald Gilmore as a witness. I don't know what more you want."

"What I want and need is a signed memorandum that authorizes modification of the contract," I told him. "If you were being represented by an attorney who said that he was taking the other party's word for something that couldn't be proven, what would you do? You'd fire him in a heartbeat. I owe my members the same level of due diligence that you would expect."

"They're not just your members," he grumbled. "They're my employees."

"That's exactly my point. We've agreed to rules of engagement regarding how we deal with the workforce. If we stay within those guidelines and stop trying to reinvent them, we can have a rational and productive relationship. If I did what you asked, the union would be failing to meet its duty of fair representation as defined by the NLRB, and we would both be in violation of the law."

"Well, I don't know about all that," he said, rising from his desk. "I'm late for a meeting. I've got to go."

I drove back to Riverside Drive, threw some clothing in a suitcase, and arrived at Tina's apartment a few minutes before six. I knocked on the door but there was no response. It was a bit early so I parked my car where I could have a view of the entrance. At 6:20 it occurred to me that perhaps she had been in the shower, so I knocked again. There was still no one home. I waited a few more minutes and then headed for the interstate.

I stopped at eleven to check into a familiar hotel in Crossville. I tried Tina on the phone but got no answer. The pieces didn't fit, especially given her mood the night before. I tried my best to get a good night's sleep but wasn't very successful.

CHAPTER 9

On Saturday morning I ate breakfast in my customary fashion, sitting in an old reclining chair that faced one of the bedroom windows in my farm house, staring out across open meadow toward a row of trees. I was upset and confused about my inability to reach Tina. Rather than spend the afternoon alone with my thoughts, I stayed busy with work calls to Jackson until Colie was dropped at my front door. We drove into town for dinner and a night at the arcade.

I asked if she was ready to return to Tennessee as I carried her back to my car.

"Yes, I think so Daddy," she said, resting her tired head on my shoulder. "Can we go to an amusement park?"

Ernest phoned the next day, requesting a meeting in Greensboro on Monday night. It meant that mountain roads and theme parks would have to wait for the return trip.

I had resisted the temptation to call Tina throughout the weekend, but after Colie was asleep I decided to give it a try.

She picked up the phone. "Hey Babe. What's up?"

"Where were you?" I asked. "You were supposed to meet me at six on Thursday to come home with me."

There was a brief silence on the other end. "I'm sorry. I was out shopping and by the time I got back it was seven. My watch is broke. I kept looking out the window and hoping you were late too, but I guess you already left."

"That's OK," I said. "You're going to have a chance to meet Colie anyway. I'm bringing her with me."

"Really? Well that's cool. I can't wait to see her."

We arrived at the Greensboro Howard Johnson's at eight on Monday evening. I knocked on Ernest's door, holding Colie by the hand.

"I see you brought company," said Ernest, smiling and patting Colie on the head.

She drew pictures and fell asleep on Ernest's bed while we talked until midnight. I scooped my daughter up when we were done and tucked her under the covers in our room.

The next day was a 640-mile straight shot down the interstate. There was a grievance meeting scheduled for Wednesday, and my attendance was expected. It was a rough haul for an adult, let alone a four-year-old. We played Dead Head and other car games throughout the ride, stopping at restaurants and gift shops. I carried her as she slept soundly in my arms to her bed in Jackson at 11:00 p.m.

The second step meeting was fairly routine, involving two reprimands and an overloaded job. I considered the most serious issue to be the verbal abuse of Shop Steward Rick Hardin by Manager Derald Gilmore, when he'd attempted to present a grievance. While there was no tangible remedy to be sought, I couldn't overlook such a blatant violation of steward rights. Gilmore was another prehistoric creature who belonged in the same museum as Poston.

The hearing only lasted for an hour, and I drove to the union hall for a committee meeting. I discussed the arrangements being made for the janitor vote and raised the slightly more controversial subject of the vice president's office, which had been vacated by Georgia's ascent to local president. The bylaws allowed for either a special election or a committee vote to temporarily fill the slot until general elections. I advocated for the second option on the same grounds I had offered Georgia the previous month.

"You got someone in mind?" asked Hollis Wade.

"I'll be straight up," I said. "There are several qualified people in this room but there are other considerations at stake. There are 115 new hires and most of them are nonunion whites from Alabama. We need them standing with us if we expect to keep taking on this company. Management hired them for a reason, and they're sitting back and waiting to see what we can do about it. We all understand human nature. These folks need to see a leader they can identify with. What do you think?"

"I think we got just the right man sitting right here beside me," said Hollis, pointing at Reverend Donald Vandiver as several heads nodded their approval.

The Reverend immediately stood up. "I thank you for the nomination, Brother Wade, and I'm honored. But what with my duties at the church, my job, my family, and what I already do for the union serving on this committee, I really don't have the time right now . . . so I respectfully decline."

"Keep an open mind, Rev," I said. "We'll talk about it. We can find a way to make this work for you."

I received a phone call from Leo Boyland that evening, inquiring about the status of his arbitration. I told him that we expected a decision soon, and there was nothing we could do but wait.

Leo said that he had relatives in Georgia who were willing to take him in, but he needed twenty dollars for a bus ticket. I asked him for an address where I could send a check.

The next morning, my phone started ringing off the hook with frantic calls from committee members and stewards. Thursday was payday. The company had stopped taking union dues out of the members' checks. I called Bob Knuckles to hear his response.

"We spoke with our attorney and he advised us that while the status quo requires the maintenance of terms and conditions in regard to employees, it does not encompass the administrative relationship between the union and company." He sounded as if he were reading from his notes. "The company does not intend to resume the deduction of union dues until we once again have a contract."

Ted Yeiser no doubt believed this would be a tactical coup de grâce at the bargaining table, leveraging the union's treasury against the economic needs of its members. It might have held sway with some unions but not with us.

I spoke with Ernest, and he assured me that the union was prepared to go as long as necessary without receiving dues from Local 281. We agreed this could even be turned to our advantage. It would show workers that collection of union dues was not our top priority and put me in the unique position of being able to offer a period of free membership to those who remained on the fence. I would continue to present newly signed cards to management as evidence of our growing support.

Negotiations were scheduled to resume the next week on August 22, and Ernest said he would revise his schedule to join me at the table. I got off the phone and typed a leaflet while Colie drew pictures on the floor. A leaflet can sometimes be the most emphatic, credible way to assume a bargaining position with management. Once the union has deliberately and publicly painted itself into a corner, the other side can harbor no illusions (Fig. 5).

It turned out to be a good couple of weeks for my daughter to be in Jackson. I had few meetings of a critical nature and was able to spend most days working with her by my side.

Old union halls make a wonderful play area for small children to explore. There are desk drawers and closets filled with long-forgotten relics and photographs, usually including stamps and official seals from bygone eras. An ink pad that hasn't completely dried out can provide hours of uninterrupted entertainment.

On Saturday afternoon we picked up the leaflets and arrived at the gate to join two stewards in greeting D shift. Colie was becoming a fixture in the community, warmly greeted by many of the workers, including members of management.

When we regrouped at seven, Colie handed me a union card. "A man said to give you this."

"Do you know what it means?" I asked.

"Yes. It means he's in the union now and you're going to fight for him."

I told Colie on Sunday that I was taking her to meet my new friend in Jackson.

"Is she the one you bought the sparkly necklace for?"

"Yes, it is. I hope you like her."

I actually had no idea how Tina would get along with Colie but trusted myself to intervene if things weren't right. We drove to her apartment where we all decided to spend an afternoon in the park.

Tina's natural sweetness came out with Colie, and they hit it off immediately. We played together in the warm sun like three children and then went to dinner.

Negotiations were scheduled for ten on Tuesday morning, but we arrived at nine because Ernest wanted to touch base with the committee. The Reverend pulled me aside at the conference room door and asked if we could talk in private.

"I've been praying about what we discussed last week," he said. "There are going to be times when my obligations with the church conflict with something that the union has scheduled and I'm going to have to put the church first. I'm not sure how that will look to the people and to the rest of the committee. I believe that when a man takes a position he should be prepared to fulfill all of its obligations."

"Look, Rev, everyone respects your spiritual calling and the role you play in the church," I answered. "It's all about helping people in the way your heart leads you to. The way I see it, what you do for the local and for your congregation are two sides of the same coin and part of the same mission. I trust you to follow your guidance and integrity in terms of how you prioritize and juggle your responsibilities. You've done a pretty good job of it so far. The truth is, I'd rather have you as a half-time vice president than any of the others full time."

"Well . . . you'll have me better than half time, I reckon. Where do we go from here?"

"The committee's in the next room. It'll take ten minutes to make it official. So that things look right and everyone's comfortable, how about staying outside till I call you?"

Ernest and the committee were already engaged in animated discussion when I entered the room. I awaited a pause and then interjected. "Last week, Hollis Wade nominated Donald Vandiver to fill the office of acting vice president until elections in December. The Rev has just informed me he is willing to accept the nomination. Does anyone wish to second the nomination at this time?"

Georgia immediately responded, "I second."

"Does anyone wish to make a motion that we vote on the nomination at this time?"

"I so move," said Georgia.

"Can I get a second on that motion?"

All hands rose simultaneously.

"The motion having been made and seconded, all in favor of Donald Vandiver serving as acting vice president please raise your hands."

Every hand was once again visible and it was done. I confirmed that minutes had been taken. Ernest just sat back and watched. He would have kept himself more discreetly in the background under similar circumstances but knew better than to interfere with my moves within a local. He respected momentum and results over methodology.

The Reverend returned to the conference room and was greeted with a standing ovation. He asked that we remain on our feet while he offered a brief prayer. Ernest looked at me and rolled his eyes. I met his gaze but offered no other acknowledgment. He had no use for the formalities of Bible Belt religion and, if anything, saw them as an encumbrance to the union cause.

Bargaining began with a gentlemanly sparring match between Ernest and Ted Yeiser over the deduction of union dues. Both felt the need to get their positions on record, but it was substantively of no value. I tapped Ernest on the arm and told him there was a preliminary matter to address. Complaints had arisen about a new cleaning solvent being used in the Spinning Department that caused employees' eyes to burn and water. I requested the Material Safety Data Sheet.

The union presented and reviewed a small booklet containing slightly modified versions of articles in the Tennessee Textiles contract that had yet to be addressed. Yeiser asked for clarifications until it was time for lunch. We returned on schedule but saw nothing of management for another hour and a half.

Yeiser finally led his group back into the room. He apologized for the delay, saying they had been in a meeting with Dominic Poon that lasted longer than expected.

He handed me a copy of the requested safety data sheet, and I noted the warning regarding eye irritation and need for protection. Before I could speak, he committed to immediately discontinue use of the solvent.

Yeiser spent the next hour reviewing the brief history between American Mills and ACTWU from the company's perspective.

He concluded by stating, "In the interests of demonstrating his good faith, Mr. Poon has instructed me to withdraw all economic proposals which are of a concessionary nature at this time. He is hopeful that the union will reciprocate and withdraw its proposals for wage and benefit increases. Let's see how the new ownership fares and perhaps we can discuss these matters again in the future."

A development of this magnitude required more than an off-the-cuff response, and we requested a caucus.

"What do you think?" Ernest asked the committee.

"I didn't think they would back down that quickly," Georgia replied.

"You made them back down," said Ernest. "Old Pooh Bear, or whatever his name is, thought that y'all would just roll over and play dead like the people who work for his family back home. He didn't know who he was going to be dealing with."

"Does this mean that we should consider taking our own proposal for a raise off the table?" asked the Rev.

"No," said Ernest. "The people at this plant have waited too long for a raise and they won't forgive us if we don't come through. American Mills may be having some cash-flow problems during its start-up phase but the family that owns it is loaded. We might need to show some flexibility about how much we get and when, but we can't come away empty handed."

I summoned management and the session resumed. Ernest expressed the union's recognition of the "significant movement" that had been made but then chided the company: "Dominic Poon should have never approached these workers asking for givebacks in the first place."

On Thursday afternoon, I entered the conference area for a group grievance on behalf of Yarn Prep employees. Apprehension over participating in union activity had been transformed into anticipation, and within a few minutes, the room was filled. Bill Cooper and Bob Knuckles cordially welcomed the group, thanking them for their attendance and interest in improving their department.

For the most part, the issues were a replay of what had been addressed during the Spinning Department meeting a couple of months earlier: broken transport wheels clogged with dust, vacuums needing repair, off-standard conditions compromising earnings, and overloaded jobs. One might think that management could have stolen our thunder by taking some initiative to resolve these simple problems in the remaining areas. As much as they hated grievances, it appeared to be the only thing that provoked action.

The meeting was over by four. As I walked to the exit I heard a voice calling me from behind. "Phil, can I have a word with you?" asked Paul Poston.

I turned back toward him and we shook hands.

"There's a matter which Mr. Poon has requested that I discuss with you." He cleared his throat and continued. "Mr. Poon feels that you're a bright fellow with a lot of initiative and he would like to offer you a job. We're inviting you to become part of our team at American Mills."

This exceeded even my levels of preparedness for the unexpected, and I waited a moment before responding. "I very much appreciate the offer, but I already have a job with an organization to which I'm committed. Even if that weren't a factor, my daughter lives in North Carolina and permanent relocation isn't an option for me. Please convey my appreciation to Mr. Poon and my hopes that we can still build a productive partnership."

I was uncertain whether Poon naïvely believed my loyalties could be purchased, or if this had been a more calculated effort to neutralize and then get rid of me.

I retrieved Colie from the steward who was babysitting and we headed to North Carolina. I wanted to cover as much distance as possible to allow for a full day in the mountains.

We awoke the next morning in a small, privately owned hotel with an overlook of the surrounding hills. Colie wanted to sample more of the attractions in Gatlinburg, so that is where we spent the day.

As we resumed our journey home, we periodically stopped at viewing areas to stretch our legs and take in the scenery. At one location, a small crowd had gathered by the forest's edge. Two bear cubs were frolicking a short distance into the woods. The mother was no doubt present but not visible.

"Do those polar bears bite?" asked Colie.

"Not if we don't try to pet them."

During my absence, the committee distributed a meeting announcement I had prepared (Fig. 6).

CHAPTER 10

I returned to Jackson in time for the union meetings on Wednesday evening. The transition from my peaceful home life to the field was always jarring and a bit disorienting. I had yet to learn the wisdom of arriving the night before an event to realign myself with the environment.

The turnout and energy in the room were impressive as seats quickly filled, and Rick Hardin pulled additional chairs out of storage. Donald opened the meeting with prayer, and I administered his oath of office to the membership's approval. He returned to his seat on the stage and the room became still. I stared at the union members, allowing their silence to perpetuate and swell for nearly a minute, then spoke in a slow and deliberate manner that permeated the hall.

"There has been a major development in contract negotiations." I paused and looked about the room, making fleeting eye contacts. "The company has taken ALL CONCESSIONS OFF THE TABLE!!"

The people roared with one voice, standing as they applauded as if to shake the rafters of the old building. It was exhilarating and yet humbling to be present in the face of such an ovation, having offered the thrill of victory to a multitude that had always been downtrodden and disempowered.

I waited for the acclamation to run its course and then continued. "The wages and benefits that you fought so hard to win and even harder to keep are now secure. But we're not done! How many people in this room think that it's time for a raise?"

There was once again applause with shouts of agreement. A middle-aged man ignored the rules of order and rose without being recognized. "What I wants to know, is how much are we gonna GET!?"

"If I knew the answer to that, it would mean I was crooked and had already made a secret deal with the company, and it wasn't going to be much," I responded. "The answer lies more in your hands than in mine. You have the power! You all remembered how to stick together and the company has backed down more times in the past few months than it has in the last ten years. If we can keep the faith and stay strong, and get some of these new hires to stand with us, we'll end up with a raise you can take to the bank and be proud of!"

I reviewed the major grievances and then opened the floor for commentary.

An hour later, I did my best to repeat the process as if doing it for the first time.

I arrived at Tina's apartment at seven the next evening. We hadn't had a chance to spend time alone since before Colie's visit, and I was looking forward to seeing her. I knocked on her door, but there was no answer. I waited a few moments and knocked again, this time a bit louder. The door cracked and then opened.

"Oh, it's you," she said.

"Who were you expecting?" I asked.

"It's no thing," she replied, turning her back and walking inside. She made her way to the kitchen where she had been washing dishes and continued as if I weren't there.

"Where do you want to eat tonight?" I inquired.

She didn't seem to hear me over the running water so I repeated myself.

"Where do I want to eat? Where do I want to eat? I'm not hungry," she replied.

"Well, I've been in meetings all day and I am."

Tina turned off the faucet and wiped her hands on her jeans. "OK, I'll come along and watch you eat."

We drove in silence to the nearby restaurant where we had previously dined and service was fast. "Are you sure you don't want anything?" I asked after we were seated.

"I already told you I'm not goddamn hungry, alright," she said with a sharp edge in her voice. "How'm I doin'? Are you hungry? Why aren't you hungry? Why the hell don't you get off my case? Why you think you always have to be so nice to me?"

"I care about you, that's all."

"Why? What you want with my black ass anyway? You think you're gonna turn me into someone who's gonna help you with all this union shit? You think you're going to turn me into a shop stewardess or something? Let me tell you something. I don't give a damn about any of this motherfuckin' union shit. The only reason I signed a card is because my daddy's in the union. I works hard and when I'm done, all I want to do is have a good time."

"Are we having a good time yet?" I asked.

"Fuck this shit. I'm leaving." She shoved her chair back with a screech and headed for the door.

I caught up with her. "I'll drive you back and get dinner later."

"Whatever . . ."

Tina exited my car in silence and walked to her apartment. I had no idea what had provoked her outburst but this obviously wasn't the time to pursue it.

There is a common misperception that unions are businesses that solicit members to profit from dues revenue. In truth, the Internal Revenue Service classifies unions as nonprofit organizations similar to charities. Both are chartered to perform a service but cannot function effectively without resources.

Federal law regulates the collective bargaining process, but individual states define the criteria for union membership. Half of them provide for "closed shops" in which all employees at union facilities are required to become members. Everyone receives the fruits of union wages, benefits, and protection, so each person is obliged to contribute.

The others have right-to-work laws and are home to some of the lowest paid workforces in the nation. The statutes mandate that every employee in a union shop is entitled to equal representation but membership is voluntary. The sole intent is to weaken unions and limit their presence. It simply costs more money to represent locals with partial membership than is collected in dues. The Southern Region of ACTWU couldn't have survived without subsidies from the national union.

The most immediate impact of local membership on the lives of union workers is that it affects bargaining leverage. Companies incessantly review membership percentage as part of their labor strategy, regarding it as an indicator of the union's influence and ability to mobilize employees.

Labor Day was a paid holiday under the contract, and management announced that the plant would stand on Sunday and Monday for cleanup
and maintenance. This was a perfect opportunity to find workers from
all shifts at home and hopefully relaxed. I planned to spend each of the
next several days visiting nonmembers from specific departments, accompanied by stewards from their areas. On Friday morning I picked up
Vernette Chandler at her house and began with the Spinning Department.

Vernette was a soft-spoken, unpresumptuous woman in her thirties
who worked on C shift and had become increasingly involved as the campaign progressed. She remained confident and levelheaded under pressure but lacked the dynamic presence and motivation that leads to higher
office. She helped me navigate the narrow residential streets lined with
old mill houses, and twisting mazes of country backroads within which
I could have disappeared and become lost forever without guidance.

We were equipped with house-calling sheets prepared by the union's
clerical staff. In addition to name and address, they listed job, seniority,
age, gender, and race. Reviewing the information before a visit gave us
some sense of what to expect.

In the rural South, it was much easier to approach black workers.
Some hadn't yet joined because they were holding on to prior resentments or simply taking advantage of what they considered free benefits.
It was rare to find someone with genuinely antiunion sentiments.

White employees, especially among the new hires, were offspring of
a more conservative paradigm. A significant number had grown up in
sharecroppers' cabins and joined their parents in the field at an early age.
To them, finding a job in a textile mill was like having their ship come
in. Many saw no reason to join black coworkers in what they viewed as
a radical organization, engaged in a struggle against the employer that
had given them an opportunity.

On Saturday, Harvey Thaxton and I knocked on the doors of card room
employees. Though sharing a common income bracket their lifestyles
varied significantly.

We parked in a driveway adjoining a neatly manicured lawn and
were ushered into a modest suburban home, well maintained with nice
furniture. The husband and wife both worked multiple jobs, were frugal
with their money, and abstinent of vice. Their values and self worth were

deeply invested in their small niche within the American dream. Ten minutes after departing, we found ourselves in a dingy walk-up apartment smelling of mold and rotten garbage, with several boisterous, unwashed children running about as their father sat unshaven at a kitchen table littered with empty beer bottles.

Following a short drive beyond the city limits, we searched for an address within a crowded trailer park and eventually came to meet a family of limited means who did their best to maintain a decent and sanitary environment.

People shared their thoughts on God's vengeance, the glories of hunting, and how they had nearly committed a felony the last time their supervisor disrespected them. But mostly, they talked about living from paycheck to paycheck, wanting to know if the union was going to get them a raise and, if so, how much.

A liberal idealist turned organizer might have spoken passionately about politics and social justice, incurring the contempt of his audience without even knowing it. I simply empathized with a sincerity born of my own experience. I told folks that while it was unrealistic to expect a life-changing amount of money from one set of negotiations, like winning a sweepstakes, I would fight like hell to put every cent possible into their pockets.

I'd decided to hold back and allow Tina a cooling-off period, having long since learned the futility of trying to reason with a moody person while still upset. It was better to wait out the storm.

I returned home that evening and was preparing dinner when the phone rang. "Was' sup? You don't call me no more . . ." a voice whispered.

"I thought you might need some space. I didn't want to pressure you."

"I just get like that sometimes. You shouldn't pay it no mind."

"Do you want to come over tonight?"

"OK. I'll be there."

I ate dinner, watched a movie (interrupted by three phone calls), and was about to wash up and retire when there was a knock on the door. I thought better of asking Tina why she was so late and invited her in, restraining my impulse to offer a hug until I could assess her disposition. It was often best to give her some distance until she decided to move closer.

I met Georgia in front of her small church at noon on Sunday. Though Weaving remained the strongest department in terms of both membership and participation, much of this was concentrated on the day shifts.

Night-shift employees tend to exercise seniority and transfer to daytime as vacancies arise within their job classifications. Comparatively few long-term employees remain permanently on night crews unless motivated by a second job or nocturnal nature. There is a smaller pool from which to develop seasoned officers, who in turn provide knowledgeable representation and encourage membership. Supervisors are often more liberal with petty abuses during graveyard hours when senior management isn't present.

The holiday weekend provided a unique opportunity to find both C and D shift workers at home and awake on the same day. Georgia knew her way through the labyrinth of country roads. She had also grown up as a sharecropper, picking cotton since the age of six. She was a dynamic and compelling spokesperson, often jumping in and taking the lead. My primary function was to secure a signed card as the discussion ended.

Reverend Donald Vandiver was good enough to sacrifice his Labor Day to accompany me. I had also arranged for him to have union leave on Tuesday so we could spend two days focusing on new hires from all departments.

The better I got to know Donald, the more I liked him. Just beneath the Reverend's exterior lived a salty, knock-around guy who had seen life from many different perspectives. During his younger years he had walked a path with one foot on either side of the law until finding his religious calling. He offered no pretense or apologies for his past but rather embraced it with the understanding that it brought wisdom and dimension to his ministry.

Donald had a beautiful young wife and four children. He earned his living in the Carding Department, preaching on Sunday mornings and Wednesday evenings to a small rural congregation. He was on call to both members of Local 281 and his parishioners. This was a man with a deep sense of conviction and responsibility, interlaced with a fun-loving nature and wild side.

As we threaded our way through city streets and down country roads, our conversations moved seamlessly between matters of philosophy and religion to women and street fighting. He was sufficiently comfortable with himself and his faith to not require bolstering with pompous airs and judgment. I was surprised and delighted to discover that he could fluently cross-reference prophecies from Nostradamus and Revelation.

Donald made the perfect partner with whom to visit this segment of the workforce. He was from a similar background and instinctively knew how and when to play the reverend card. If we encountered resistance, he would interject with statements such as: "Ma'am, I'm not just the vice president of my local, I'm a reverend. If I didn't believe in what I was saying before Almighty God, I wouldn't be standing here talking to you." It always resonated and was sometimes a turning point in the discussion.

On other occasions, Donald assumed the religious perspective for purely ingenuous reasons. If someone revealed they were suffering from illness or personal tragedy, he would switch gears to pray with them for twenty minutes and even employ the laying on of hands. The people I worked for would have been embarrassed by these displays and counseled Donald to reserve his spiritual activities for the church. I was impressed by the dexterity and humanity with which he moved between his two realms of service.

The Alabama-raised mill workers would be a tough nut to crack, having come from a true vestige of the Old South. Paul Poston and Ted Yeiser had selected their hiring pool well. I couldn't maximize the potential of Local 281 without getting at least some of them on board.

We spoke with a lean and muscular loom fixer who told us, "I have a cousin who works in the coal mines of West Virginia. I understand the need for unions there, with all the safety hazards and mine cave-ins. But I don't think there's any need for a union in a place like a textile mill."

I talked with him about numerous safety violations we had corrected during the past few months and how much less money he would now be making if the union hadn't blocked the concessions, but to no avail. I might as well have suggested that he convert to a new religion.

We knocked at the apartment of a woman who hysterically burst into tears a minute into our presentation. "What's wrong, Ma'am?" asked the Rev. "Did we say something that offended you?"

"No," she wailed. "It's just that my brother was killed in a union strike in Michigan back in 1964, and this brings it all back up."

"Which union was it?" I asked.

"The Teamsters," she replied with tears still streaming down her face.

"Well, we're not them and this is a different time and place," I said, "but we understand your feelings and are sorry for what you went through."

We bid her good day and moved on. Neither prayer nor solidarity would be of any use in this situation.

This was a far different dynamic than speaking with long-term employees who preferred to receive the benefits of representation without the responsibilities of membership, or were holding on to an affront by their shop steward from five years ago. We were in a process of education where eroding stereotypes and creating goodwill translated into a successful visit, even without a signed card. After two ten-hour days, we came away with six new members, while many others were at least left questioning their preconceptions.

Bob Knuckles called on the morning of September 11, asking to meet off the record and offering to include Georgia.

I arrived at his office a few hours later, while Georgia was still making her way up from the weave room. Knuckles sat behind his desk, leaning so far back on his reclining chair that I wondered if his enormous weight would cause it to tip over. I had the impression that he was not only comfortable with his girth but that it gave him a sense of power and masculinity.

A voice at the door said, "hey hey," and Georgia entered the room.

"I have a sensitive matter to discuss with you," he said. "I need your assurances that what gets said in this room stays in this room for now. If you disagree with anything I say, I don't want to see it plastered all over some leaflet tomorrow."

"You've got our word," I replied. "We're off the record."

Knuckles cleared his throat and explained that sales were falling far short of projections and the new company's cash-flow situation was rapidly deteriorating. He said that management wanted to consolidate the workforce into three eight-hour shifts working six days a week, and eliminate the twelve-hour crews.

"We're kind of between a rock and a hard place," Knuckles continued. "We can't do this without the union's support or we'll violate the status quo. Phil, I really need your help on this one."

"How critical is your need?" I asked.

"It's very critical, or else we wouldn't be sitting here talking like this. We're nearing the threshold where our costs are going to exceed the extent of our bank loans and operating budget."

"Why?" I asked. "What's really going on? You guys started a new company four months ago by investing millions of dollars in equipment and adding over a hundred jobs. How could things have gone downhill so quickly?"

Knuckles leaned forward and rested his elbows on the desk. "For the record, I wasn't part of starting the new company. I'm just one of the newly hired employees. All I can tell you at this point is that we've fallen far short of our business plan, and there needs to be some immediate damage control."

Multiple scenarios raced through my mind as I stared back without expression. Seniority would govern the transfer of twelve-hour employees to the expanded eight-hour crews. Their earnings would actually increase, with at least one day of overtime scheduled on a weekly basis. The workers subject to layoff as a consequence would all be new hires, catapulting the local's membership to way over 50 percent. While I felt bad for anyone who'd relocated in response to a job offer, only to be released within a matter of months, based on what I was hearing a workforce reduction seemed inevitable.

I stepped outside the office with Georgia for a brief caucus and returned.

"How quickly does this need to happen?" I asked Knuckles.

"Time is of the essence. The sooner the better."

"Then here's what we need to do. Georgia and I are prepared to recommend this to the rest of our committee before negotiations tomorrow. Once they're on board, I'll schedule a union meeting, recommend it to the membership, and put it to a vote.

"What you're proposing represents a radical change in people's lives, especially in terms of childcare arrangements and second jobs. This is the best I can offer. I can't join you in implementing such a sweeping change without a mandate."

Knuckles expressed his appreciation and said he understood our constraints.

"I'd like to help you pull this off," I said. "I think it would be useful if the discussion could include alternative start and stop times for the shifts."

"I believe that Paul would be flexible on that point."

Negotiations had been scheduled for 9:30 the next morning. I arrived a few minutes early and told Ted Yeiser I would need some time with the committee to discuss the eight-hour shifts. The committee members stared at me in silence for over a minute after I shared the details of the meeting with Knuckles.

Finally, Donald Vandiver spoke up. "How do we know this isn't just something the company is saying to get what they want from us? The new owners came in here a few months ago with millions of dollars to throw around. Where did it all go? I don't trust these people."

"I don't trust them either, Rev," I answered. "The thing is, it's more than just talk. A company doesn't change its entire shift structure and lay off workers it hired a few months ago just to make a point. The cost of doing something like that, if business conditions demanded the opposite, would outweigh the gains.

"I'm not saying that we back off any of our bargaining positions. On the contrary, if the company is having cash-flow problems, we should do what's necessary to help them conserve and hope there's something left over for a raise."

Georgia reminded the committee that the plant hadn't run during the past three Sundays and that, according to her supervisor, the trend was likely to continue. "The twelve-hour people can't make it on thirty-six hours a week," she said. "I know I can't. Forty-eight hours with time and a half on Saturday sounds a whole lot better to me."

Percy Ray Long had remained on the bargaining committee but offered little input since resigning as president. But now he shared his thoughts. "I've been dealing with this company longer than any of y'all. I've seen owners come and go, one after the other. No one's ever been able to make a go of this sorry plant. I'm personally not surprised by any of this. I think we need to do whatever to keep this place running and try to get a raise. . . but the members deserve the last word."

The committee voted unanimously to recommend the proposal and schedule a vote on Friday. Georgia located the management team and invited them back into the conference room.

Ted Yeiser conveyed his gratitude to the union for its willingness to assist. I reminded him that we couldn't make any promises beyond a meeting and recommendation, then requested as much detail as possible regarding the underlying reasons.

"There are, of course, many variables at play in the start-up of a new business," he explained. "Textiles are an especially cyclical business and customer demand cannot always be accurately forecast. Unfortunately, our sales to date have fallen far short of expectations and we're getting close to the point of not having sufficient revenue to adequately service our debt."

"Do you think, to put it bluntly," I asked, "that Dominic Poon overextended his position and was too aggressive in his initial hiring strategy?"

"I'm not saying all that," Yeiser responded. "I'm simply saying that the company is presently challenged by a disappointing return on investment."

Glancing around the table, I noticed Knuckles shaking his head and exhaling as he took notes. I knew two things on a gut level. We were being told the truth—but not the full story behind it. I would endeavor to unravel the situation through backdoor channels.

Yeiser apologized that he had to catch a mid-afternoon flight out of Memphis and asked that we work through lunch. He suggested it would be a waste of everyone's time to further discuss economics until the company had greater clarity regarding its level of solvency. It was difficult to refute that logic, so we devoted our attention to bridging gaps in some of the contract articles.

After taking the committee to a late lunch, I returned home to prepare the meeting announcement (Fig. 7).

I decided to surprise Tina during her dinner break and offer another chance to return with me to North Carolina over the weekend. I needed to know whether or not to book a flight for myself.

I found Tina outside on the lawn, taking in the pleasant September night. She broke into a big smile when she heard me call and walked to the gate. I tossed over a bag with two burgers and fries. "You trying to fatten me up so no other guys will look at me?"

"You got me all figured out."

"You do try to treat me good," she whispered, leaning her body against the fence. Our lips met through the chain-link and I felt hers open soft and wide as they did when she was willing. We kissed for several minutes and I felt her fingers reach through the fence and touch between my legs. At that moment, I wanted her more than life itself.

We both stepped back a few inches and looked at each other, breathing heavily.

"Listen," I said. "There's going to be a union meeting on Friday and after that, I'm leaving for home. If you want to come to the hall, I could be there with my bags packed and you can come with me."

"I'd love to come with you," she smiled. "But how about you just pick me up at my place when you're done with the meetings?"

I returned to my car feeling optimistic, but mused to myself that Tina always seemed to be at her sweetest and most receptive when there was a chain-link fence between us.

The voting process on the janitor issue extended through the next two days. Employees from the various departments were assigned staggered report times to the conference room so that partial operations could continue.

On Thursday evening, Georgia and I presided over the counting of ballots. Workers surprised everyone by voting to dispense with the contracted janitorial service and return jobs to the bargaining unit. After making a good first impression, the outside agency had apparently become slack and allowed conditions in the canteens and restrooms to deteriorate.

I returned home and discovered a message from Leo Boyland, once again inquiring about the status of his arbitration. He answered when I called his number. We had yet to hear from the arbitrator, whose response was now several weeks overdue. I explained that trying to pressure someone who held full and final authority wasn't a good idea.

Leo had found a job at a poultry plant in rural Georgia, where one of the national brands cut and packaged chicken parts. It was a long way down the social ladder from a machine operator at a union facility, but at least he was no longer on the street. It appeared that he was doomed to remain in this exile pending a favorable outcome to his case.

"They hold back the first two weeks of my pay, and I'm not getting any money until the end of the month. Do you think you could send me something to get by until then? I'll pay you back when I get my settlement. . . . I promise."

I agreed to put forty dollars in the mail the next day. I felt genuinely sorry for the guy. He hadn't brought this on himself.

Turnout was heavy on Friday evening at both the 5:00 and 6:00 p.m. union meetings as the agenda directly impacted everyone's life. The response to the eight-hour shift proposal was mostly positive. Employees on the rotating twelve-hour shifts had relied on working every other Sunday (paid at time and a half) to maintain earnings and meet expenses. The transition to eight-hour shifts was seen as an opportunity to restore and perhaps increase income levels.

While the issue didn't directly impact workers already on eight-hour crews, they supported the interests of their fellow union members and what was presented as an opportunity to help keep the plant viable without taking anything out of their pockets.

Due to the unexpected and hurried nature of the process, the vote was taken by a show of hands. Workers accepted the eight-hour shifts and then chose to maintain the existing start times, beginning with first shift at 6:00 a.m.

As I drove to Tina's apartment, I contemplated that the past week had borne redemption to the promise of union workers having a voice in regard to their working conditions which is unparalleled in other environments.

I arrived at her door by 7:30 as arranged, knocked, and was greeted with silence. I stood there for a minute. I could hear the voices of a couple screaming at each other in an adjacent unit. I tried again, this time with repeated rapping, but there was no response.

"Fuck this," I said to myself as I got back in my car and headed into the night toward my real home.

CHAPTER 11

I spent two days with my daughter, taking her to the zoo in Asheboro on Monday instead of day care, and then dropped her at her mom's apartment. When I asked if she was ready for another trip to Jackson, Colie replied, "Not this time, Daddy. Ask me next time. Is that OK?"

I assured her that it was, saying that I missed her when I was away but wanted her to do whatever made her happy. Commuting on business trips to Tennessee was a stretch for a little girl, and I was careful not to push past her comfort levels. Workers aren't the only ones who deserve a voice in their circumstances.

I headed west the next day, stopping for the night in the mountain town of Cherokee. I called Georgia from the hotel room to get a sense of what might be in store on my return. She told me the company had posted an announcement that the eight-hour shifts would go into effect on October 2.

I spent several hours the next day on a leisurely drive through the mountains, gradually winding my way back to I-40 east of Knoxville. I saw a sign for "Clingmans Dome," advertising it as the highest point in the Smoky Mountains. I drove up a long and narrow entrance road, parked, and then continued by foot until I was standing atop a rocky plateau overlooking the mountain range. I stared down through the wispy cloud cover to a clear view of endless summits sprawling below. It was worth the detour and what would be a very late arrival back in Jackson.

Second- and third-step grievances were scheduled for the following afternoon. Bob Knuckles called me beforehand and asked if I could arrive early for a private meeting.

Once I had taken my customary seat across from his desk, he unceremoniously declared, "I wanted to give you a heads-up that the company has suspended its plans to convert to an eight-hour operation until further notice."

He explained that senior management had decided on a different strategy involving significant changes in style and product lines, which required continuation of the existing schedule.

"Give me a fucking break!" I said, unable to constrain myself. "You've got to be kidding! I put out a leaflet supporting this move, stand up in front of the membership and recommend it, put it to a vote on your timetable . . . and now you've changed your mind?!

"This is going to make us all look like a bunch of fucking idiots. People actually liked the idea and got their hopes up. The last thing either of us needs now is for folks to once again feel disappointed and let down. I put my credibility way out on a limb for you guys and got left hung out to dry."

Knuckles exhaled, shook his head, and spoke softly. "I'm as fed up with this shit as you are. The best I could do was clue you in so that you and the committee wouldn't get caught completely off guard."

"Let's talk off the record," I suggested. "If you want my continued cooperation I need to know what's really going on. You have my word that I won't share anything and that what you tell me will remain confidential."

"It is confidential. If you breathe a word of what I tell you, it'll mean my job."

I restated my assurances as Knuckles stared past me toward the wall. "It all comes down to the Sulzer looms," he finally said. "This particular model was designed to be attached to concrete floors, not the old wooden floors we have here. The level of vibration is interfering with our quality and efficiency. We had the customers lined up. The problem is, we either can't make deadline or the orders get rejected because of defects. Our warehouse is overflowing with truckloads of returned inventory.

"We've actually increased efficiencies with the old looms, but the business they generate isn't enough to meet payroll costs, let alone service our debt."

"Unbelievable," I said. "Do you mind telling me who was responsible for inspecting these looms and making the recommendation to buy?"

Knuckles paused and looked me in the eye. "Derald Gilmer."

"You mean, after all his huffing and puffing, he's the one who finally brought the house down?"

"Well, the final decision was Paul's, but he relied heavily on Derald's experience and expertise with weaving equipment."

"So, what's plan B?"

"The operations team has been meeting round the clock. They think they've identified certain products that require lower grades of cloth that hopefully can be manufactured on our Sulzer looms within customer specs. But given the production cycles, and interaction between the different departments required to run these styles, we need to keep our present shift configuration.

"The owners are also making discreet inquiries behind the scenes to see if they can secure additional funding by bringing in new investors. Now you know everything I do. Look, Phil, I haven't always agreed with your methods or your message to the workers . . . but I've come to believe that your word is good. If any of what I just told you gets out, there'll be somebody else sitting behind this desk next week."

I sincerely thanked Knuckles for his candor and reassured him of my discretion. "You've got to understand one thing," I told him. "I've got to disassociate myself and the union from this decision-making process. You're going to see a leaflet that's more in keeping with the tone of a few months ago, rather than where we seem to have recently taken the relationship. Your superiors aren't going to like it. Maybe you can spin my response to them in a way they can relate to. This is frankly a business decision I have to make."

I glanced at the clock and saw that it was time for the grievance meetings. I shook Knuckles' hand and walked down the hall to the conference room.

The committee members greeted the news as warmly as I had. For those on the twelve-hour crews, it wasn't just a matter of credibility but of their own paychecks. No matter how hard-hitting my message was, they could expect with certainty to get blamed by some of their coworkers.

"Do you think this is something the company had planned from the beginning, to make the union look bad?" asked Georgia.

"No I don't," I said. "Sometimes this job comes down to street sense and knowing how to read between the lines. I believe that Knuckles was being straight up. The business really is in trouble and the new owners are going crazy looking for a way out."

Cooper and Knuckles knocked on the closed door. We spent the next two hours in a fairly routine grievance meeting involving disputed write-ups, job-bidding issues, and the impact of substandard equipment on earnings.

The next day Bill Cooper responded affirmatively in writing to all but one of the cases. He concluded his answers by stating, "Our intent is for all members of management to listen, answer, handle, and solve problems." This was a far cry from his "we'll look into it" responses back in June.

The infrastructure of the local had been transformed, membership levels were responding, and a productive bargaining relationship was being forged with a difficult employer. If the company could survive its present crisis, I envisioned a successful conclusion to the project by year's end.

I left the mill and returned to the union hall to write a damage-control leaflet (Fig. 8).

Realizing that the new hires were fated to remain with us, I requested that Donald Vandiver be excused for union business on Tuesday and Wednesday to make house calls.

Percy hadn't been present at the recent grievance meeting, and I called him that evening to ask why. He told me his doctor had placed him on long-term medical leave and apologized for not having advised me. "You had best find someone to take my place on the committee until I return," he suggested.

I had lost track of Tina's work schedule, but it seemed time to give her a call.

"Hey, what's up," she answered the phone casually, as if nothing was amiss.

I decided to ease into our discussion. "How you doing?'

"It's all good. You?"

"I'm OK, just really busy. There's a lot of new shit going on at the plant. The company just told me they're canceling the change to eight hours."

"That's fine with me. I likes my night shift. Work twelve hours, get it all over with, and then have a few days off. I'm OK with that."

"You were supposed to meet me last Friday night to come back to North Carolina with me. You weren't there again. What's going on?"

"Oh, I'm sorry about that. . . . I was over at my sister's, playing with my little nephew, and we just got to talking . . ."

"Look, just be straight up. Is there some reason why you don't want to come home with me? If there is, just tell me. I'll understand. I ain't about pressuring people to do something they don't want. I just thought you'd enjoy being on the road and seeing where I live."

The other end of the line went silent. After about thirty seconds, I called her name gently and then again a bit louder.

"It's just that some of the girls I work with . . ." She paused. "They say if I come home with you, your white friends are going to get one look at me and then tar and feather my black ass and run me out of town."

"Do you really believe that's what I'm about?"

"No, not you. I know you're not like that. But that don't mean your white friends aren't."

"Do you think that someone like me would be friends with racists like that?"

Tina thought for a moment. "I don't know. Sometimes you don't think peoples is a certain way until they show it. I don't think I'd be too popular back where you're from."

I knew she was finally being sincere and there would be no dissuading her, having come to the realization that Tina was not one to challenge her fundamental beliefs and conditioning.

I told her the offer would always be open and asked if she wanted to get together. She said this wasn't a good night and asked me to call her the beginning of the week.

On Saturday I drove to the printer to pick up the leaflet. The owner greeted me warmly as I'd become the most significant client his business had ever serviced.

I treated myself to lunch at the Ramada on the way back. Once seated at a table, waves of exhaustion overtook me and my perception blurred, as often happened when I hit the pause button and my body allowed itself a brief opportunity to rest. With the help of a sandwich washed down by several cups of coffee, I jammed myself back into overdrive and met three stewards at the plant gate to leaflet B and D shifts.

My Sunday schedule was empty, and by evening I was going out of my mind with boredom and loneliness. Many organizers would have long since chosen a bar as their local refuge, but my abstinence excluded me from the prevailing medium for social interaction in this culture. I decided to try Tina.

"Do you want to get together?" I asked.

"Yes," she replied without elaborating.

"What do you wanna do?"

"I'm working tomorrow, but you could take me for a walk in the park before my shift. I likes going to the park with you and being outside."

I only had a meeting with Bob Knuckles and some phone calls on my calendar, so I agreed.

The next afternoon I stood with Tina next to a rock overhang with the autumn sun shining upon us. The weather was beginning to cool, and she was wearing a faded denim jacket and jeans, with a slinky black tank top underneath, revealing several inches of her waist. I couldn't help glancing at her cleavage and following the skin up her chest and slender neck to flowing dark curls brushing her shoulders.

"How come you're not wearing the necklace I got you?" I asked.

"I lost it gambling," she replied without hesitation.

I didn't believe her but decided to play along. "What game were you into?"

"I was shooting craps."

I'd learned the wisdom of not challenging deliberate falsehoods as that only leads to further lies. It's better to feign belief and leave the ground fertile for future revelations.

It was obvious that Tina felt conflicted about our relationship. I had brought a new and larger reality crashing into hers, and it made her uncomfortable. Tina knew how to survive the grim circumstances of real life in ways the affluent world traveler could never imagine, but her view of the horizon was far more limited.

She was used to being appreciated for sex and otherwise gruffly dominated. In the beginning, my attention was flattering and a turn-on, but my efforts to behave like a gentleman triggered only confusion. When a person's fundamental identity is steeped in shame, it inevitably causes them to question the motives, and even worth, of someone who regards them as an equal.

Tina was my only avenue for occasional comfort and a fledgling social life while assigned to "Jupiter's Moon." I decided to take a few steps
back emotionally and see what happened.

We had a pleasant walk in which nothing significant was shared,
and I dropped her at the plant in time for her to report and me to leaflet. As we sat in the parking lot, I asked when she wanted to hang out
again.

"I traded shifts with one of the girls on D crew, so I'm not working
on Wednesday. I'll come to your place."

I knew better than to ask what time.

Donald Vandiver and I met at the union hall the next morning to resume
our visits to the predominantly white employees who had been hired
in June. As always, I thoroughly enjoyed the Rev's company. He was a
complex man of unexpected contradictions, and we continued to share
our experiences and philosophies about many areas of life.

"Did you know that Jackson, Tennessee, was made famous by Hollywood?" he asked as we tried to find our way through a network of neighborhood streets. "Did you ever see the movie *Walking Tall*?"

"Yes, I did. You mean the one about Sheriff Buford Pusser, right? It's
a great movie. I've seen it several times."

"Well," said the Rev, "the actual events depicted in the movie took
place in the county just south of here, but the movie was filmed in Jackson.
Those courthouse scenes, they were shot at the Jackson courthouse."

(The 1973 movie was based on the true story of a newly elected sheriff who battled organized crime and political malfeasance in one of the
most corrupt areas of Tennessee. He had been beaten and shot, his wife
killed in an assassination attempt, but he refused to back down and ultimately prevailed.)

"Did you ever meet Buford Pusser?" I asked.

"Everyone from my generation who grew up in these parts has rec-
ollections of Sheriff Pusser," Donald answered. "I remember one time
I was sitting in my parked car when the sheriff came rolling down the
street in his patrol vehicle on the other side. There was this gang of about
five young men who started cat-calling after him and making insults.
Sheriff Pusser pulled over, got out of his car, and whooped the snot out
of all of them. That was the only way to get respect around here."

"Did he really clean up the county, like the movie showed?" I asked.

"He locked up his share of scoundrels for sure, and things did seem to change around here . . . at least for awhile."

We parked in the driveway of a small mill house and rang the doorbell. A man in his thirties, broad shouldered and wearing a sleeveless white T-shirt and torn jeans, answered.

"Who the fuck do y'all think you are, coming to my house?" he screamed.

"I'll have you know, sir," said Donald, "that I'm a reverend and take offense at your language."

"I didn't know that," the man said in lower tones. "I apologize for cussing . . . but y'all still better git off my porch, now, before I come out there."

"Take note, sir, that we're not afraid of you . . . but we'll honor your wishes and leave. You missed out on some information that would have been important to you whether or not you chose to join the union," Donald calmly replied as we turned away.

After lunch, Donald led me to a section of Jackson, far removed from the major thoroughfares, of which I hadn't been aware. He suggested that we park on the outskirts and enter the neighborhood on foot.

"There's no telling what will be left of your car if we park beyond this point," he advised.

"What is this place?" I asked as we got out and locked the doors.

"It's sort of like the white ghetto of Jackson. You name it, it goes on here. Even the police are afraid to enter this neighborhood after dark."

I stared down the road past a stone wall into a community of small wooden houses interspersed with trailers.

"Are you sure you want to do this?" Donald asked. "There's no telling what we're in for."

"If folks who work at the plant live here, then we can't avoid it."

It was a brisk and sunny autumn day, and we were both wearing dark colored windbreakers and sunglasses as we walked down narrow streets with cracked pavement, looking for our first address. We knocked several times but there was no response. The employee sheet was shuffled to the bottom of our pile and we continued our search for the next person.

My experiences in New York had given me the instincts to sense the potential for crime and violence on a city street. It was unrelated to anything witnessed or heard, but rather a feeling based on intangibles. I was on high alert and poised to react. We were out of place in terrain where it was best to remain invisible.

We knocked on the door of a trailer, positioned at a random angle to the adjoining residences, but again there was no response. We continued on and encountered the same result at several more addresses. Despite open curtains and cars in the driveway, our overtures were greeted with dead silence.

We stood atop a small wooden porch gazing about and saw that the streets had become empty. The several teenagers who'd been loitering on a street corner had disappeared. Suddenly, Donald burst into a wide grin. "They think we're the doggone FBI or state police," he said. "Look at how we're both dressed, shades and all, knocking on doors like we own the place. The word's gone out and everyone is laying low. Nobody's going to talk with us today."

"You're right. Let's get out of here."

Ernest called me that night around nine. He explained that Bruce Raynor had a longstanding relationship with Frank Gress, a minority owner of Tennessee Textiles, and now American Mills, through the investment firm in which he was a partner. We were moving into the era of leveraged buyouts and corporate mergers, and it was important for someone at Bruce's level to have connections with the players.

Frank Gress had contacted the southern regional director, wishing to discuss the company's financial situation and negotiations. An off-the-record meeting with Gress and Dominic Poon was scheduled at the Nashville airport on Friday morning, and my presence was required.

Donald and I reconnected the next day to continue our rounds. We slogged through one visit after another, but the Rev's impeccable knowledge of nooks and crannies within the city and surrounding counties, and the shortcuts between them, contributed to our efficiency. By midday I was confident we had crossed a critical threshold and achieved majority status within Local 281.

We shared stories from our younger days when we had both flirted with the other side of the law. It made for an interesting study in contrasts between urban and rural environments, with the commonalities of violence and betrayal.

"I came real close a couple of times to getting hauled off by the collar into one of Buford Pusser's pokeys," said the Rev. "All I can say is that the Good Lord had me chosen for a higher calling and kept me from harm's way."

I confided how trapped I'd felt during my fourteen years as a taxi and bus driver. I would spend hours fantasizing about robbing a bank, planning it down to every detail and contingency, much as I now organized a campaign. I told him that in the final analysis I always decided against it because I knew enough to realize that the rewards didn't justify the risk.

"The Lord was looking out for you too, my friend," he said. "He also had you in mind for better things."

Shortly after nine o'clock that evening, there was a soft tapping on my door. "Who is it?" I instinctively shouted.

"Who you think?" I heard Tina answer.

We embraced briefly as she entered my living room, and then she turned and walked into the kitchen, sitting at the table. Tina reached into her purse and, smiling, held up two large joints in the palm of her hand. Usually radiant with a perfect complexion, her face showed signs of fatigue, and her eyes were bloodshot.

She asked me for a match and lit one of the sticks. The embers glowed on one end as she inhaled the smoke slowly and deeply into her lungs. She waited a few seconds and then released her breath, the thick cloud of fumes swirling about my head.

Tina held the joint up to me as she gazed in my eyes.

"You know I don't," I said quietly, "but you go ahead. I'm cool with that."

"Your loss. This some good shit." She drew another long breath of smoke.

She finished the joint in silence, returned the other to her purse, and walked into the bedroom. The swaying of her hips from behind made me forget everything except how much I desired her.

I made a brief detour to the bathroom to freshen up, then approached the bed by the dim light of a small lamp, seeing Tina's clothes scattered about the floor. She was lying face down beneath the blankets, fast asleep. The next morning I awoke to find the covers drawn back and an empty house.

I planned to spend the night at a hotel near the Nashville airport to meet Bruce Raynor and Mark Pitt as they arrived early the next morning for the off-the-record.

I lacked one item in my wardrobe, and that was a tie. It would be many years before business casual hastened the decline of the men's clothing industry. The other players would be dressed for business, and I needed to look the part.

I had a sharp-looking blue pinstripe suit that I sometimes wore to contract negotiations, but without a tie, perhaps reflecting a lingering ambivalence I still felt toward the corporate world in which I was now a participant. It was time to take the last step in the transformation of my attire.

I had become a regular customer at the JC Penny in Jackson, as I continued to explore and upgrade other parts of my wardrobe. I donned the suit jacket over a button-down shirt, visited the store, and sought out a salesman with whom I'd previously done business.

"Ah, good to see you again," he greeted me. "Is there something I can help you with today?"

"I'm looking for a tie to go with this suit I bought from you earlier this year."

He guided me to the tie rack, where I made my selection. I was thirty-eight years old, and this would be the first tie I ever owned. I looked at the salesman with a straight face and said matter-of-factly, "I have no idea how to tie this. Could you show me?"

Without missing a beat and maintaining the utmost discretion, he replied, "Come right this way. I'd be happy to show you."

He arranged the tie around my neck, under the collar, and then removed it, as I did my best to memorize his movements. I had visions of myself engaged in mortal combat with this neckwear early the next morning and running late for the important meeting.

"Could you do that one more time," I asked, "and then just loosen and slip it off, so I can pull it back over my head and tighten it tomorrow? I appreciate your patience."

"Not at all," said the salesman, adeptly camouflaging whatever his true thoughts might have been. "It's my pleasure. We appreciate your business."

During the past two years, I had experienced a crash course in how differently people are treated when they have money in their pocket. An individual perceived as affluent receives the benefit of the doubt under circumstances where a person of lesser means would incur scorn. While one is appreciated as a bit eccentric, the other is branded crazy. A crook driving a new vehicle can more easily talk himself out of a traffic citation than an honest man behind the wheel of a jalopy.

I removed the suit coat when I returned to my car, replaced it with something more casual, and headed for the plant gate to distribute leaflets to the remaining shifts. As I stood on concrete with the fence to my back, wind tousling my hair, exchanging greetings with the workers, I realized this would always be the world in which I felt most comfortable.

The 6:00 a.m. alarm shattered my dreams the next morning and rudely brought me back to the airport hotel where I'd arrived late and endured restless efforts at sleep. I stood in my suit before the long wall mirror and carefully adjusted my tie, grateful that the knot had retained its shape.

I drove to the terminal and greeted the two directors as they disembarked from the same flight. Neither of them had eaten breakfast so we strolled to a restaurant on the promenade. Bruce wore an expensive blue suit perfectly tailored to his slender proportions, with a white shirt and amber tie, his trousers held in place by suspenders. Thinning grey hair made him appear much older than his forty years.

Once situated, Bruce was delighted that the menu offered steak and eggs, which he ordered and Mark followed his lead. Having already eaten, I requested coffee with a roll. We began to brief each other from our respective vantage points.

Bruce shared what he had learned during his conversation with Frank Gress. Dominic Poon's family had opposed his venture into the American marketplace and, now that the business was in trouble, refused to provide additional resources.

"It sounds like the story of a rich kid who rebelled against authority by buying a textile mill to call his own," I interjected.

"I guess that's one way to put it," Mark said.

Bruce opened his hard-shell briefcase and pulled out the newsletter I had distributed during the summer. "What really amazes me, Phil, is your endless ability to invent new issues to organize around."

"I didn't invent any of them. All the issues were real, as well as the resolutions."

Bruce laughed. "C'mon Phil. Don't kid a kidder. It's perfectly OK for an organizer to contrive issues to get the people fired up. We all do it . . . and you do it especially well. But don't tell me you didn't invent some of these."

"I didn't," I answered calmly. "The fact is, this place was a total cluster fuck when I got here. I investigated, separated the real issues from the bullshit, and built the local around making changes."

"Give me a fucking break," said Bruce, genuinely annoyed as he put away the newsletter. "Nobody could have rallied people like this without fabricating issues along the way, and I don't care that you did. I just wish you'd be straight with me."

I decided to let it go. I had never organized around contrivance and hype, but it didn't really matter what Bruce thought of my methods so long as he remained pleased with the results.

We walked through the terminal to a private lounge in which Bruce had membership and seated ourselves at a round table within a small conference room. Dominic Poon and Frank Gress joined us a few minutes later.

Gress was a short, rotund man in his fifties, with slouched shoulders and the casual manner of one who has earned his fortune and had nothing to prove. Turning to me, he said offhandedly, "So, this is the agitator . . ." He seemed more curious than disapproving.

Poon initiated the meeting by saying that the company had gone downhill since he had bought it and that he was "pissed off" over having personally lost $3.5 million since making the investment. He had to make a decision about whether to invest an additional $1 million by Monday if the plant was to continue operating.

"I understand how you must feel," said Bruce. "I'd be pissed off if I lost $3,000."

Poon faced Bruce and launched into a rant about how it was primarily the union's fault. "You are agitating my employees trying to collect members. You make us waste time and money arbitrating this stupid case. You make employees vote on whether I can subcontract the janitorial work. By paying three and a half million for this company, I earned the right to decide who should be janitor. Give me one reason why I should decide to let the union stay."

He said he had bought the plant planning to make it a place where the workers wouldn't want or need a union. Management had counted on productivity increasing but instead it had declined significantly. There was no mention of the fifty-four Sulzer looms that I'd learned were at the root of his business plan and its subsequent failure.

Gress interjected and asked if the union would be willing to invest part of the million dollars which was needed and become a part owner in the company. Bruce explained that we weren't a business and that representing employees who actually worked for us would be a conflict of interest.

Gress then asked why I had felt it necessary to be so hard-hitting in my approach to the new company during its start-up phase.

"First off, I don't think anything I've done has cost the company a penny in production. In reality, I channeled employee input to identify chronic problems that were costing you money and increasing your exposure."

Bruce tried to put the discussion back on track by noting that while it hadn't been our decision to terminate the contract, we would be prepared to reinstate the terms of the Tennessee Textiles agreement, thereby providing an area of stability and certainty to the troubled business.

"It is beyond that now," Poon responded. "You are a businessman. I will tell you three things I need if I am going to make the decision to invest another million dollars and allow the union to stay.

"You need to reduce my contributions to the pension and forgive the debt to the plan I inherited from Tennessee Textiles. We need to do something about productivity and increase efficiency. I need to be able to terminate whoever I feel necessary to run the plant the way I want. There are people who don't need to be working here, and right now I can't do anything about it. I can't even decide who should be the janitor."

We took a caucus, and I stepped out of the conference room with Bruce and Mark to discuss his demands. Back at the table, Bruce told Poon that we might be agreeable to terminating future pension contributions if a suitable 401(k) could be substituted, and suggested that we negotiate wage increases which were directly tied to productivity.

"But there's no way we can agree to let you fire anyone you want," he said. "We couldn't agree to this legally as the employees' representative, even if we wanted to. You have the right to fire for just cause. If you document the cause, we won't fight you on every decision."

"You have not given me any reasons why I should allow the union to stay," said Poon. "But it doesn't matter anyway because I'm probably not going to invest any more money."

The meeting adjourned with Poon agreeing to contact Bruce on Monday regarding his final decision about further investment and to see if there was more to discuss. We all shook hands politely, and I accompanied Bruce and Mark to their flight gates.

I wanted to check back into the hotel and sleep for a week. Instead, I got in my car and drove 460 miles until I reached Black Mountain.

CHAPTER 12

I had hoped to get some rest on returning to my house in North Carolina, but instead experienced another restless night. As I grew more exhausted, my adrenalin levels escalated, making it increasingly difficult to sleep. My body simply wouldn't allow me to lapse into a state where I couldn't react to crisis at a moment's notice. It had served me well throughout my life, but I'd never been able to locate the off button.

Colie arrived at my door the next afternoon carrying a little pink suitcase decorated with flowers. "Can I come with you to Tennessee, Daddy?" she asked as she stepped inside.

"Yes," I answered, lifting her up for a hug. "I was hoping you'd come back with me this time."

"Can we go to an amusement park?"

"We'll do lots of fun things," I promised.

I felt a gnawing sense of urgency to hasten my return to Jackson, given the uncertainties raised by the recent meetings with Knuckles and at the airport. As my time with Colie would be spent traveling, I decided to leave the next day but plan the route for her entertainment.

While packing, I received an agitated phone call from Georgia, informing me that the company had put out a letter to employees attacking the union. As personal fax machines were still a modern marvel several years off, I told her to leave a copy for me at the union hall and suggested that she and the other leaders use their common sense in refuting it.

Colie and I enjoyed a leisurely departure and stopped after several hours to spend the night at my usual spot in Black Mountain. The next morning we headed west and then south into the Smoky Mountains. Our first stop was Cherokee, where we visited the Trail of Tears museum, a memorial to the 1830s removal of Native American tribes from the

Southeast and the genocidal forced march to Oklahoma. There was a theatrical reenactment, simple enough for a child to comprehend. I wasn't certain whether Colie would find this upsetting, but she emerged deeply moved and thoughtful.

We continued south and then east to the Tennessee line. I wanted to show her Clingmans Dome. Afterward, I planned for us to have lunch and visit Dollywood Amusement Park. We drove the winding entrance road up the mountain, parked, and climbed the rock escarpment to the overlook I had found so impressive.

It was a cool, sunny October day with a light wind, and several other families were present. I sat on the ground with my legs folded as currents of fatigue and dizziness passed over me. I allowed myself to briefly succumb, closing my eyes and drifting off . . .

I opened my eyes to a parent's nightmare. Colie was standing on the edge of the cliff, gazing out above the sheer, several hundred-foot drop below. There was no barrier, and her toes were more than an inch over the ledge. My first instinct was to scream her name but realized that the last thing I wanted to do was startle her. With my heart pounding, I said calmly, "Colie, take two steps back."

She ignored me and continued staring off at the mountain peaks below. I repeated the request, slightly louder but masking my distress. "Colie, this is your daddy. Take two steps back. Do it now . . . please."

She still didn't respond. Teasing each other was within the bounds of our relationship, and I knew that in her mind this was a game. "Colie, this is your daddy talking to you," I said again. "Take two steps back. Do it now or we're not going to the amusement park."

Her feet made two tiny shuffles backward, the smallest possible movements that could qualify as steps. "Now turn around and walk to your daddy."

She came to me and I picked her up in my arms. "Are we still going to the amusement park?" she asked.

"Yes," I answered, exhaling with relief and giving her a hug.

I didn't chastise her as many parents would have. There is a difference between obedience to avoid punishment and learning from experience. One sows the seeds of future rebellion, the other of wisdom and self-confidence.

After several hours of roller coasters and arcade games at Dollywood, we pushed west to Crossville and took a room.

I stopped at the union hall as soon as we arrived in Jackson to review the company handout that Georgia had left for me. The letter was titled "LET'S SET THE RECORD STRAIGHT" and had been attached to paychecks and posted on bulletin boards. I began reading it with disbelief and amusement. The document was two pages front and back, the lines single-spaced in a small font. My eyes blurred as I tried to take it in.

The diatribe blamed the union for every ailment the company suffered and accused us of arbitrating the discharge of Leo Boyland to recover his weekly union dues. The premise was absurd in that his next ten years of dues would hardly reimburse the union for its share of the costs. The third paragraph concluded:

> Their field representative brags about how he has won
> you over and how many of you he has in his corner. I
> believe this young fellow is in for a surprise.

The style clearly identified it as the work of Paul Poston. I was astonished once more at how little he understood his workers or how to connect with them. The content was irrelevant as I knew with certainty that few would take the time to read past the first couple of paragraphs. He should have learned something after months of fuming over my leaflets.

That evening, I swung by Georgia's house accompanied by my sleepy daughter. "What are people saying about the company's letter?" I asked her.

"Not much," she replied. "Everyone seems to be keeping quiet."

"That's because they haven't read it."

"Well, I did read it, from beginning to end," said Georgia," and there's one thing in there that really made me mad. They refer to you as a field representative."

"What's wrong with that?" I asked.

"It gives the impression that you just some no account person that works out in a field. I don't like they should talk about you like that."

"It doesn't actually mean that," I told her. "It means that I go into the community and work directly with the local instead of sitting in an office behind a desk."

I had scheduled a mid-afternoon meeting with Bob Knuckles to follow up on several outstanding issues and grievances. I didn't anticipate a long or contentious encounter so I asked permission to bring my daughter, explaining that we had just arrived and not yet unpacked.

"Well, hello there, little lady," smiled the big man as I led Colie by the hand into his office. She climbed onto a chair beside mine as the meeting began.

"Have you heard anything new about the status of the plant?" I inquired.

"They don't tell me a damn thing anymore," Knuckles said with frustration. "You probably know more than I do at this point. I'm like the plant mushroom. They feed me bullshit and keep me in the dark."

Suddenly his gaze fell on Colie. "I apologize for my language, sir. I forgot that we had a lady in the room."

"Don't worry about it," I replied. "She's heard worse from me."

Colie remained oblivious to the encounter, absorbed in drawing a picture of mountains with birds flying. She had long ago learned how to occupy herself while accompanying me to meetings about matters which were of no concern to her.

By the time I awoke the next morning, the tape on my answering machine was full. The local newspaper, the *Jackson Sun*, had reported that the company was poised to file bankruptcy.

Georgia's shift was working but I called the front office to summon her from the weave room. "The people are going crazy down here," she told me. "They want to know if it's true, and if it is, what's the union going to do about it."

I told her that I'd have to read the article and get back with her. I put Colie in the car and drove to a convenience store to find the paper. The story in question was on the lower half of the front page beneath the headline: *American Mills to file bankruptcy, Chamber says. Plant personnel manager calls the report from Chamber out of line.*

The chairman of the Chamber of Commerce Board was quoted as saying he had been informed by the state that American Mills planned to file for Chapter 11 later that day. Bob Knuckles was indignant in his response, calling the information "bogus" and saying the chamber had no authorization to make such a statement and was hurting the employees of American Mills. "I don't know where they got this. They need to keep their mouths shut until Paul Poston, Dominic Poon, or myself call them."

Based on what I'd learned the previous week, I didn't have a good feeling about where events might be headed. I tried to remain optimistic and conveyed this to the committee that afternoon. "I can't make any guarantee about what these idiots are going to do next," I told them. "The plant has been losing money but it's hard to imagine that Dominic Poon is ready to walk away after four months. There's too much at stake. What companies normally do in this situation is renegotiate their bank loans and look for new investors.

"I understand that everyone is nervous. I would be too if I was in your place. If the worst happens, Dominic Poon will still be wealthy and everyone else will be looking for work. All we can do now is wait and try not to feed rumors that will lead to panic."

"Do you think we'd have been better off to have just accepted their concessions to begin with?" asked an unusually subdued Hollis Wade.

"Not really," I answered. "That extra money looked good in your paycheck but compared to the rest of the company's problems, it meant next to nothing."

"I don't believe for a second that they're gonna shut this place," said Georgia. "They just playing on our fears so next time we go the table, their lawyer can tell us why they still can't give a raise."

"I don't think it's that either, to be perfectly honest," I responded. "The new company has been mismanaged and now it's in bad shape. I just think the game's not over and they still have options to explore."

I retrieved Colie from "her desk" at the union hall, and we went to dinner.

"Should we get something for that nice girl who's your new friend?" asked Colie.

I thought for a moment and realized that Tina was working that evening. "That's very sweet of you to think of that. Let's do it."

We barely had time to unpack at our house and get to the mill in time for the Weaving Department's first break. One of the weavers had stepped outside for a cigarette and, as soon as she saw us approach, went to fetch Tina, who emerged smiling a couple of minutes later.

"I didn't expect to see y'all tonight. What y'all got for me, Sugar?" she said, eyeing Colie with a paper bag in hand.

"We thought you might be hungry so we brought you supper," said my daughter.

I tossed the package over the barbed wire. Tina leaned against the chain-link and began talking to Colie, asking her about the trip and how she'd been doing. I wasn't certain whether she was more taken by the closeness of our relationship or that I'd chosen to make her a part of it.

The woman who had been smoking by the door strolled to the fence and started engaging Colie, who was always interested in checking out new people. I glanced in their direction and then put my finger through an opening, lightly stroking Tina's breast. She grinned, and I pulled back with my heart racing. The break period ended and we had to abruptly part company.

The morning of October 6 began routinely enough, with phone calls and the typing of new grievances and a leaflet.

At our previous session, Bob Knuckles had informed me that the company wanted to introduce several job changes involving workloads and efficiencies and that he expected to have the information available by this afternoon. I made arrangements with one of the stewards to watch Colie and drove to the mill for our 1:00 p.m. appointment.

I greeted Knuckles with a handshake across his desk before we seated ourselves. "Do you have the information on the proposed job changes?" I asked.

Knuckles appeared preoccupied as he stared past me and across the room, until finally his eyes settled in my direction. "All hourly employees are being laid off in approximately half an hour," he said. "The department managers are assembling employees for the announcement even as we speak. Let me share with you what's being read to them and posted on the bulletin boards."

He picked up a single sheet of paper that had been lying face down on his desk and slowly read aloud.

NOTICE

DUE TO A SHORTAGE OF CAPITAL AND A CASH FLOW PROB-
LEM, WE HAVE NO CHOICE BUT TO LAY-OFF ALL EMPLOYEES
EFFECTIVE FRIDAY, OCTOBER 6, 1989.

ALL ATTEMPTS TO OBTAIN ADDITIONAL CAPITAL HAVE
BEEN UNSUCCESSFUL, SO FAR.

WE EXPECT THIS LAYOFF WILL BE TEMPORARY, AS WE
ATTEMPT TO FIND ADDITIONAL FINANCING AND RE-
ORGANIZE THE BUSINESS. WE REGRET THE INCONVEN-
IENCE TO YOU.

Hiding my reaction, I asked, "Do you think American Mills is going out of business?"

"I didn't say that," Knuckles replied. "We've lost our ability to meet payroll beyond the time already worked this week. We're ceasing operations until the owners can get this mess sorted out. That's all I'm in a position to tell you."

"I read your interview in the *Jackson Sun*. What's the latest on the bankruptcy?"

"I don't know much more than I did yesterday. I'm assuming, based on today's actions, that there's probably some truth to it. I'm not meaning to string you along, but it appears I haven't been invited to the inner circle.

"I hope it's alright that I didn't invite Georgia up here with us. I felt it would be best to leave her down in her department where she might be of some assistance to her coworkers."

I told him I agreed and asked if representatives of the Employment Security Commission had been contacted to meet with employees for the purpose of explaining their rights and benefits. Knuckles assured me that arrangements were being made and that I would be notified once they were in place. I excused myself to be in position at the plant gate as employees streamed out.

I didn't know what to expect from the swarm of agitated workers with whom I would momentarily be deluged. I might be perceived as a source for answers I didn't have or become a target for their fear and frustration. This was not the time, however, for a leader to retreat to a safe distance to await the abatement of the storm's fury, but rather to wade into its midst and become the eye of the hurricane . . . a center of calm around which the tempest can circulate and become ordered.

The first to leave were already crossing the street to the parking lot when I arrived at the gate. Within a few minutes the exodus was in full force. Dozens of workers approached me with questions, but I was relieved not to be seen as an easy target for blame. Some of the older workers had a

surprisingly philosophical attitude echoing the theme, "I've been expecting for years that sooner or later something like this would happen."

As I later drove to pick up Colie, I was grateful for circumstances that
had placed her elsewhere on what had first appeared to be a routine day.

I spoke with Ernest and Mark that evening. Mark wished to determine if the events in question triggered employee protection under the
WARN Act.

"What's that?" I asked. "I haven't heard of this before."

"Most people haven't," Mark replied. "It's short for Worker Adjustment
and Retraining Notification, a federal statute that just went into effect in
February of this year. It requires an employer to provide at least sixty
days' notice in advance of a plant closing or a long-term layoff affecting
at least a third of its workforce. It sounds like this affects everyone."

"What are the consequences if they don't provide the notice?" I asked.

"Well, according to this regulation, the company is responsible for up
to sixty days of back pay and benefits. Of course, this is all brand new.
There's not a whole lot of case law built up at this point."

"Right now, the company is saying that this isn't a plant closing and
that the layoffs are temporary."

"I hear you. For the moment, all we can do is monitor the situation
and stay in touch."

I awoke on Saturday morning and prepared breakfast, relieved that
my daughter chose to eat hers in the living room watching cartoons,
thereby affording me a bit of much-needed space.

I stepped out into the yard so that the television wouldn't intrude
upon my reflections. The impact of the previous day's events was starting to catch up with me. Over time, I had developed the ability to feel
nothing when confronted with the worst of news. It allowed me to continue functioning at peak efficiency without interruption. But during my
first moments of peace and respite, the delayed responses would flood
my awareness like waves crashing through a levy.

The *Jackson Sun* filled its pages with several features examining the mass
lay-off from different perspectives. "Increasing competition from foreign imports and aging equipment" were cited as the precipitating fac-
tors during a decade of "financial turmoil" for the mill.

A second-page article bore the banner: *Mill employees left in daze by surprise layoffs.* Two women who had worked at the plant for most of their lives were used to portray the plight of the workforce. The story concluded by noting that one of the employees was hopeful but uncertain of being called back to work. "It could be one month, one year, or never," she remarked.

To the reporter's question "And if it's never?" she responded, "Lord have mercy. I don't know what I'll do."

The coverage expanded into a retrospective of the plant's century-long history. It was built in 1906 by Judson Moss Bemis, along with a surrounding neighborhood of mill houses complete with company store. The resulting township was aptly named Bemis. This romanticized version of local history depicted a "close-knit" community: "When jobs were hard to find, Bemis obliged. When friendship was needed, Bemis embraced. The whole town was one big playground to the kids." Jackson had annexed Bemis in 1978.

I typed a letter for mailing to all employees, letting them know that the union would remain available as a resource, and took Colie with me to the printer to make copies. The rest of the weekend was ours to share.

On Monday Colie and I arrived at the union hall, where the committee was assembled. After a brief meeting, I enlisted their aid in addressing envelopes to the nearly five hundred bargaining-unit employees of American Mills.

"Why are you mailing so many letters?" my daughter asked. "Is there going to be a party and you're inviting people?"

I walked her back to a corner at the rear of the large hall that she had turned into her play area. "Something really sad has happened at the mill," I said. "The men who bought the company ran out of money and can't afford to pay the workers anymore . . . so they had to send everyone home. I wrote them a letter so they'll know I haven't forgotten about them and they can call me if they need help."

"Why . . . why they run out of money?" she asked. "Can't they go to the bank and get more money?"

"The bank is angry because it already gave them a lot of money, and it doesn't want to give them any more. A rich man from China came here to buy the mill, but he didn't really know what to do with it. He bought a bunch of big machines that he thought would make the mill better . . . but they were the wrong type of machines and some were broken. He couldn't earn enough money to pay for the machines and to give back the bank's money, and now his treasure chest is all empty."

"That's really sad," said Colie, her eyes filling with tears. "How are they going to feed their kids? Will they ever get their jobs back?"

"I don't know . . . but I hope so. Everyone is working together to try and fix things. For right now, the government will give the workers some money to live on."

The final paychecks were scheduled for distribution at the plant on Thursday. Realizing this might be my last chance to engage the workforce en masse during this period of turmoil, I hastily prepared a leaflet. The content was similar to the letter recently mailed but it afforded the personal touch of directly presenting the message and being available for discussion.

A long line of workers formed along the chain-link fence, winding through the gate that led to the front office. Those who weren't among the first to arrive waited for over two hours. Television cameras filmed the slow migration into the factory and newspaper reporters milled about seeking interviews.

I patrolled the line of workers accompanied by Georgia, Donald, and my daughter, distributing the leaflet to both workers and journalists (Fig. 9).

The *Jackson Sun* reporter returned to her desk in time to meet deadline for the evening edition, which featured the headline: *Owners scramble for cash to reopen mill. Plant hopeful of finding enough investors.*

The article quoted Paul Poston: "We're working around the clock. We don't have any commitment yet, but we don't give up easily. Chances are good that enough investors will come through to reopen the Bemis plant. I don't want to create false hope but I don't want to make it dismal and doom either."

The reporter had toured the plant, observing "city-block-long rooms . . . filled with row after row of idle looms and other machinery . . . clocks stopped at the time when power in the various parts of the plant was turned off last weekend."

Bob Knuckles told the *Sun* he expected the plant to reopen but noted that the 54 new looms were "taking longer than expected to get up to a desirable production level."

The paper ran a story the next day providing its first coverage from the union's perspective: *Union officials hopeful about plant's chances*. A young reporter named Tom Corwin wrote:

> Statements from the Amalgamated Clothing and Textile Workers Union Local 281 echoed those made by plant officials earlier Thursday but added a note of caution.
>
> The Rev. Donald Vandiver, vice president of the local, said, "As a minister, I would like to assist people who need help in any way, particularly with counseling. The main goal of the union is to encourage the people to keep their hopes up until the plant re-opens, I hope, in the very near future."

An employee meeting was scheduled at the National Guard Armory for the afternoon of the following Tuesday. Representatives of government and relief agencies would set up booths to assist workers with unemployment claims, emergency assistance involving food, utilities, and health care, in addition to educational and retraining opportunities.

I met with Bob Knuckles and the various organizations to assist in organizing the most comprehensive presentation. A Rapid Response Team was established in accordance with Department of Labor regulations, consisting of four members of management, Georgia, Donald, and two other committee members. Events had thrust the entire community into a classic "hope for the best and prepare for the worst" scenario.

I was confronted with the conflicting obligations of remaining on the ground while the shock waves rolled through Jackson and returning my daughter to North Carolina when promised. Colie had prepared herself for two weeks away from mom and the familiarity of her permanent world, and I didn't wish to inflict the uncertainties that now permeated my work on her.

I decided to fly her home on Saturday and return on Monday. Colie was thrilled by the prospect of a plane ride and avoiding the long drive home.

CHAPTER 13

When I arrived back in Jackson, I encountered only dead calm and an eerie absence of activity. It was as if the entire community had collectively drawn its breath and was waiting to exhale. There were no messages on my answering machine, and I was unable to reach either management or committee members. I called Tina to see how she was holding up.

"I be good," she said in her soft phone voice, as if nothing in particular was going on.

I asked how she felt about the layoff and her job, and whether she was able to make ends meet.

"I don't care if that sorry mill stays shut forever," she replied. "I'll just collect me my unemployment, relax, and have a good time. I can always find a new job when I'm ready. I'm a good worker."

She seemed to be in one of her gentler and upbeat moods, so I asked on impulse if she would like me to stop by for a visit.

"Sure. You can come over if you like."

I arrived at Tina's apartment half an hour later. She was in the process of tidying up so I stood by and chatted with her as she finished.

A man burst through the front door, strode into the living room and stopped several yards from where we were standing. It was a pleasant day, and he was in shirt sleeves. I took in the faded tattoos that lined his thick arms. He was of medium height with a stocky build and broad shoulders. I didn't have a clue about his intentions. Clearly he wasn't a thief, but was otherwise bad news.

He addressed Tina as if I weren't there. "I got something for you. What you got for me?"

I looked over at Tina and asked quietly, "Do you want this guy to be here?"

The man repeated himself a bit more loudly. He didn't appear angry, just insistent. "I said I got something for you. What you got?"

Tina touched my arm lightly. "I think it would be better if you go."

"Are you sure?" I asked. My heart was racing as my mind worked overtime to focus the barrage of discordant fragments into a cohesive picture.

"Yeah," she said. "You need to leave now. I'm sorry."

My awareness and comprehension of the moment suddenly crystallized. This was her crack dealer and he expected favors in return. A menu of options streamed through my consciousness. I was unarmed, exhausted from the flight, and emotionally unprepared for a confrontation. But then, neither honor nor compassion demanded intervention. This man and the world he represented were more a part of Tina's daily existence than I was . . . and she had made her wishes clear. She wasn't afraid, but rather embarrassed and compromised by my presence.

I walked past the intruder, reciprocating his indifference toward me, and out to the parking lot. I sat in my car and stared at the closed door to Tina's apartment. I didn't have any work scheduled, and my emotional-delay mode was disengaged. I forced my hand to turn the key and backed out of my space. I drove in a fog toward Riverside Drive, waging war with every disparaging voice awakened in my psyche.

I couldn't foresee continuing our relationship and believed the final thread had snapped. It was now obvious what had happened to the gold necklace.

I propped my head against a couple of pillows and lay across the bed with my shoes on, hoping to sort things out and reestablish my equilibrium within the allotted time. I was grateful there were no meetings scheduled, providing nearly a full day to sink to the bottom of the ocean and explore its depths before returning to life.

I contemplated that placed within a stadium packed with fifty thousand people, if one of them happened to be a woman with a tormented childhood, who ran away at fourteen, and was a recovering drug addict who once rode with a bike gang, we would inevitably find each other. We'd be drawn together like moths to flame. If she was also sweet natured and sensitive, I would be smitten, and we'd end up in bed within hours. I wouldn't be so naïve as to fall in love, but would remain captivated as long as it lasted.

Survivors recognize each other. It's a small, exclusive club with a high price of admission and no exit clause. Nobody chooses the hardships into which they're born, but there is a choice to survive and not be broken—damaged perhaps, but never broken. We are bound by an understanding of that which all others would rather not know, and this becomes the foundation of our attempts at intimacy.

This had been yet another spin on the merry-go-round, and I'd been hurled off when least expected. I needed to remain strong with my wits about me for the sake of those I cared about. With a violent act of will, I propelled myself out of bed and donned my workout clothes. I had some of my most pristine reflections during physical exercise.

The gathering at the National Guard Armory began at 1:30 p.m. the next afternoon. I arrived with my emotional turmoil neatly packaged and stored in the recesses of my mind to be retrieved later for further examination. Booths staffed by representatives of the Employment Security Commission, United Way, and other relief agencies lined an enormous room. The media was again on-scene in full force.

For several generations, textile workers had formed a unique industrial subculture within American society. Their family roots were usually agricultural. They were often barely literate individuals who had honed a skill within one of the industry's manufacturing niches. Some of the workers would remain at a plant their entire adult lives, while others drifted into itinerancy, confident that their skills would be in demand at any town built around a textile mill.

The process of carding and spinning cotton fiber into yarn, which is then woven into cloth, is unique in the manufacturing world. The skills learned over a lifetime as a doffer, weaver, spinner, or loom fixer have no application in other industries.

The erosion of the domestic textile industry in the wake of foreign imports had been underway for years before my arrival and more than a decade before NAFTA heralded its ultimate demise. In 1989, the weaker companies foundered while the more resilient downsized and continued to prosper.

For a younger and inherently intelligent employee sucked into the whirlwind of layoffs, government agencies offered opportunities and funding for education and retraining that wouldn't have been available under normal circumstances. The more ambitious and fortunate would scrape by on unemployment (with perhaps a part-time job off the books) and emerge as electricians, skilled mechanics, and office workers. A few would be accepted at a community college and persist until achieving a degree.

These options were meaningless to a fifty-five-year-old fixer of spinning frames with a third-grade reading level. The future held only a descent from the respect and pay afforded the more highly skilled members of a workforce, to the most menial of vocations with half the wages and no benefits. Desperate and humiliated men would take to drink and spousal abuse as mortgages went unpaid and families disintegrated.

The purpose of the meeting at the armory was to help individuals assess and make the most of their choices if the worst came to pass.

I was again interviewed by the *Jackson Sun* and while encouraging workers to take advantage of the various programs, restated my longer-term optimism.

To my surprise, Bob Knuckles took back some of his earlier predictions. "Cohen seems to be more optimistic than I am. I don't know of anything that's happening to expedite the mill reopening. I don't think we need to give our employees any hope, because I don't see it there."

I was uncertain whether he had simply been unable to resist contradicting me in print, or was now privy to unfavorable developments.

Knuckles apologized to me the next morning for the tone of his remarks. "It was depressing seeing all of our employees gathered under these circumstances. Everyone's got a lot to lose here, including me. I let my feelings get the better of me and probably spoke a bit out of turn. You never know what these damn reporters are going to quote or how they're going to use it out of context."

I spent the remainder of the week in limbo, frustrated by the need to wait for events to unfold rather than initiating them. I continued to meet with committee members and community leaders, interspersed with newspaper and television interviews.

There was sufficient room in my work schedule to reflect upon recent developments and revelations in regard to my relationship with Tina. I reviewed the several months of our involvement and reached the conclusion that while her crack use had at first been recreational, it had escalated over time.

I realized that I was a visitor in her world and not entitled to expect that she or her reality change on my account. The encounter I'd recently witnessed was a tragic reflection of her life, and not a betrayal or affront to my self-respect. It was my choice to either accept who she was or move on.

My weekend was entirely unscheduled, and the respite was unwelcome. There was no internet or satellite TV to facilitate the passage of time. My home and loved ones were seven hundred miles to the east. Jackson had nothing to offer me in terms of diversion or culture. My focus began to dissipate and the insight of contemplation became lost in the redundant spinning of mental wheels.

I picked up the phone and called Tina. She seemed happy to hear from me, acting as though nothing amiss had occurred, and invited me over.

I'd reconciled my emotional conflicts over the previous week's interaction, having been exposed to far more aberrant behavior by those close to me on the streets of New York. But one prevailing concern remained—the health risks to which I might be exposing myself. These were peak years in the public awareness campaign regarding HIV and it appeared that precautions might be appropriate under the circumstances.

Tina greeted me in good spirits and invited me into her living room. I unobtrusively turned the lock on her front door while entering. I allowed sufficient time for us to relax and connect until it felt like a good moment to broach the subject.

"You know, both of us have been around," I said. "I guess that's part of what makes us both interesting. I've been hearing all this shit on the radio and TV about the AIDS epidemic and using precaution. What do you think about all that?"

"I don't know," she responded. "I haven't thought much about it. I ain't queer or nothing."

"They're saying that it doesn't just affect gay people but also straights," I said, feeling as though I were swimming against the current. "Do you think that maybe we should use condoms or something when we're together, you know, just to take care of each other?"

Tina's facial expression and body language contracted as if a lever had been pulled. "What you saying? That you think I'm dirty and gonna make you sick?"

"That's not what I'm saying . . ." I interjected but her words rolled over mine.

"You just see me as some piece of trash you picked up off the street, don't you? Then what you doin' here if you feel that way!?"

Tina's shoulders were hunched and she had the look of a cornered animal in her eyes. I reached out to touch her reassuringly but she pulled away. She stared at me bewildered for thirty seconds, walked into the kitchen, and began washing dishes. I followed and stood behind her.

"I'm sorry if I hurt your feelings," I said over the running water. "That wasn't what I wanted to do."

"That's OK," she replied with a sharp edge in her voice. "Now it's all clear to me."

"What do you want me to do? Where do we go from here?"

"I ain't goin' nowhere. Maybe you should be goin' back home."

I lightly stroked her back and then walked out her door, locking it behind me as it closed. As an organizer, I realized that I'd made a critical mistake by failing to accurately gauge the tolerances of another before speaking. As a man, I knew with certainty that this was the curtain scene of a strange and troubled, but sometimes sweet, relationship I would never forget.

Given the emerging public profile of the crisis, I began laying groundwork to build a network of community and political alliances. I started the week by meeting with representatives of the Department of Labor, Chamber of Commerce, and JPTA (Jobs Training and Protection Agency). Their general consensus was that efforts were in progress that would result in the plant reopening, the details and timing of which they either had no knowledge or weren't at liberty to disclose.

I called Ted Yeiser, hoping to find out more about where the situation was headed. He informed me that it remained the owners' intent to solicit investment and use this as a basis for restructuring loans. I reminded him that the employer had failed to meet its notice obligations pursuant to the WARN Act, and that in the event of a permanent closing or protracted layoff, the union wished to engage in effects bargaining. (The NLRB requires companies to negotiate with unions over the "effects" of a shutdown, including payment of accrued vacation, disposition of other benefits, and severance.)

Yeiser acknowledged the request to bargain but disputed that there had been a WARN violation, citing loopholes pertaining to "unforeseen business circumstances" and temporary closings. We scheduled a meeting for November 9, during which the parties would either continue their efforts to negotiate a contract within the context of recent developments, or fulfill their responsibilities in the event of a less fortunate outcome.

I prepared a union meeting announcement for the coming week. It would be an opportunity to maintain cohesion and generate input regarding the difficult decisions that might lie ahead. The leaflet began:

Our Future

Our Rapid Response Team contacts with the Department of Labor and members of the Jackson business community lead us to believe that American Mills will reopen. Their opinions are based upon talks with the owners of American Mills. We wonder why the Company is being so tight lipped with its workers, while sharing its future plans with the Department of Labor and Jackson businessmen.

The committee and I spent the next day at the union hall, launching the new mailing and organizing a regimen of follow-up phone calls. Their continued dedication and willingness to serve under difficult circumstances deeply moved me. Entrusting the cartons of stamped envelopes to Georgia, I drove to Knoxville for a meeting with Mark and Ernest, then continued the trip home.

CHAPTER 14

I spent three full days at my house in North Carolina. I had several close friends with children the same age as Colie, and we visited them in turn. It was a welcome relief to reconnect with the part of my life that had existed before union campaigns. The night before I was to leave, Colie surprised me by wanting to know if she could return to Tennessee.

"Are you sure you're ready to be away from your mommy again, so soon?" I asked.

"I'll be OK," she answered, sitting on the bed in her sleep clothes. "Day care is boring, and we do fun things together. The only thing is, I hate the mountains."

"Why?" I asked, somewhat surprised. "What is there about the mountains that you don't like?"

She thought for a moment. "They make me cry."

I tried to assess what my daughter was trying to tell me. "Do you mean that they're so beautiful that it hurts your heart, and that makes you cry?"

"Yes," she answered with a tear rolling down her cheek.

"Do you want us to not go through the mountains anymore?" I asked.

"No," she said, yawning and lying down with Mr. Tomato in her arms. "But it might make me cry."

We took the straight shot back to Jackson on the interstate to hasten my return during this uncertain period. I also thought it might be wise to give Colie a breather from the mountains in light of our recent conversation.

Time on the long, monotonous seven-hundred-mile haul always passed more quickly when my daughter was with me. We played Dead

Head and other travel games, while she programmed our music from among her favorite tapes in my country music collection. She especially enjoyed "Coat of Many Colors" by Dolly Parton.

Children enable us to experience the mundane aspects of life as if they were brand new and exciting. All you must do is tune in and see through their eyes. Stopping for lunch at a restaurant with a gift shop or buying gas at a convenience store with an unusual person behind the register become unexplored vistas in the adventure of life. The motel room just off the highway exit is transformed into a resort instead of a sterile domicile of insomnia for the business traveler.

We arrived in Jackson on the afternoon of Wednesday, November 1, in time to return calls to committee members, Mark Pitt, and the media.

I brought Colie with me to the union meeting the next evening. As one cluster of workers after another entered the main hall, it was clear that the mailing and phone calls had generated impact. The absence of work and shift configurations had allowed for scheduling one concentrated gathering. By 6:00 p.m. all available seats were filled and late arrivals were left to stand along the walls.

I was again relieved that the union hadn't become a default target of resentment or unrealistic expectations. People had questions about their benefits and options that had remained unanswered at the armory, and looked for some insight into what might be in store for the plant.

A meeting was scheduled the next morning with Jackson Mayor Charles Farmer. As I led Colie by the hand from our parking space on Main Street to City Hall, she asked, "Dada, who are we going to meet with today?"

"We're meeting with the mayor."

"Who's that?" she wanted to know.

"He's sort of like the King of Jackson."

Colie nodded her head with understanding.

I ushered her through the glass doors of a fairly modern building, and a receptionist directed us to a conference room. It was rather unusual for a professional representative to bring a small child to meet with a city's mayor, but I figured that if he wasn't human enough to appreciate the circumstances, then neither would he be genuinely concerned about the families of displaced workers.

Mayor Farmer walked through a door across the room just as we entered. We converged at the conference table, where I shook his hand and introduced my daughter, explaining that she was traveling with me on business. He seemed pleased to make her acquaintance and shook her hand as well.

The mayor took a seat at the head of the table, while Colie and I sat across from each other on either side. She immediately got out her drawing materials and began to occupy herself. I asked Mayor Farmer if he was privy to any new information about the company's efforts to refinance and resume operations.

"There are things in the works that may well prove very favorable to American Mills employees," he answered.

When I requested details, he only responded, "I'm not at liberty to discuss anything further at this time, but I am hopeful that the outcome will be positive."

He asked me to refrain from referencing this exchange with reporters. I didn't press him further as this was an introductory meeting and instead changed the subject. "Would you be in a position to use your influence to secure state funding or loans that might facilitate the plant reopening?"

The mayor said he would pursue the recommendation and any other measures that would provide assistance.

The meeting lasted for half an hour, and he again shook my hand, saying that I could call on his office anytime. I evaluated our encounter as having been pleasant and superficial—but a worthwhile first contact. Colie handed Mayor Farmer a picture. He smiled, thanked her, and then left the room with the artwork in hand.

"What did you draw for him?" I asked Colie as we exited to the street.

"It was a picture of a castle," she said seriously. "Since he's a king, I thought he would like a picture of a castle."

After lunch, we attended the first meeting of the Labor-Management Committee that had been formed nearly a month prior as part of the Rapid Response process. In addition to the four union committee members and four representatives of management, I was present as technical advisor and joined by an official from the Department of Labor. The perfunctory session focused on defining the group's membership and became ensnared in a protracted discussion about choosing a neutral chairperson. Eventually Madison County Judge Walter Baker Harris was selected.

Tom Corwin from the *Jackson Sun* was present as an observer and afterwards interviewed the participants. His story appeared that evening beneath the headline, *Team to help American Mills workers slow to form.*

The article began by noting that "Officials of the Amalgamated Clothing and Textile Workers Union are disgruntled and dismayed at the slow progress of the team." The coverage profiled Judge Harris and included an interview with the mayor:

"Farmer said he would go to bat for the laid-off American Mills workers and try to get state or Tennessee Valley Authority funds to either re-open the mill, study it or attract investors."

The absence of daily activity at the plant allowed an unscheduled weekend to share with my daughter. The integral components of a union campaign—investigation and resolution of grievances, building the local union structure, visits to the facility—were all in a state of suspension. I remained in limbo along with the rest of the community.

Colie and I ate breakfast and watched cartoons until she became bored. "Can we go somewhere fun today, Dada?" she asked.

Casey Jones' house was hardly worthy of a second visit and with that, we had exhausted Jackson's menu of attractions suitable for a child. An impulsive notion popped into my mind. We were situated about an hour north of Mississippi, one of the few states I'd never visited and about which I'd always been fascinated. It represented the cultural antithesis of the New York streets from which I had emerged. I was especially intrigued by Tupelo, often romanticized in country songs and literature. It was another hour south of the state line and I envisioned it as a landlocked version of Charleston.

"Would you like to go on a trip to a city we've never been to before?" I asked. "It's called Tupelo and it's in the land of Mississippi."

"OK," she replied. "Will there be fun things for us to do there?"

"I don't know. Let's find out."

I threw on my street clothes, and we were soon speeding south to Mississippi.

We entered the city limits of Tupelo and drove from one side to the other, which didn't take long as it was much smaller than expected. It seemed more like a shabby industrial town than a metropolis worthy of artistic mention. We explored drab residential neighborhoods and faded two-story commercial districts. By comparison, Jackson was the hub of civilization. To our right, we passed a shack about half the size of a hotel room, with a sign proclaiming it as the birthplace of Elvis Presley. I momentarily thought to stop, for lack of alternatives, but there were no parking spaces on the street, and traffic was behind us.

Eventually I spotted a shopping mall and entered the parking lot. Having been confined to the car for three hours, we were both ready for any form of distraction.

Referring to this enclosure as a mall is somewhat of an indulgence, though it was perhaps the most noteworthy historical attraction of our visit—a missing link between the old-fashioned Main Street, lined with rows of privately owned small businesses, and a modern shopping center. It was as if we had gone through a time portal and found ourselves in the 1950s. The establishments lacked imagination and inventory, with few belonging to a recognizable chain. There were no childhood amusements, with the exception of a rocking horse that required a quarter. I searched in vain for a restaurant with a decent menu until hunger obliged us to settle for what was available.

We visited a toy store and I bought Colie a pair of plastic roller skates with yellow wheels. She put them on and spent the next hour rolling down the aisles of the Tupelo shopping mall. Families who appeared as though they'd walked off the set of an Andy Griffith episode glowered at us with disapproval. My little girl laughed and beamed with delight as she whirled past them.

We rested on a bench and enjoyed some of the world's worst ice cream, and then headed back to Jackson. It was soon dark, and I pressed forward, alone with my thoughts beside my sleeping daughter.

I was surprised to receive a call from Ted Yeiser on Monday morning. He informed me that the owners of American Mills were in a Memphis courtroom, filing for bankruptcy under Chapter 11. I agreed to remain discreet pending a public announcement, and sought more information about the projected outcome of the proceedings and the impact on the plant's future.

"To the best of my understanding," American Mills has entered into a Liquidating and Occupancy Agreement with a company called United Foods, Inc. If the plan is approved by the bankruptcy court, UFI will lease the equipment and premises from American Mills and resume operations as a new company."

"I assume they're going to recognize the union and continue bargaining," I said.

"I honestly don't know what to tell you there," Yeiser replied. "I wasn't involved in drafting the agreement. In fact, I'm no longer retained as legal counsel by the company. I simply wanted to offer you this heads-up as a courtesy. If the truth be known, American Mills owes me a sizeable invoice for legal services, and I anticipate taking my place in a long line of unsecured creditors."

"I'm sorry to hear you got stiffed along with everyone else," I said. "I appreciate your keeping me in the loop."

"I wish you good luck with this new situation," said Yeiser. "Please convey my best to Ernest."

As we got off the phone, I had to admit that despite the reputation which preceded him, Yeiser had never conducted himself dishonorably in our dealings.

I contacted Bob Knuckles to see if there might be information to glean from that quarter.

"Listen, there are only ten employees left on the American Mills payroll, he grumbled, "and I'm pretty near the bottom of the food chain. You probably know more about what's going on than I do."

"Why is a food company making a bid to take over a textile plant?" I asked. What sort of business are they planning to run?"

"Beats me," he answered.

"I just got off the phone with Ted Yeiser and learned that he's no longer in the game. Who's going to be representing American Mills or its successor in labor relations? Are we still meeting a week from Thursday?"

"I've heard nothing about new counsel being retained," said Knuckles. "We might want to think about putting this off for another week, but I'm not sure who will be there representing the company."

We tentatively agreed on a postponement until November 16, pending the availability of other parties. I then spoke with Ernest to apprise him of the new developments, and was told he could adjust his schedule. In the process, I learned that the lease on my staff vehicle was expiring and that another car was waiting for me at the regional office.

My work calendar for the week was empty. There was little to do except remain alert and prepared to react at a moment's notice. I stayed in touch with the committee and community contacts, and fielded calls from the press.

On Tuesday I answered the phone and it was Leo Boyland. To be honest, amid the deluge of recent developments, I'd almost forgotten about his situation. I informed him of what was befalling the plant and his former coworkers, and that we were still awaiting the arbitrator's decision. Leo told me he was otherwise OK but had just returned from a ten-day layoff at the poultry plant and needed food money to tide him over until his next paycheck.

"How much do you need?" I asked.

"Whatever you can spare, but forty dollars would really help. I'll pay you back everything once I get my money from the arbitrator."

I agreed to send the funds. Whatever else might be said about Leo, he hadn't been responsible for the circumstances of his discharge or the arbitrator's delay.

Colie and I left for Atlanta on Thursday. I apologized that this would preempt our visit to an amusement park but she looked forward to the journey as yet another first visit to a new city.

The next morning I dropped off one car and picked up another, a white Ford Taurus—not exactly my style but it cut the right professional image. Memories of my prior circumstances were still too recent for me to complain about receiving a free vehicle. Ernest had told me that when the lease expired, I'd be given a menu from which to select a new car.

I introduced Colie to the clerical staff at the regional office, and then we fired up the Taurus and got on I-85 North. The interior was spacious and met with her approval.

During our drive to Atlanta the previous day, events had been unfolding in a Memphis courtroom. Attorneys for the creditors of American

Mills had appeared in a hearing before Judge William Brown, raising strong objections to the operating agreement with United Foods, Inc. Upon the judge's approval of the arrangement, United Foods would begin production at the facility with options to either buy or walk away at its discretion. The firm would assume ownership of raw materials and inventory but none of the existing debt or obligations of its predecessor.

Creditors argued that their interests weren't adequately protected under the terms of the arrangement and would be entirely subject to the whims of a third party. The most contentious of the opposing entities was Gibbs Machinery, which had sold American Mills the fifty-four Sulzer looms and now felt entitled to repossession, having been paid only $360,000 of the $2,378,085 sales price. The *Jackson Sun* quoted Gibbs' attorney, Jennie Latta, as stating, "United Foods is trying to learn the textile business at the expense of creditors . . . and the factory's workers."

UFI officials refused to publicly disclose the nature of the planned business enterprise prior to approval of the agreement.

The director of the Bureau of Business and Research at Memphis State University expressed misgivings about the company's intentions: "I'm not sure what they're up to. In almost every one of these cases, they're figuring out some way to make money. They're not doing it to help Jackson or any other humanitarian reasons."

The final witness had been Mayor Farmer, who testified in favor of United Foods, referring to it as "expert in fixing things up."

The news media continued to run features on a daily basis. I'd given my North Carolina phone number to *Sun* reporter Tom Corwin, and naturally he called. He needed to answer some of my questions before I could respond to his.

I learned that United Foods was a locally owned and publicly traded frozen food company. It was based twenty miles northwest of Jackson in Bells, Tennessee, where J. O. Tankersley had founded it in 1945. The company presently maintained operations in several states and was run by Tankersley's two sons, who controlled a majority interest. It was a bottom-feeding enterprise, specializing in the acquisition and sometimes flipping of distressed and bankrupt facilities.

Corwin informed me that an attorney for one of the creditors claimed that UFI only planned to rehire 150 employees and requested my comments.

"One doesn't presumably buy an operation of that size to run it at 25 percent capacity," was all I could offer from a distance. I reiterated the union's intention to resume bargaining with American Mills and to engage the officials of United Foods.

The hearing was scheduled to resume on Monday, November 13. This had turned out to be an inopportune period for me to be away from my assignment, but one can't foresee every eventuality within a complex drama.

CHAPTER 15

I exited I-40 a few miles east of the Jackson city limits on the afternoon of Tuesday, November 14, to buy gas at a convenience mart. I located the row of newspaper vending machines alongside the building and perused them until I found a copy of the Sun. The front-page headline read: *United Foods gets OK to reopen mill. Applications now being taken for temporary startup.* The article, again written by Tom Corwin, reported that the bankruptcy judge had granted temporary approval to the operating plan but that final determination had been reserved for a subsequent hearing on December 1.

United Foods announced it would immediately begin taking applications for an initial 140 hourly and 20 management positions, meet with selected applicants at week's end, and resume partial operation of the textile business the following Monday. The company's executive vice president, Don Dresser, said that UFI had begun looking into taking over the plant the weekend after it closed.

Judge Brown had rendered his decision over the objections of Gibbs Machinery, which continued efforts to reclaim the fifty-four Sulzer looms for which it hadn't been paid. Gibbs operating manager, Bob Ollis, cited poor planning by management as the root cause for the short existence and rapid demise of American Mills. He noted that ". . . the Sulzer looms tended to vibrate and move around on the wooden floors . . ." of the old mill and that equipment upgrades had been required in other areas to improve yarn quality to the specifications of more advanced looms.

I raced through the winding streets of Jackson at twice the speed limit, unlocked my front door with bags left in the car, and called the Knoxville office, relieved to find that Mark was available. "This is getting kind of ridiculous," I told him. "I'm finding out about events affecting the fate of our local by reading the newspaper like any other member of the general public. We need to insert ourselves into this bankruptcy process ASAP."

"I'm already with you," he replied. "I've spoken with our legal department in New York, and they've made arrangements to retain a labor law firm out of Memphis. They'll be filing motions to suspend the temporary operating agreement and have the union listed as an unsecured creditor on behalf of employees. We'll be present at the hearing on December 1."

"What about charges with the NLRB for failure to bargain?" I asked.

"I expect we'll be doing that as well but we should have a better idea of how to frame the allegations after Thursday's meeting with management. Ernest and I will be flying in. We're still on for that, right?"

"Last I've heard, yes, but Bob Knuckles says he still has no idea who's going to be representing the company."

There were several messages on my answering machine from committee members. United Foods had begun accepting applications at noon, openly declaring that employees would be selected at management's sole discretion without regard to seniority, and offering reduced wages and benefits. Candidates wouldn't be limited to individuals who had previously worked at the mill. A copy of the application form and cover letter with declaration of terms had been left on my desk.

I rushed back to my car and sped to the union hall. The letter, bearing the logo of United Foods, Inc., had been stapled to applications and mailed to employees. It began: "Dear Friends and Neighbors, We invite you to apply for work at Bemis Mills, a new division of United Foods, Inc."

It went on to explain, "Bemis Mills will hire employees in several steps as we take the mill to full capacity." The company would notify those selected for hiring during the "first step" on Thursday and then meet with them in small groups over the next two days.

The threads of information I'd been gathering during the past month assumed a pattern as I reviewed the document. It was obvious that this plan had been initiated within days of the plant closing. The management of American Mills, as well as the civic and political officials with whom I'd met, had deliberately obfuscated the truth to both the union and public. I now understood what lay beneath Mayor Charles Farmer's cryptic remarks that "things were in the works," during our cordial and innocuous meeting. His assertions to the press about actively soliciting state funds to reopen the plant had been entirely disingenuous.

United Foods was attempting to take over the business as if there had never been a union. In fact, the union hadn't once been mentioned in statements to employees or the press. It was clearly their intention to move forward under this premise, confident that the transition would be immersed in courtroom dramas that could be dragged out indefinitely, during which time anything could happen. The local union would slowly dissipate and lose its identity, the officers driven by necessity to find new employment, and the national union would eventually make a business decision to cut its losses and allocate resources elsewhere. If, several years later, the litigation endgame resulted in the payment of awards and penalties, it would be shrugged off as the cost of doing business.

There was no doubt in my mind about the outcome of the selective hiring process. Committee members were contacted and advised to fill out applications to secure their legal standing, but not to expect a phone call on Thursday. I explained that while the union's program of legal intervention would hopefully lead to an early reversal, they should prepare themselves for a bitter conflict.

Waiting for events to bear testimony to writing on the wall can be a fatal delay in desperate circumstances. The momentum was ours to recapture. I scheduled a press conference for the next morning and prepared a leaflet for immediate mailing (Fig. 10).

Donald Vandiver returned my call that evening and I read him the leaflet. "Them's pretty strong words," he cautioned. "Don't you think we ought to at least wait and see what comes out of the meeting on Thursday?"

"There's no time to waste here on diplomacy, Rev," I said. "They've already stolen the initiative. A man comes up to you on the street and insults you, you try to talk and reason with him. A man comes up to you with a knife, you try to kill him."

"I understand what that's about," he acknowledged. "Whatever comes to pass, you know I'll have your back."

The press conference had been scheduled for 10:00 a.m. at the union hall in order to make the midday broadcast. As I glanced in the mirror during my morning ablutions, a ragged face with unkempt hair stared back at me. I had slept poorly, unable to unwind from two days of hard travel and the news that greeted my arrival. I drank an extra cup of coffee, knowing from experience that my game would switch on the moment I shook hands with the reporters.

The escalation of a bankruptcy case into a labor dispute had caught the media's attention. The primary function of a newspaper is to sell copy and nothing increases readership more than the drama of conflict. The press is ultimately in the entertainment business every bit as much the motion picture industry.

Tom Corwin arrived first, accompanied by a photographer. Corwin was a friendly, open-minded young man who asked intelligent questions. It felt as though we were building a relationship and that I was winning him over. The television van showed up a few minutes later.

Following the interviews, I raced across town to retrieve leaflets, grabbed a sandwich, and returned to the hall to meet with local leadership and address envelopes. The committee's punctuality and grace under fire impressed me. They remained focused and methodical, keeping their questions brief and listening without interruption to the answers. It was a far cry from the hysterical conclave I'd encountered at this office eight months earlier. What I felt for these people exceeded the "solidarity" of labor movement rhetoric. They had earned my love, loyalty and respect. I knew that I would stop at nothing and risk everything on their behalf.

Tom Corwin's article in the evening edition appeared beneath the headline: *Decision on textile plant not a 'done deal.' Union to keep pressing for worker rights.*

He capitalized on the colorful approach with which I'd sought to infuse the controversy. From our half-hour discussion, he extracted the commentary: "It's very clear that American Mills and United Foods are attempting to use the bankruptcy process for the intended purpose of busting the union. . . . We're not looking for a nice lawsuit settlement out of this. Our end result goal is to get United Foods/American Mills to adhere to NLRB standards in regard to all aspects of the collective bargaining process."

Corwin had challenged me with assertions from United Foods that it "may close the mill if forced to take on additional liabilities, such as bargaining with the union."

"That's the stereotypical bluff of every employer that is trying to run a non-union plant. That's the way they threaten the workforce; that's the way they threaten the community."

The article documented my concern that if United Foods was successful in its efforts, it might begin a trend and that companies and unions alike would closely monitor the litigation's progress. "Whichever way it goes, it's going to be a shot heard 'round the South."

I awoke on the morning of November 16, uncertain about what to expect as I prepared for the scheduled bargaining session. The phone rang, and the caller introduced himself as American Mills comptroller Richard Moore. I found this a bit unusual as the man had never been involved in labor relations and I'd only encountered him in passing on several occasions.

His tone seemed awkward and apologetic as he explained that he was the sole employee who remained on the payroll of American Mills. The other members of management had either been hired by United Foods or moved on. As the bargaining session was between ACTWU and American Mills, he would have to present himself as the company's representative. He further elaborated that the meeting couldn't take place in the plant conference room because this was now a United Foods facility and wanted to know if we could meet instead at the union hall.

"Please don't take offence," I said, noting his discomfort and that he was a pawn rather than a protagonist in these matters. "Do you have authority to negotiate, or even an understanding of the collective bargaining process and the issues that need to be resolved?"

"I'll do the best I can to be of assistance and respond to all legitimate requests from the union," he answered.

Given the short notice and lack of immediate alternatives, I agreed to his unorthodox request.

Mark had previously alluded to the retaining of Agee, Allen, Godwin, Morris & Laurenzi, an employment law firm representing unions and the rights of individual workers. I drove to the union hall for a preliminary meeting with him and Ernest, along with a partner from the firm named Mark Allen. I updated them about who we would actually be meeting with and where.

The attorney was a clean cut gentleman of similar age to the rest of us, with a casual and unpretentious demeanor, who had been practicing labor law since graduation. He opened his briefcase and presented a motion that one of his partners had filed with the bankruptcy court:

> Comes now the Amalgamated Clothing and Textile
> Workers Union and its Local 281 and herein files its
> Motion to Suspend Temporary Approval of Liquidating
> and Occupancy Agreement and Objection, noting in
> support thereof as follows:

The motion emphasized that as "the exclusive representative of the employees of American Mills, Inc.," the union should have been notified and given opportunity to participate in the November 13 hearing, and that United Foods and American Mills were in violation of the law, having changed the terms and conditions of employment without bargaining.

A letter had also been faxed to Don Dresser of United Foods, advising that ACTWU and its Local 281 were now represented by Allen's firm. The document constituted a formal request to bargain and an admonition to maintain the status quo regarding terms and conditions of employment, including seniority and recall.

We reviewed the situation from the perspective of the National Labor Relations Act and prepared charges on the union hall typewriter in anticipation of how the next two days were likely to unfold.

A Labor Board charge briefly lists the allegations against the respondent and sections of the Act violated. The NLRB assigns a primary investigator to initiate a process of soliciting testimony and material evidence, which transpires over a period of weeks or even months, depending on the complexity of the case. The regional director then instructs a committee of attorneys and agents to review the file, and if the allegations are deemed substantive, a complaint is issued.

The parties are given an opportunity to negotiate a resolution subject to the Board's approval. The respondent has the option of challenging the complaint in a trial before an administrative law judge. The outcome of litigation can be appealed to the actual National Labor Relations Board in Washington, a five-person panel appointed by the president of the

United States. Their adjudication is subject to further appeal in federal district court and, in rare situations, to the Supreme Court.

The charge prepared at the union hall was filed against United Foods and American Mills as joint employers. It cited their refusal to bargain, along with unilateral changes to the terms of layoff and recall. It would be submitted to Region 26 of the National Labor Relations Board in Memphis.

Committee members joined us at noon and received an explanation of the legal actions being undertaken and changes in meeting format.

At exactly 1 p.m., a frail looking man of less than average height walked tentatively through the door of the large meeting area. The comptroller's sparse grey hair covered a narrow and humorless, but not disagreeable face. He was attired in a tweed sport jacket with well pressed trousers. The casting director of fate couldn't have selected a more appropriate bean counter for our drama.

We were casually arrayed around two long folding tables which had been hastily arranged lengthwise for the negotiations. "Let me make one thing clear," said Richard Moore as he entered the room. "I'm not going to tolerate any physical abuse."

I glanced at Mark and then several of the committee members. "I'm afraid you've seen too many movies," I told him. "That's not what we're about. No harm is going to come to you in here and no one is going to disrespect you in any way. You have my word."

The timid comptroller appeared to muster some confidence and came forward to shake hands and assume his lone chair on one side of the table. He said that as of midnight on November 15, all American Mills employees had been terminated except for him. Most of the salaried employees had been retained by United Foods, but the hourly workers would have to submit employment applications and await the results. He had personally not been hired but would remain with American Mills during the transition.

"I understand that you're here with authority to bargain regarding the effects of plant closing," said our attorney.

"But the plant is reopening on Monday," objected Moore.

"Let me phrase it another way," said Mark Allen, maintaining his composure. "I'm referring to the ceasing of operations by American Mills, Inc., and its effect upon employees. Do you have authority to bargain on behalf of the employer in regard to mandatory subjects as defined by the National Labor Relations Board?"

"I'm afraid I still don't have any idea what you're asking for," said Moore.

"What we're talking about is unpaid vacation money, the pension fund, insurance benefits, for openers," Ernest interjected, not being one to long restrain his frustrations. "What does the company propose in regard to making full restitution of vacation pay accrued in 1989? What are its plans to sufficiently fund the pension to insure future benefits? Have COBRA notifications been sent out in regard to medical benefits? Does American Mills intend to make people whole, or will these liabilities be assumed by United Foods?"

"I have no idea," replied Moore. "I'll be happy to take your suggestions back to our attorneys."

"It's clear you have no idea what this meeting is supposed to be about," said our attorney. "I understand the awkwardness of your position, but the union doesn't negotiate by conferring suggestions through a messenger. What I am going to give you is an information request to take back to whoever actually remains in control of the entity known as American Mills. You're welcome to stretch your legs or get some coffee. This will take me about half an hour to prepare."

It would be many years before professionals routinely arrived in conference rooms with laptops slung across their shoulders. Mark Allen pulled a pen from his shirt pocket and began preparing a six-page document on his legal pad.

In addition to requesting detailed employee information, including entitlements in various benefit categories, the union sought copies of all correspondence and agreements between American Mills and United Foods. As the representative of employees and plaintiff in multiple legal actions, the union was on solid ground in demanding an expedited response. The nature of the relationship between the two companies, along with the underlying process and reasoning on which it was built, would hopefully soon be exposed.

The members of the union committee rushed off in different directions, and I followed up with reporters as promised. The *Jackson Sun* featured another Tom Corwin story as its headline that evening: *Plant deal meets resistance. United Foods accused of trying to bust union.*

I discussed the deliberately pointless meeting and the deception of American Mills management, who just the previous week had claimed there was nothing to report concerning progress to reopen the plant. "This is an attempt to make an end-run around the union. . . . We'll stop at nothing; we intend to fight them to the screaming limit in court and every other way."

United Foods and American Mills representatives were unavailable for comment.

The American people have varying levels of comprehension and sympathy in regard to organized labor, but nothing is more reviled than corporate deception and contempt for the law. As the press grew increasingly comfortable with reporting the controversy from this perspective, the union's fight against the collusion of two underhanded companies evolved into a popular issue within Jackson and surrounding communities.

I felt as though a relationship of informality and goodwill was being developed with both Tom Corwin and television reporters. My passion and willingness to step out on a limb generated more column inches than the dry, predictable rhetoric of management. The practical application of media coverage to the overall campaign remained to be assessed. At the very least, company efforts to effect a clandestine transition had been exposed.

United Foods management had scheduled small group meetings with its selected employees to run the course of the next two days. Rather than await the receipt of information through legal channels, I decided to conduct reconnaissance on the ground.

As anticipated, despite long and in many cases exemplary work records, none of the committee members had been rehired. Several of them stood with me at the personnel gate to take note of those who entered the plant. I was adamant that there should be no hostility expressed towards employees reporting for orientation, even in the case of low seniority nonmembers who were filling jobs they'd held for years.

"You can't blame a person for accepting a job, especially under these circumstances," I told the committee as we huddled in the biting November wind shortly before the first arrivals.

"They're not the enemy and treating them as such plays right into the company's hands. Union busters always count on a division of the workforce and the anger of the local union to drive the wedge. We have to stay a step ahead of them . . . anticipate what they're expecting and do the opposite.

"Our best chance is to do everything we can to unify the workforce and, at the very least, try not to alienate people and push them over to the company's side. The folks about to walk through that gate are getting screwed also. Last month they had a decent job under a union contract. Today, they're returning like dogs hoping for a bone. When the time comes, we'll need as many of them as possible to stand with us."

"Hey, hey," said Georgia. "Y'all hear what the man is saying? We're not here like common hoodlums looking for a fight. We're here to watch and learn what tricks the company has up its sleeve. Look . . . here they come now."

For the next two days, we cordially greeted and spoke with workers as they entered and left through the gate. While the meetings were in progress, we did our best to alleviate the boredom and ignore the cold by sharing jokes and anecdotes. Occasionally, someone made a run for coffee or sandwiches.

Committee members identified the employees who reported, and Georgia took notes, indicating race, gender, and union membership. Of the 138 hourly workers who had been rehired, only twenty-nine were union members. There were no shop stewards included, with the exception of one individual whose activity had been marginal. The largest demographic was white males.

One of the union members lingered with us on his way out, glancing about in the hope that he wasn't being observed by management. His level of support for the union might not have been apparent over the years, due to a quiet demeanor, and lack of involvement precipitated by the need to work two jobs.

"What did they tell y'all at the meeting?" asked Georgia.

"They talked a whole lot of shit . . . about how this is a new company with new rules . . . about the mistakes of the old company and how they was going to turn things around. They congratulated us on being the first ones hired and said that would make us the most senior employees at the plant."

"Did they say anything about the union?" asked Betty Trice.

"No, they didn't bring it up and nobody asked. All they said was if we had any questions or complaints, we should talk with management.

Look, I got something for you. I managed to leave with an extra copy of the employee handbook."

He slipped me a thick, stapled pamphlet and walked to the parking lot, looking back over his shoulder.

The committee members and I greeted the next group of workers and were once again left standing in each other's company on an empty street. The sky was overcast and the wind was picking up. I wished I had worn a sweater under my jacket. I began browsing through the handbook, grateful there was something to occupy my attention for the next hour.

"What's it say in there, chief?" asked Donald. "Anything good?" he smirked.

"You'll love this part," I replied, reading aloud.

EMPLOYMENT AT WILL

It is the policy of the Company that all employees are employed at the will of the Company for an indefinite period. Employees may resign from the Company at any time, for any reason, and may be terminated by the Company at any time, for any reason, and with or without notice. The at-will nature of an employee's employment may not be modified or altered except by an express written agreement signed by both the employee and the President of United Foods.

"So, they're pretty much saying, in not so many words, that there ain't no union and Just Cause is a thing of the past," remarked Georgia.

"That's about the size of it," I replied, "until we shove it back down their throats."

"Amen to that brother," said Donald.

"Look at the bright side," I continued. At least they've acknowledged in writing that employees aren't indentured servants and retain the right to quit if they become miserable enough."

"I'll bet there's no grievance procedure either," said the Rev.

I flipped through the booklet until arriving at the final page. "No, what they have instead is a 'Complaint Procedure,'" I answered, quickly scanning the text. "It says that an employee is free to raise a 'complaint,' first with his supervisor and then with his department manager. If the 'problem remains unsettled,' it is brought before 'The Employee Relations Committee' for a final decision."

"And who's on this committee?" Donald interrupted.

"The Personnel Manager, a coworker chosen by the employee, and a supervisor. I wonder how many 'complaints' will be resolved in the employee's favor?"

"They'll probably just 'terminate the employee for any reason' for having opened his mouth, before it even gets that far," reflected Betty.

We passed the handbook around, the review and discussion of which took us through the remaining hours. Georgia drew our attention to the "Dress Code," which prohibited items of attire that were not in "good taste," including shorts and cut-off shirts.

"I suppose they'll consider it in 'good taste' when people stink like pigs in the summer," she noted.

In addition to intelligence gathering, the union's vigil at the plant gate served another purpose. It demonstrated our continued presence and resolve, providing tangible substance to what the workers had been reading in the newspaper.

Tom Corwin continued his coverage in the *Sun* with an article titled, *Union joins scuffle over United Foods' mill takeover.* The piece elaborated on the union's legal position regarding the NLRB charges and the motion filed in bankruptcy court. It also reported that American Mills would no longer be participating in the labor-management committee that had been established to provide assistance to displaced workers.

A Memphis newspaper ran an inside story, omitting the controversies and featuring a lengthy interview with Mayor Farmer, who extolled the virtues of the takeover, referring to it as "extremely pleasing."

There would be few opportunities to affect the course of events before the hearing in bankruptcy court at the end of the following week. The advent of Thanksgiving weekend on Thursday preempted other considerations and marked a lull in hostilities.

I checked my appointment book and remembered that I had previously scheduled another meeting with Mayor Farmer for Monday at 1:00 p.m. My efforts to solicit his allegiance had been an exercise in futility, but with nothing else planned, I decided to insert my presence into his world once again.

The mayor was waiting for me in the municipal conference room when I arrived, and he rose to greet me. "I see that you didn't bring the little lady with you this time," he commented as we shook hands.

"No, she's back home with her mother, getting ready for the holidays." We took our seats.

"And where is home exactly? You may have mentioned, but it's hard for me to keep track of details. I meet with so many people during the course of a week."

"North Carolina, near Chapel Hill," I answered.

"Oh, you must be a Tar Heel fan! Are you looking forward to the game this weekend?"

"Actually, I don't follow sports," I replied, losing patience with the pleasantries.

I wondered to what extent this lightweight even comprehended that we were now entrenched on opposite sides in a bitter labor and community dispute. I saw no advantage in maintaining the facade of diplomacy. "You weren't truthful with me at our last meeting regarding the plant's future. I would appreciate knowing why."

"I wasn't at liberty to discuss the details at the time. I would think that you would be delighted now that the outcome is known and people are back at work."

"The organization I represent has been illegally displaced, along with some of the most senior and experienced employees, many of whom happen to be my friends. I find nothing to be delighted about. Read the newspapers. Perhaps the next person to be displaced will be the mayor in the general election."

"That will be for the voters to decide," the mayor replied, maintaining his banal disposition.

There had been nothing to lose by initiating the exchange, but there was no point in prolonging it. Perhaps a seed had been planted that would later sprout into a political reevaluation of his position.

I prepared a leaflet announcing a union meeting for the following week, appealing to both the displaced and rehired workers. It was essential that the members of Local 281 remain a cohesive force within the community. The outcry of union professionals would ring hollow without them.

In contrast to their predecessors, the owners of United Foods were sophisticated and cunning. The inevitability of conflict had most certainly been factored into their business plan. I intended to offer the anticipated battle, but with an approach for which they would not be prepared.

The meeting announcement rallied workers against UFI's employee handbook:

> WAKE UP! The nightmare is real. You've just had a taste of life without a Union. Some of you have given your lives to this mill and not been called back. Those that have been called back find themselves treated like kids in reform school:
>
> —WORKERS CAN BE FIRED WITHOUT CAUSE
> —INSULTING WORK RULES
> —INSULTING DRESS CODE
> —"NO SLACK" ATTENDANCE POLICY
> —"LATE" AFTER ONE MINUTE
> —NO SENIORITY—NOW OR LATER
> —NO BENEFITS
> —NO GRIEVANCE PROCESS

UFI was operating the plant with eight-hour crews. I concluded the announcement by scheduling additional meetings at midnight and 8:00 a.m. for the convenience of second and third shift employees, aware that attendance would be light but wanting no one to feel excluded.

Tom Corwin's coverage sprawled across the front page of the *Jackson Sun: Mill reopens amid union frustrations*. UFI officials again refused to comment, giving me another opportunity to continue defining the story: "Many of the most senior employees have been bypassed. They're still on the unemployment line."

The article noted that out of two dozen local officers and stewards, only one had been rehired.

I received a call from Mike Zucker of the union's Corporate Affairs Department in Washington. At my request, he had been conducting research on United Foods, a heretofore unheard-of company within our organization. The clothing and textile union had no prior reason to amass information about a producer of frozen vegetables.

UFI wasn't simply in the business of acquiring distressed facilities at bargain prices. Within that niche, it had developed a history of targeting organized plants and successfully eliminating the union. The investigation had uncovered multiple instances, including the demise of longstanding Teamster locals. Having a chance to exercise this unsavory specialty in their own backyard must have been irresistible to the Tankersley brothers.

I drove to the printer the next morning to oversee the cut-and-paste layout of the new leaflet and waited as the copies were run. The owner was now accustomed to dropping everything else on my account to generate instant turnaround.

I stopped for a sandwich to eat in the car while racing to the union hall for another press conference and to meet with committee members for what we now called an "envelope party." The timing seemed auspicious as reporters could receive a copy of the just-printed leaflet.

On the way back to my house that evening, I pulled into a convenience store to see if the latest edition of the *Jackson Sun* had hit the stands. I was stunned by the headline: *Mill worker questions truth of union's charges.*

The article featured an interview with one of the recently rehired employees, a middle-aged white woman named Linda Morris. It began by quoting her objections to the union's position: "They're just interfering with getting the plant running. What they've said is just not true."

She disputed the allegation that United Foods was discriminating against union members, claiming that during her hiring process, "The word 'union' was not mentioned once."

The article continued, "She also took issue with a union claim that many of the senior employees were not rehired, saying that she was rehired and had nine years' seniority."

The story resumed on page 2 and wrapped around a smiling picture of the employee. It listed the union's objections to the employee manual, borrowing the bullet format used in the leaflet along with some of the text. I was quoted from the recent interview, characterizing the rules as "repressive and offensive even by standards at the turn of the century."

This was followed by additional commentary from Ms. Morris, who said that not only did she see "nothing wrong with the new directives" but that some represented a "definite improvement."

I turned back to the front page, glanced at the byline and noted that this had been the work of Tom Corwin. The evening news on Channel 7 echoed a similar theme. It was frustrating that neither reporter had contacted me for a response to the criticism. It would have been an effortless rebuttal.

Management had no need to inquire about the union membership of applicants as the cards were on file. Linda Morris considered herself "senior" based on nine years of service. She wouldn't have been viewed in that light by the thirty-year veteran who should have been recalled to fill her position.

Linda had never belonged to the union and obviously hadn't been curious enough to read the contract. Had she taken the time, she would have found herself hard pressed to specify the "improvements" offered in the United Foods handbook compared to the Just Cause provisions of the collective bargaining agreement.

Despite their lack of substance and foundation, I knew that her published remarks would be damning in the eyes of the general public.

I was tempted to call reporters the next morning, but my instincts cautioned against it. It would be better to allow Linda to have her fifteen minutes of fame and then hopefully disappear once again into obscurity. Through acknowledgment, her platform might become that of an ongoing participant.

Instead I contacted Franklin Long, president of the Jackson Central Labor Council and a long-time resident, to see if he could offer any insight as to why the reporters had suddenly reversed their perspective in such a heavy-handed manner. "What you've got to understand," he said, "is how closely tied the owners of the *Jackson Sun* and Channel 7 are with the Chamber of Commerce. They probably got with their editors and issued new instructions regarding coverage of this issue. Honestly, I'm surprised it took them this long."

"What do you think it means going forward?" I asked.

"I hate to say it, my friend, but I think you've already seen the shape of things to come."

I packed my suitcases and drove toward the Nashville airport to fly home for the holidays. Halfway there, traffic slowed to a halt. My phone calls had already put me behind schedule and I envisioned missing the flight, spending Thanksgiving alone in Jackson away from my daughter.

Pulling onto the shoulder and passing stalled cars at forty miles per hour, I eventually came upon an accident scene and eased back into the crawling traffic before law enforcement noticed. Minutes later, I was compensating for lost time as the speedometer pushed eighty. I arrived at the terminal gate running with luggage in hand and only seconds to spare.

CHAPTER 16

I was unable to offer Colie a traditional holiday celebration so I took her to a fancy restaurant that served Thanksgiving luncheon. I then returned her to her mom's, where she could eat more turkey.

Hollie informed me that she had made arrangements to visit her brother in Washington with Colie. I was disappointed at having time with my daughter cut short, but this wasn't the sort of thing we quarreled about. Her mother had never disparaged me or attempted to interfere with our trips to Tennessee. It would have been bad form to object.

I visited friends and attended social gatherings but found little pleasure or comfort therein. I'd driven and run like a maniac to get home for the holidays only to discover that my contemplations remained in Jackson. I realized that my only roots were deep within and that I no longer truly lived anywhere.

My return flight was on Sunday evening. I needed to be in position in case the week began with yet another round of unexpected developments.

I shuffled into the kitchen on Monday morning and noted with relief that there were no messages on my answering machine. As the day progressed, I began receiving calls from newspaper and television reporters seeking updates and requesting additional information regarding the legal cases. I responded normally and made no mention of the Linda Morris story. The *Sun* refrained from further coverage, while there was a thirty-second spot on the evening news.

The previous week, Franklin Long had invited me to address the Central Labor Council, informing me that six other unions administered locals in the Jackson area. In light of what had been revealed about the broader profile of United Foods, I accepted the invitation and considered a context for my presentation while driving to the meeting.

The political and social tides in our society had turned against unions in the early 1980s when Ronald Reagan (who had launched his political career as a union president) decimated the Air Traffic Controllers Union. Since then, union busting had been in high season. Meanwhile, the industrialization of third world economies had precipitated a growing epidemic of American plant closings. The labor movement had weakened and become increasingly vulnerable as our manufacturing base eroded and private sector union membership declined from 33 percent in the 1960s to 14 percent in the late 1980s.

I believed that other unions could be rallied against the common predator that had entered our midst.

Two hours later I returned home with assurances of support but uncertainty about the potential impact. The various union locals combined were only a minor demographic within the community.

There were approximately fifty people in attendance at the Local 281 meeting the following afternoon. Given that most of the membership had been out of work for nearly two months and the absence of personal contact, I was somewhat surprised and gratified by the showing. Reverend Vandiver began the meeting with prayer, and Georgia welcomed the members, requesting that questions and comments be held until the update was concluded.

I explained what I had learned about United Foods and the legal strategies initiated by our attorneys. I reiterated the union's commitment to stand by those who had spent their lives working at the plant and shared the pledges of support we had received from other unions.

Several hands rose when the floor was opened for discussion. I called first upon an older white man who'd worked in the card room with Donald and been a member of Local 281 for nearly as long as I had lived. "I was getting set to retire in two years," he said. "What's gonna happen to my pension? Am I gonna get anything or is that all gone now?"

"The pension benefits you've already earned are protected and insured by the federal government," I told him. "Even if the fund went belly up or these crooks stole it all, you'd still get your money. The thing is, the amount will be frozen and won't continue to grow based upon additional years of service, unless the courts force the company to bring you back under the terms of the old contract."

I pointed to a younger black man who was short in stature but appeared agile and muscular under his jacket. He had not previously been a familiar face at the hall. "OK, look here," he began. "I worked at this mill for seven years, which I know is less than most of the folks in this room. But I've been a member of the union that whole time. I filled out my application, and I didn't get called back either. From what I hear, there's people working in my department with less than a year.

"Y'all been talking the talk and that's good. I like what I been reading in the newspaper and frankly, that's why I'm here today. But I wanna know when the talk is gonna turn into walk! When we gonna be out there with the picket signs and start showing this company what we're really about?"

There were murmurs of approval and a brief smattering of applause.

"I'm a step ahead of you," I answered. "I've already said exactly the same thing to our lawyers and the people from the union who sent me here. But they all want us to hold off until we go to court on Friday.

"This is a conservative part of the country. They don't want us to do anything that might give United Foods the opportunity to play to all the negative stereotypes about unions and influence the judge against us. The court hearing is our one chance to get things straightened out quickly. If that doesn't work, this is going to turn into a long, ugly fight. There'll be plenty of time for picket lines and other things as well."

"What other things?" asked the young man.

"If I told you, someone in here would run their mouth and word would get back to the company. For all we know, they could have someone planted in this room, just like they planted someone in front of the reporters. Be patient, brother. You'll get your chance . . . either to work or fight . . . I'm not sure which."

"Do you think we're gonna win on Friday?" one of the women called out.

"I'm not sure what to expect. That's why we've also filed charges with the Labor Board. But our lawyers think we have a shot, so I've got to go with that."

I remained at my desk after the meeting had adjourned to speak with individuals who wished to raise something in private. A short, husky

white man approached, appearing to be about my age and wearing a
black leather jacket. He was another union member with whom I'd had
little contact during the American Mills phase. He waited politely until
the others had dispersed and then stood over me.

"I wanted you to have a look at this picture," he said.

The photograph was slightly out of focus and showed what appeared
to be a piece of distressed architecture. "That's what's left of the canning
plant in California where my brother-in-law used to work," the man explained. "They'd been with the Teamsters until United Foods took over
the company.

"United Foods did sit down to negotiate a new contract, but it was
all a sham and they forced the Teamsters out on strike. As soon as that
happened they brought in scab labor to cross the picket line and began
running the plant without a union. The Teamsters finally realized it was
a lost cause and someone burnt the place to the ground. That's what
you're looking at."

"Was the plant ever rebuilt?" I asked. "Is it running now?"

"No. The damage was too bad. It still looks just like it is in the photo."

The day before the court hearing seemed a good time to expand my political contacts into the state and national arenas. I had scheduled a morning meeting with State House Representative Matt Kisber and one later in the day with Congressman John Tanner, accompanied by Donald
Vandiver. The presence of an articulate minister would be favorably received by Bible Belt politicians and might offset their preconceptions
about labor unions. I was smartly attired in a navy blue sport coat I had
recently purchased.

The state official graciously welcomed us and listened patiently, providing assurances that he would investigate further and exert whatever
influence was deemed appropriate. My expectations weren't excessive,
but neither had there been anything to lose in reaching out. Even one
well-placed politician's advocacy might prove useful at the right time.

I treated Donald to lunch, and we drove to Congressman Tanner's
office, which was located seventy-five miles away. I considered the distance to be a positive factor, as it meant we would not be meeting with
another member of the Jackson business community.

The congressman asked numerous questions which, along with his
congenial manner, engendered a spark of optimism. I was uncertain

how much he would prioritize our cause, but didn't sense insincerity. Following a ninety-minute discussion, I rose to shake his hand.

"I believe that you forgot to cut the patch off your jacket sleeve," he pointed out with deference. There was in fact a rectangular name-brand patch sewn above the cuff on my right sleeve. I'd assumed it was intended to be decorative, similar to trousers, which often have permanent patches affixed to a rear pocket.

"Yes, you're right," I responded. "I was in such a hurry this morning that I forgot to remove it. Thank you for pointing it out."

As we returned to the parking lot, I asked the Rev, "Are you really supposed to cut these off?"

"Yes, you are," he smiled, "usually as soon as you get the jacket home."

Mark Pitt made a detour to my house that evening on his drive to Memphis. "I've brought something from the Knoxville office that should make your life a bit easier with all the group mailings you've been doing," he said, standing in my doorway. "Give me a hand bringing it in from the trunk."

We walked to his car, and he handed me a cumbersome monitor screen as he gathered up wiring and a computer terminal. "Where do you want this?" he asked as we entered the living room, and I directed him to my workspace on the kitchen table.

He briefly exited again, returned with a printer, and began to dexterously assemble the components. "I had my secretary prepare a data base with all the employee addresses," he told me. "You should check it for accuracy and to see if anyone got left off. Now, when you have to do a mailing, you can just print out address labels and be on your way.

"Oh, I almost forgot." He reached into his briefcase and placed a large box of labels on the table. "This should also be really useful when it comes to organizing information as you investigate the various charges. You can assemble it the way you want and then print out reports."

I stared with consternation at the equipment that now sprawled across my personal work area. "I don't have a clue how to use any of this," I said.

"It's not that hard," Mark chuckled. "Here, let me walk you through it. I'll start you off with the address list and I can show you the rest another time."

During the era preceding the advent of Windows, the process of interfacing with computer files was far more intricate than future generations would ever imagine. I observed Mark's nimble exercise of the protocols with all the comprehension of a cat watching television.

"See, it's all fairly straightforward," he said, as the bargaining unit list appeared on the screen. "You should be good to go from here."

I told him I'd call if further instruction was needed and changed the subject. "Has there been any contact with United Foods?"

"After ten days of phone tag, I finally got up with Don Dresser yesterday," Mark replied. "I requested that we set up a meeting to discuss recognition and bargaining but he wasn't interested. He complained about UFI being accused in the press of trying to bust the union and how he wasn't going to put up with that. He said he'd see us in court."

I arose at dawn the next morning to eat a hasty breakfast, knowing that I had to be walking through the doors of the Memphis courthouse by 9:00 a.m. I donned my pinstripe suit for the first time since the Nashville meeting, slipping the well-preserved tie noose over my head.

The union's law firm planned to put Georgia on the stand, so I stopped by her house at seven to provide transportation and review her testimony. Several carloads of stewards and other union members would also be joining us. The union considered it important for both the judge and media to see the faces of people whose lives hung in the balance, and to provide an opportunity for the core of Local 281 to remain engaged in the process.

"I believe this is the first time I've ever seen you in a suit and tie," Georgia remarked as I whipped around the entrance ramp onto the interstate. "You look very distinguished."

"I appreciate that, but I've never quite thought of myself as distinguished."

"What do you think of yourself as?" she smiled and looked toward me.

"I'm an outlaw," I said half jokingly. "I know how to fight and use it to help other people. I'm just someone who's seen too much and decided to do something about it."

"You're no outlaw," said Georgia. "Those guys who stand on the street corner selling that crack cocaine . . . they're outlaws. Them that took over our mill . . . they're outlaws as well. But you . . . if I was to have to stand before God right now and be judged, I'd swear that you were the one person wearing a suit in Jackson today that I know for sure is no crook."

I turned to Georgia with a look of gratitude.

"Phil, honey, watch the road and while you're at it, slow down!" she exclaimed. "I want to live to have my day in court."

Corporate bankruptcy hearings are an unparalleled multi-ring circus within the realm of jurisprudence, far more complex than the classic trial where two opposing parties vie for supremacy. In addition to the debtor in possession, attorneys for numerous creditors make their appearance, filing motions and offering testimony in favor of their clients' interests.

The Chapter 11 proceedings had been assigned to U.S. Bankruptcy Judge David Kennedy. A dozen attorneys were present in the courtroom along with officials of the organizations represented.

United Foods and American Mills had been awarded temporary approval to resume operations at the mill pursuant to the Liquidating and Occupancy Agreement presented to the court on November 13. The purpose of the current hearing was to determine if the arrangement would be allowed to continue. The L & O Agreement was in itself an interim measure in lieu of a final reorganization plan, which would be voted on by creditors at a Confirmation Hearing in January.

Donald Vandiver entered the courtroom, smiling graciously in his neatly pressed suit, followed by several of the stewards. He handed me the latest edition of the *Jackson Sun*, and I braced myself for the headline: *Textile workers' fate hangs on hearing. United Foods wants to keep plant open.*

I was relieved to find that the coverage was unbiased, though lacking the human interest and drama of recent weeks. Tom Corwin included commentary from six of the primary litigants, presenting an unsentimental but fairly balanced portrayal of issues before the court.

Sam Morris was the attorney appearing for the union—a clean-cut man in his thirties with short curly black hair and a manner similar to the partner I'd worked with a couple of weeks earlier. He offered me copies of exhibits tendered at the previous hearing, which included the L & O Agreement, and supporting documents addressed to creditors and UFI shareholders. As I scanned the pages, the specifics of the proposed reorganization came into sharper focus.

United Foods would initially function as an "agent" of American Mills, "converting existing raw material and work in progress into inventory." The proceeds would reimburse the company for costs, with the remainder paid to Bankers Trust, which held the secured interest in these goods. UFI would have sole discretion over hiring and establishing terms of employment.

Following this transitional phase, Bemis Mills would become a division of United Foods, which would lease the building and equipment from American Mills for seven years at the rate of $150,000 per month, paid to a trustee for disbursement to creditors. UFI would retain options to either terminate the lease at any time or purchase the facility.

Various creditors and the union presented a wall of opposition to the plan's approval but for disparate reasons. The creditors sought to claim the portion of tangible assets to which their debt had been secured, rather than receiving small disbursements over a seven-year period. If their motions prevailed, operations would cease in favor of a full liquidation. The union's objective was for United Foods to continue running the plant but in a manner that fulfilled its collective bargaining responsibilities.

Our legal position was based on Section 1113 of the Bankruptcy Code, which had been legislated to prevent the process from being used as a vehicle to circumvent collective bargaining. The statute mandates that a bankrupt company remain bound by an existing labor contract, or status quo, and the obligation to bargain.

Under exigent circumstances, the employer can seek relief from the court in regard to provisions that might compromise the reorganization, but only after having made a reasonable effort to negotiate modifications with the union. The language and implementation of the Liquidating and Occupancy Agreement amounted to an undisguised renunciation of these requirements.

Sam Morris, Mark Pitt, and I took seats on the left side of the courtroom and were joined by twenty-five stewards and senior members from Local 281. The two employers and their creditors shared the right. The intervening aisle was like a railroad track separating neighborhoods of two social classes.

The union was neither first on the agenda nor foremost in the court's mind as the hearing began with the objections of ITT Commercial Finance Corp. which had outstanding loans to American Mills totaling $3.85 million. Two dozen local activists who had arrived hungry for righteous battle sat stupefied through two hours of accounting and legal minutiae. It was difficult to resist whispering jokes about the pompous bank executives, which caused consternation to our attorney but appeared to go unnoticed by others in the courtroom.

Even that which is experienced as eternal eventually comes to an end. Judge Kennedy graciously smiled at the ITT representatives, thanked them for their presentation, and called a brief recess.

When we returned from the lobby, Mark and I remained standing together in the aisle. Union professionals have little tolerance for remaining seated and inactive.

Bradley MacLean was the attorney representing United Foods, and I was unprepared for the first witness he called to the stand—Tennessee Lieutenant Governor John Wilder. During his introductory testimony, it was revealed that he had been serving on the United Foods Board of Directors for nine years. I realized that the network of political support reached much higher than the mayor's office or Chamber of Commerce.

Wilder was a short, plump man with wispy grey hair and rounded shoulders. He attempted to characterize the UFI takeover as a benign enterprise whose primary motivation was to save jobs and uphold the economic base of the Jackson community. He testified that the previous day he had visited the mill and encountered "a smiling group of workers. They were happy people who looked forward to the success of the new business."

As Wilder elaborated upon his depictions of employee utopia, Mark turned toward me and whispered sarcastically, "We were like one big happy family . . ."

"We were all just like one happy family," concluded the lieutenant governor.

Mark glanced in my eyes and snickered under his breath. The cliché performance might have amused me, except that Judge Kennedy seemed enamored of his distinguished witness and taking every word at face value.

Wilder was cross-examined by the attorney for Gibbs Machinery and then by the union. Sam Morris hammered him about his knowledge of United Foods' hiring practices and criteria.

"I am aware that they are hiring former American Mills employees, and I am aware that the ones they have hired have been about half black and about half white, and about the same number of union members that were employed by American Mills," Wilder responded.

The members of Local 281 briefly filled the courtroom with shouts of "No! No!" as the judge exclaimed, "Please. In respect, please."

Morris continued with his interrogation. "Let me ask you about that, Mr. Wilder. You said that the current employees represent the same percentage of union members as previously?"

MacLean objected but was overruled on grounds that relevancy could be later established.

"I'll tell you what I was advised before I came to this hearing today, that there are about 25 or 30 percent of the employees now hired that are union employees," the lieutenant governor answered.

"Who gave you that advice, Mr. Wilder?"

"I think it's Mr. Dan Tankersley."

I was impressed by our attorney's tenacious cross-examination but uncertain about its impact on the court.

MacLean's next witness was Mayor Charles Farmer. He again portrayed United Foods as a beneficent savior that had intervened in the spirit of community service, glorifying the positive effect this would have on the area's economy. Judge Kennedy smiled graciously at his commentary and periodically nodded his head in approval.

When the hearing reconvened after a break for lunch, the union found itself on the sidelines once again. Assistant U.S. Trustee Julie Chinn raised a conflict-of-interest concern regarding American Mills attorney Henry Shelton. A partner in Shelton's firm also sat on the United Foods Board of Directors. The judge elected to decide the matter at a future hearing but assured Shelton he wouldn't lose his fees.

The union was finally given an opportunity to present its own witnesses. Mark Pitt elaborated on the long collective bargaining history at the mill involving successive owners, which had abruptly ceased with the advent of United Foods.

Morris next called Georgia Bond. She testified that while jobs were being provided to Jackson residents, the question of who received those jobs was being ignored. Employees who'd served the mill for twenty or thirty years remained at home, struggling to pay their bills, while people imported from Huntsville, Alabama, seven months before worked their jobs.

Pointing to her coworkers in the assembly, she said, "If not for them, there wouldn't have been a plant for United Foods to come in and purchase."

Morris asked what she thought of the lieutenant governor's portrayal of employee morale when he visited the plant.

"Management probably told the workers that someone is visiting the plant and you should greet them with a smile," she responded.

Georgia personified a good local union leader throughout her testimony, maintaining a level head and emotional restraint. I was proud of her. She in no way resembled the militant hothead Mark Pitt had warned me about during our first meeting.

The next creditor to offer testimony was Gibbs Machinery regarding its motion to reclaim the fifty-four Sulzer looms for which payment had not been rendered. The company's attorney called its owner, Jimmy Gibbs, to take the stand. I was intrigued with this fellow as I looked back across the aisle and watched him rise to his feet. He was tall and broad shouldered with an athletic build visible even under his black suit, and wore a western-style string tie with polished boots emerging from neatly pressed trousers. His rugged, chiseled features contrasted with the bland countenances of the other creditors and their attorneys. He looked more like a man in the oil business than one engaged in the barter of used mill equipment. As he strode purposefully to the front of the courtroom, I sensed that one would be ill-advised to cross him, either professionally or personally.

Gibbs explained that the $2 million he was owed for the looms represented 15 percent of his working capital, which he couldn't afford to have tied up in a seven-year leasing arrangement. He was in the business of buying and selling liquidated equipment through cash transactions that didn't involve prolonged terms of credit.

His attorney, Jennie Latta, asked if he had been given details of the reorganization prior to the bankruptcy filing. Gibbs said that he was present at a meeting held in United Foods' headquarters on October 25 with Dominic Poon and the other major creditors. The officers of UFI had distributed and explained a twenty-six-page document outlining the plan.

Latta then inquired if he had attended any prior meetings to address the specific interests of his own business. Gibbs testified that he had met with Dominic Poon the day of the plant closing in an effort to discuss terms of payment for the looms. Poon had attempted to assure him that his "primary reason for wanting to shut the mill down was to basically force the two partners out and to bust the labor union."

There was agitated whispering on both sides of the aisle as Judge Kennedy requested silence.

"I have no further questions at this time, your honor," said Latta.

"Are there requests from counsel to cross-examine this witness?" Kennedy asked.

Sam Morris had been poised to rise like a runner awaiting the start of a race and being the first to declare intent, was granted permission by the court. He asked Jimmy Gibbs to elaborate on his meeting with Dominic Poon.

"I asked him why a man from his family of great wealth could not go ahead and buy my looms, and his statement was that his intention was to get his other partners out, and he said if he kept the plant shut for four months, some legalities I don't understand about labor unions, he could bust the union."

"Did you understand him to imply that he was planning to reopen then?" Morris continued.

"Yes."

"With non-union labor?"

"Yes."

Gibbs further asserted to having been told by Poon that United Foods had no idea how to run a textile mill and that within six to eight months, he planned to "walk back in and take it over," resuming timely payment of his debts.

Agitated discussions inundated the courtroom as the judge tried to restore order, finally pounding his gavel. Morris concluded his cross by eliciting a few more details, and Kennedy, noting that evening was now upon us, adjourned the hearing until Tuesday.

I personally had no idea whether to believe Jimmy Gibbs or if desperation and payback had motivated his testimony. It really didn't matter. We were engaged in a battle of appearances in which truth was not a participant. This had been the sort of unexpected miracle the union needed to regain the upper hand in regard to public perception. A crowd of journalists rushed to surround me as I exited the hearing.

I drove with Georgia to Jackson with the setting sun in my rearview mirror. "You did a great job today," I told her. "You were a real star."

"I put my hand on the Bible and took an oath to be honest, and that's how I answered the questions," she replied. "That was something, what that Gibbs fellow said, wasn't it? He sure shed some light on their dirty little scheme."

"Yes he did. I think he gave us back some credibility with the press. It remains to be seen how much it influences the hearing."

"All I can tell you is that I'm for what's right. I have always been for what's right. I believe if you stand up for what's right and don't back down, all will be revealed in its time and things will turn out the way they should."

"I hope it goes down like that," I said. "Sometimes being right before God and being right before a judge are two different things. I would love to see this over next week, with the senior people back at their jobs and us back at the bargaining table. If not, we're going to have to win this a different way."

"What way is that?" asked Georgia.

"On the street," I answered.

I didn't set my alarm when I turned in that night and slept until noon, using the weekend to recharge for the grueling days ahead. I cleared my mind over breakfast and drove to the newsstand. I inserted the coins and removed two copies as was my practice, believing that my enhancements to circulation warranted a complementary edition.

The headline above Tom Corwin's article loomed in two-inch type: *Mill deal portrayed as plot. Creditor says owner hopes to regain factory, bust union.* The story noted:

> The hearing came to an end with a bang when Gibbs took the stand to testify about a conversation he had with Poon soon after the plant closed. . . .
>
> Gibbs' testimony about Poon's intention to get rid of the union "corroborates everything we've been saying about how this whole deal came about," said Phil Cohen, International Representative for the union.

Dominic Poon was quoted in response. "That's nonsense. Do you think I'd say something like that? I'm an educated person. I think logically."

Don Dresser, on behalf of United Foods, proclaimed, "The mill is up and running and we're extremely proud."

Television and radio newsrooms likewise focused on the testimony of Jimmy Gibbs and its vindication of the union. The tide of media coverage had once again turned abruptly, this time back in our favor. I had no way of knowing for certain what had transpired behind the scenes at various news organizations, but imagined that courtroom events had sufficiently defined the story so as to supersede other considerations.

The materials I had received from Sam Morris included the proposed operating plan that was distributed by United Foods to creditors at the October 25 meeting. This occurred during the period when American Mills management was actively telling the union and community that it was soliciting new investors to perpetuate the existing company and Mayor Farmer claimed to be seeking government assistance.

There was a section titled, "Current Status of American Mills, Inc.," which began, "American Mills, Inc. is insolvent. . . . The statements show that the company sustained losses at a rate somewhat in excess of $200,000 per week."

It provided a detailed critique of the five-month rise and fall of American Mills, citing an "unrealistic" business plan, insufficient credit, and corroborated what Bob Knuckles had shared in confidence back in October:

> American Mills' business plan was premised upon obtaining 54 used Sulzer looms, installing them promptly, and putting them into service at full capacity within a short period of time. The looms were not operable when received. American Mills has spent in excess of $450,000 repairing and rebuilding the Sulzer looms. More work will be required. They have not yet been run at anything close to full efficiency. There is currently some question regarding whether the Sulzer

looms can be run at capacity due to the vibrations they create in the wood flooring and structure of the mill.

As I stared at the booklet bearing the United Foods logo, my euphoria over the recent media coverage began to ebb. I reflected on the previous day in court and didn't care much for Judge Kennedy. He impressed me as a highly educated man from a privileged background with little comprehension of the realities faced by the majority of people in our society. I believed that with the predisposition of a vain and superficial personality, he would gravitate toward simple answers and the course of least resistance.

Sam Morris was an articulate, forceful advocate but didn't possess the ruthless cunning of his adversary. While he eloquently appealed to the letter of the law in the courtroom and within his motions, UFI was appealing to the values and sensibilities of the judge.

I was not content to await the fruits of litigation in lieu of further action. I contemplated the entrenched position in which United Foods had strategically placed itself, considering whether there might be an area of vulnerability that had been overlooked. The union needed a way to draw blood with a surgical strike to the jugular . . . on a field of battle that didn't offer the luxury of indefinite procrastination.

I got in my car and drove to the plant, which was closed for the weekend. The reorganization proposal was beside me on the passenger seat. I circled around the empty brick building and passed the rear gate, which was used for deliveries.

The initial phase of the Liquidating and Occupancy Agreement was already in progress. Once United Foods had completed the manufacture of existing inventories into finished goods, it would begin to purchase its own raw materials. I wondered how much support we could expect from the Teamsters if we ran a picket line.

I returned to Riverside Drive and called Galin Meals, the president of Teamster Local 217, whom I had met at the Central Labor Council. (The Teamsters have a different organizational structure from ACTWU. Its locals generally encompass numerous employers and local presidents function as staff.)

Galin informed me that most Teamster contracts covering truck drivers contained a prohibition against crossing union picket lines, which in some instances extended to supervisors who might otherwise handle shipments to areas of dispute. UPS drivers would likewise not cross a picket line to make deliveries. He told me that we could also expect cooperation from some of the nonunion fleets—motivated either by sympathy or the desire to avoid confrontation.

The Teamsters' attorney in Nashville reinforced Galin's assessment and commitment for support. I contacted Georgia and Donald and asked them to begin compiling a list of all freight companies that historically had serviced the mill.

I successfully navigated the streets of Memphis on Monday afternoon and entered the office of our law firm for the first time. It was a large suite which exuded the presence of an established and successful practice. ACTWU was in the process of spending more money on legal fees than it could ever hope to recover in future union dues from Local 281.

Sam Morris greeted me at the door accompanied by Deborah Godwin, a partner who was working with him on the Labor Board case. We were scheduled to give affidavits and present evidence at Region 26 of the NLRB, the day following our return to bankruptcy court.

I walked past the attorneys and saw Mark and Ernest seated at a table engaged in animated discussion. I was glad that Ernest had flown in. His perspective from the field was closer to mine than that of anyone I'd thus far encountered in the union.

As I approached the two directors, a slender young man emerged from the restroom and took a seat among them. Ernest introduced me to Mike Zucker from the Corporate Affairs Department. He was short, wiry and his curly black hair was neatly cropped. His handshake was that of an intellectual rather than a man confident of his physical strength.

Mike's initial appearance hid what lay beneath. He was tenacious and formidable in the investigation of companies, identifying essential business relationships and weak links between them that could be penetrated and exploited. He was the union's equivalent of an intelligence analyst, who provided field agents with the information necessary to fulfill their mission. The polite and soft-spoken researcher was as tactically relentless as Ernest and I, from a different but complementary vantage point.

Sam and Deborah joined us and reviewed our legal strategies, distributing recently prepared Motions and Objections for our reference.

"Where do we stand in regard to pursuing a Transmarine remedy with the Board?" Mark interrupted.

"I think our foundation is fairly solid," said Deborah. "It would be difficult to argue that our meeting with the company's comptroller constituted bargaining over the effects of a plant closing. Under the 1965 precedent established in Transmarine Navigation, everyone who was employed before the layoff should be entitled to a minimum of two weeks' pay and benefits as compensation. I'll bring this up with the Board on Wednesday."

The analysis grew increasingly redundant, and I was eager to share my conversations with the Teamsters but restrained myself. We finally took a break to stretch our legs and refill coffee cups. On returning to the table, I seized the opportunity: "I appreciate the persistence and hard work of our attorneys. But we could be right as rain and still have these cases drag on for years through the appellate process. I don't have a good feeling about this bankruptcy judge. I'm not certain that he comprehends, or even wants to comprehend, the union's concerns.

"We need to find a way to hurt this company decisively right now . . . to force them to make a business decision that dealing with us is in their best interests. We need to put a gun to their heads and march them to the bargaining table. Hopefully the legal cases will help us to leverage our position once we get there."

"And how do you propose to do that?" Sam asked.

I saw Deborah rolling her eyes as she glanced at Mark as if to communicate, *I guess we'll have to put up with the ramblings of your hothead organizer before we continue.*

"I've been in touch with the Teamsters," I said, looking toward Ernest, explaining what I had learned and the commitments of support that had been offered.

"United Foods is a blood enemy of theirs, and this will be a chance for payback. The mill can't run without cotton. This is our move but we have to do it soon, before there's nothing left of the local."

"That's very interesting," said Sam. "You've obviously done some good networking. But I think we need to hold our horses for the time being. I agree with you that we have a conservative judge and we don't want to do anything that might piss him off while the case is still undecided."

"Look, the hearing is tomorrow," I said. "I wasn't planning to drive back to Jackson tonight and set up a picket line on third shift. I'm talking about contingency planning. If the judge orders the resumption of collective bargaining, then maybe none of this will be necessary. Frankly, I'm not all that optimistic."

"We happen to have a pretty strong case here," said Sam, tapping his files. "It's supported by some very solid case law and precedent. Have you had a chance to read through some of it?"

"Yes, I have, and the arguments are compelling. The thing is, while you've had your eye on the letter of the law, I've had mine on the judge's face. We need to be prepared for what comes next if things don't go well tomorrow."

Ernest was a master at sitting back while others debated until inserting himself at a decisive moment. He didn't mince words and had little tolerance for excessive diplomacy. "I like the plan," he said. "We need to wait for the judge to make a decision, which may or may not happen tomorrow, but if he rules against us, we need to be prepared to hit the ground running.

"Start buying materials to make picket signs and line up your key people. Prepare a memo to me with an outline of your conversations with the Teamsters. If we're going to do this thing, I want to make sure that Bruce is behind us and that he has the necessary support from New York. It might pave the way for some discussion between the unions at a national level that will reinforce what you're already doing."

Mark and I entered the courtroom together the next morning and were met by Georgia, Donald, and several other stewards. There was no need to continue filling the chamber with a full contingent as it obviously wasn't going to affect the verdict. Ernest and Mike were already airborne toward their next destinations.

The judge offered company representatives an opportunity to respond to the testimony of Jimmy Gibbs, beginning with Paul Poston, who had remained the plant manager. He claimed that the fifty-four Sulzer looms were essential to maintaining the arrangement with United Foods. Poston testified that upon acquisition of the looms, he had found them to be in worse shape than anticipated. The expense of repairs and duration of startup delays had exceeded the tolerances of the business plan, exhausting operating capital and precipitating bankruptcy.

He was cross-examined by Gibbs attorney Jennie Latta, who produced a letter written by Derald Gilmer upon inspection of the looms prior to purchase. She read aloud from the correspondence which described the state of disrepair: "A lot of small parts were missing. There was no maintenance done on these machines for a long time." Poston remained expressionless and offered no response.

Sam Morris next had his turn, grilling the taciturn manager about the rehiring process. He asked if the union had been discussed during negotiations between American Mills and United Foods.

"It came up at one meeting," Poston replied. "We said we had a union that we hadn't recognized."

I wasn't certain whether Poston was intentionally lying or if the old textile relic was just utterly oblivious to distinctions within collective bargaining law. It annoyed me that Sam Morris didn't pursue the discrepancy.

American Mills attorney Harold Shelby called Dominic Poon to the stand, who reiterated that the new looms were at the heart of the plant's viability. In sanctimonious tones, he told the court he had never taken a dime in salary and was prepared to forfeit his entire investment.

The judge exercised his discretion to inquire and asked Poon about the veracity of allegations made by Jimmy Gibbs that the pending deal was merely a scam to bust the union and exclude his partners.

"It's up to the court to decide," he responded. "I would say that's not what I said."

Morris pressed Poon for additional information, but he remained obsequious and unforthcoming. We adjourned for lunch in anticipation of United Food's Don Dresser being the next appear.

Mark and I stood together at what was becoming our customary station in the aisle between front rows as the afternoon session commenced and UFI's executive vice president was sworn in. After having engaged him in the media for six weeks, this was the first time I'd actually laid eyes on him.

Dresser was a tall man with fit build who exuded the authority and smug confidence of an iconic executive, with an expensive suit draped perfectly over a white shirt and conservative tie. He had sufficient affability and charisma to beguile anyone receptive to the corporate myth.

UFI attorney Bradley MacLean led his witness through the customary preamble, inquiring about his position, responsibilities, and previous experience. Dresser recounted the litany of his scholastic background, beginning with the Ivy League college he had attended.

"Why, that's an excellent school," Judge Kennedy interjected, turning to the witness and smiling pleasantly. "I have several friends who graduated from there. They have an exceptional business curriculum." The judge went on to share details of his own alma mater.

Dresser resumed his recitation by naming the university where he had completed his graduate studies before continuing on to another institution and earning a law degree. He said that he had practiced law in Washington before assuming his current position with United Foods.

"My . . . so you're also an attorney," the judge beamed in admiration, before chatting about where he had gone to law school.

Dresser continued by listing his professional accomplishments prior to joining UFI, which brought further remarks of appreciation from the judge. The two men were facing each other at a forty-five-degree angle and appeared more to be having a personal discussion than addressing the court.

"If these two guys could get some privacy, I believe they'd suck each other off," Mark whispered from the side of his mouth.

I didn't believe that Dresser had expected to so charm the judge but he made the most of it, smiling and chuckling along with him as if they were relaxing at a country club.

Once the protracted introduction concluded, MacLean turned his attention to the primary focus of his examination, which was using Dresser to explain the financial logic and structure of the proposed reorganization. He began asking questions to elicit a detailed enumeration of the debtor's assets and liabilities, and the methodologies by which United Foods could convert these into both a profitable enterprise and seven-year payment schedule to creditors.

Dresser reached into the interior pocket of his suit jacket and then other pockets. "It appears I've forgotten my calculator," he smiled at the judge. "Do you mind if I leave the stand and return to my seat for a moment? I believe I have one in my briefcase."

"By all means," the judge obliged with a flurry of his hand.

Dresser arose and walked to the rear of the courtroom still grinning, pumping his elbows as if he were power walking. His demeanor was that of a man enjoying a pleasant social gathering at which one could not possibly have a care in the world.

A couple of minutes later he returned, smiling and holding up a calculator as he resumed his seat before the bench. His attorney led him through a complex and well-rehearsed accounting sequence intended to impress the court. Dresser testified that if United Foods was required to recognize and bargain with the union, it might walk away from the deal entirely.

Sam Morris cross-examined Dresser with a torrent of questions about the company's hiring criteria, as he had done with other management witnesses. Dresser testified that jobs were offered to people with "the expertise to run the equipment"—who were productive, efficient, and "had the ability to perform more than one job."

I whispered to Georgia and Donald that this definition applied far more to them than the individuals recalled in their stead.

Morris questioned the dapper executive regarding the company's refusal to provide information about the current workforce. MacLean objected on grounds that the request was "overly burdensome" and not in accordance with federal law.

"Your honor, all the union requires are copies of reports already on file, as mandated by the National Labor Relations Board," responded Morris.

Judge Kennedy lacked familiarity within this venue and was susceptible to argument. While he didn't rule in the company's favor, he allowed for ongoing debate over the merits of the objection. The afternoon dissolved into evening, and the hearing was again continued to the following Monday, with Dresser to remain on the stand.

The judge concluded by admonishing the union and United Foods to meet informally in an attempt to resolve differences, declaring from the bench, "I want you all to sit down and have some face-to-face meetings before we reconvene."

Mark invited me to join him for dinner at a Cajun restaurant on Beale Street. He led me to stools lining the bar, where meals were also served. I'd never been exposed to Creole food and so ordered the same as Mark. The dish contained a blend of seafood, in a spicy red sauce, which included crayfish. I was curious, but as unfamiliar with the crustacean as was the judge with matters of collective bargaining—unaware that the shell had to be peeled away before consumption.

I attempted to chew on different portions of the crawdads but with equally unsatisfying results. I picked one up in my hand and chomped on what appeared to be a meaty section, like a prehistoric humanoid who had reached into a stream. I failed to comprehend why these were considered a delicacy.

I returned somewhat hungry to my hotel room and lay on the bed, reviewing the day's long proceedings. United Foods wasn't defending against the objections of the union and Gibbs Machinery by arguing the law but rather by avoiding it. The company's position was based on the simple ultimatum that either it would dictate the terms under which the mill was run or not go forward. It was a bluff intended to compel the court's final determination. The costs associated with a protracted labor dispute far outweigh the price of reaching accommodation with the union.

The *Jackson Sun* published two articles by Corwin, titled, *Mill owner, union asked to talk, find compromise* and *United Foods faces difficult road to takeover of mill.*

The next morning, Mark and I entered the Region 26 office of the National Labor Relations Board to present statements and evidence. Deborah Godwin, the attorney who had assumed lead in this venue, accompanied us.

An investigation of charges by the NLRB begins with sworn affidavits being provided by witnesses, accompanied by relevant evidence. The process is somewhat less formal than taking depositions in a lawsuit. The investigating agent asks questions that encourage open-ended responses, and witnesses are permitted to volunteer information they consider relevant.

During this period of history, testimony was scribbled on legal pads by the agent and subsequently typed onto an official form. The witness was permitted to review the effort for accuracy and to request changes, which would be handwritten into the final document and initialed. The purpose of the affidavit was to accurately reflect the content of the statement, the veracity of which would be determined later.

Mark and I chronicled decades of bargaining history that had continued uninterrupted through the American Mills acquisition, until the plant was abruptly shut and then reopened under present circumstances. We discussed Dominic Poon's animus toward the union, as expressed at the airport meeting and later corroborated by Jimmy Gibbs' testimony. The agent was given a list of Local 281 committee members and stewards, noting that only one had been rehired.

The first cornerstone had been laid in what was to evolve into a lengthy and elaborate process. The union would present members of the workforce as witnesses and add to the list of allegations. The Board would take affidavits from management and evaluate their evidence in conjunction with ours. The union's representatives and attorneys would in turn have opportunities to address disparities between opposing statements. Both parties would file position papers and briefs as the investigation unfolded.

Over lunch, I asked Mark if we were making an effort to set up a meeting with United Foods as Judge Kennedy had requested. I'd bought a plane ticket to fly home on Thursday but was prepared to cancel if there was even the possibility of a meeting.

"I called Dresser last night and twice today but he hasn't gotten back with me," he said. "Go home and see your daughter."

CHAPTER 17

I held Colie's hand as we emerged from a familiar restaurant and walked down Franklin Street toward the arcade, feeling bad that we had spent only one day together in over a month. I remembered how comfortable the laid-back college town had felt during my bus driving years, rendered colorful and interesting by its alternative and artistic communities. It had been a welcome contrast to my previous universe of noise, pollution and violence encased in never ending concrete. But this evening, my experience of everything felt surreal, like a stranger drifting through a reality where he no longer belonged.

Three inebriated and grinning college students wearing Tar Heel sweatshirts approached us, holding up their index fingers in the "we're number one" gesture. I pushed my way through and told them to go fuck themselves.

"Why were you mean to those boys?" my daughter asked.

"Because they're idiots," I told her.

Mark and I entered the Memphis courtroom on Monday morning for resumption of the bankruptcy hearing and Don Dresser's cross-examination. Before the session was called to order, Bradley MacLean presented Sam Morris with the requested employee information, indicating the 138 hourly employees that had been selected from a list of 830 applicants.

We huddled together for a few minutes, scanning the report. One of the weavers was a woman who had first been hired by American Mills on October 2, four days prior to the shutdown. I wondered how she had so distinguished herself in this skilled craft during her brief tenure as to be considered a more valuable employee than Georgia.

Judge Kennedy reminded Dresser that he was still under oath, and Morris recommenced with his cross, continuing to focus on hiring criteria. Dresser freely admitted that seniority wasn't a priority factor and that the company was considering applicants other than the hundreds of American Mills employees who remained on layoff, having posted want ads in several out-of-town newspapers. "We're going to evaluate our needs as they come up and hire the best available employees," explained the executive vice president.

The judge neglected to admonish Dresser for having failed to meet with the union as requested and announced the lunch recess, after which he would render his decision.

Judge Kennedy granted United Foods final permission to continue operating the plant according to the terms of the L & O Agreement, on the basis that it represented the only available option. He denied the motion of Gibbs Machinery to reclaim its looms, citing the essential nature of the equipment to the plant's operation.

The judge reiterated several times that he did not want to rule on labor law issues in his courtroom, conveniently overlooking Section 1113 of the Bankruptcy Code, which Congress had enacted specifically for that purpose. He went on to say the union should be more concerned with the 138 employees who were working than with those who weren't.

The Confirmation Hearing was scheduled for January 8, during which the long-term reorganization plan and details of the leasing arrangement would come under closer scrutiny.

The rain had cleared as I drove back to Jackson, not especially surprised by the verdict. It had been the union's misfortune to appear before a judge who subscribed to the theory that the affluent and well-bred must by definition represent the moral pillars of society; the underlying thesis of hypocrisy since humanity first emerged from cave dwellings.

The Confirmation Hearing still lay ahead and with it new opportunities for appeal and objection. My thoughts turned to organizing the fight that for weeks I'd known would be inevitable.

The headline in the *Jackson Sun* proclaimed, *United Foods Inc. wins judge's OK to keep running mill. Union, creditor opposed agreement.* The article concluded with an interesting quote from American Mills' attorney Henry Shelton: "It's not Christmas and Mr. Dresser's not Santa Claus. But it's the only deal we got."

Ernest and I spoke that evening and agreed we would begin with an "informational picket," a public protest and demonstration of resolve that doesn't otherwise impact business operations. The objective would be to focus media attention away from the legal machinations and back on the workers whose lives were upended. The strategy would allow us to guide our troops through a process of escalation toward stronger measures as they gathered nerve and learned how best to use it.

We planned to wait until after the Christmas holidays to initiate the truckers' boycott. This would allow for discussion between the upper echelons of ACTWU and the Teamsters, while hopefully leaving United Foods unsuspecting as it resumed operations in the New Year.

There was a union meeting scheduled for Tuesday which had been organized via word of mouth instead of publication. The list of likely participants had already been defined, and we wished to exclude both the indiscreet and company informants.

I explained that what had transpired in the bankruptcy hearing was only the beginning of what would be a prolonged legal process in several venues. If we wanted to shake things up in the present, it would require taking matters into our own hands.

"Some of you grew up with your parents working at this mill and when you came of age, you in turn walked through its gates to support your own families," I exhorted the membership. "Now, after twenty or thirty years of blood, sweat, and tears, they toss you out in the street like yesterday's dinner scraps, and bring in scabs to run your jobs! This is their style. They've done it twice to the Teamsters. The question is: Are you going to let them do it to you?"

A woman screamed out, "Hell, No!" and others joined her in chorus.

"Then, let me tell you what's going to happen. The lawyers will continue to fight it out in court but we're going to take this fight to the streets. How many people here are with me on that?"

A wave of hands rose in the air and some of the members stood with shouts of approval, with one man proclaiming above the rest, "That's what I'm talkin' about!"

I arranged a schedule for people to assist with making picket signs. We agreed to regroup at the union hall at 9:00 a.m. the following Monday, when they would be briefed about strategy and conduct before assuming formation in front of the plant. I told them to expect reporters and television cameras.

"Does this mean I'm gonna have my picture in the newspaper?" asked a heavyset woman with an attractive face and long braided hair.

"Stick with me, beautiful," I said. "I'll make you a star."

A document prepared by Mike Zucker was passed around the room for signatures, addressed to the managing director of ITT Capital Resources Group. The correspondence politely requested that the financial institution exert its influence in a manner that was ethical and consistent with community interests, while conveying the risk posed to its own interests by escalating labor problems. The underlying message would be underscored by worker signatures and reinforced by media coverage of the picket line.

The next afternoon I met with Reverend Albert Doanes, a local minister with deep ties to the NAACP and social justice movement. I had enjoyed his down-to-earth, insightful manner at an earlier meeting and considered him a contact worth cultivating. The minister had been following the news coverage, but I filled him in on missing details. I shared the union's upcoming legal and organizing strategies, including the Teamster alliance, about which I implored discretion.

"You know that Jackson has a long history of labor conflict," he informed me.

"I wasn't aware of that," I admitted. "Do you know any of the details?"

He answered that there had been a series of strikes involving several Jackson locals during recent decades, most of which had turned violent and bloody. I remembered the solemn portrait hanging in the union hall.

"You need to be careful," Reverend Doanes admonished. "You're heading down a dangerous path."

Neither of us had a pressing schedule that day, and we relaxed and spoke for several hours, during which I received some interesting context regarding Jackson and its surrounding counties.

"You've got to understand that this is probably one of the most backward sections within the continental United States," he reflected. "Demographically and culturally, this area is really more a part of Mississippi than Tennessee, except that the Civil Rights Movement pretty much passed it by.

"Mississippi was at the heart of the movement and the exposure altered the values and perceptions of poor and working black people. But the closest Dr. King ever came to Jackson was Memphis, and that might as well have been a world away. This area became isolated as history passed it by, and the local institutions and beliefs which shaped it remained pretty much intact.

"Take something as basic as birth control. Within the black community, there is a commonly held notion that pregnancy can only occur when both partners climax at the same time. People resist the use of contraception in favor of staggering their release. There are couples in their forties with six kids who can only afford to feed two, that still swear by this method."

I now understood why Tina had been so shocked and deeply offended when I suggested the use of condoms.

Deborah Godwin filed a second NLRB charge, which included allegations that, in addition to discounting seniority during its hiring process, the employer had willfully discriminated based on union activity. The individual officers and stewards were cited as examples.

I met with Joan Williamson, the token shop steward who had been rehired, to solicit her assistance in gathering evidence. As circumspect as UFI management had been in expressing their true intentions, there must have been times when their guard was down.

"You know if they were going to say something, it wouldn't have been around me," she said.

Joan remained loyal to the union and was willing to give an affidavit regarding the changes in working conditions she had experienced under new management, but wasn't optimistic about her efforts to talk with coworkers.

"These people just scared for their jobs," she told me. "Most of them weren't members to begin with, and those that were . . . well they're scared too. They seen what the company done to the others. And then they had to sign this paper that the company could fire them for any reason. . . . It's like we're back on the plantation and the boss man's standing there with his whip, giving us the evil eye.

"But I'll do my best. Lord knows, we need to see the union back in there. I'll call you if I find something out."

I acquired poster board and colored markers, and spent time at the union hall making picket signs with members of the committee. I wanted our message to be less boring and predictable than one might expect at a labor demonstration, and tailored to the unique situation. In huge letters we scrawled (some more neatly than others):

IT'S OUR MILL!

UFI/AMI—BARGAIN OR BATTLE!

SENORITY—A LIFETIME OF WORK!

WE WANT OUR JOBS!

UFI/AMI—YOUR SCAM WON'T WORK!

WE WANT OUR MILL BACK!

The Local 281 newsletter logo, with lightning bolts exploding from the ACTWU emblem, was enlarged at the bottom of each sign.

Even under the most desperate of circumstances, there is a camaraderie and joy shared by union people working together in the field. We were both freedom fighters dedicated to a grueling mission and silly children working together on an arts-and-crafts project. We joked, shared stories from our past, and discussed strategy. A person who loses the ability to laugh in the face of danger will soon be broken.

Tom Corwin called to ask if there had been any recent developments worth writing about.

"I need your agreement that you won't publish or request comments from the company until after the events I'm going to tell you about take place," I told him.

Tom offered his assurances, and I informed him of the picketing scheduled for Monday. There were similar discussions with television and radio stations. I trusted that reporters would maintain the confidence. Credibility was as much a part of their stock and trade as it was in mine.

On Saturday morning I checked my mail and discovered an envelope from Arbitrator Gordon Ludolf. The correspondence began with a cover letter in which he apologized for an extensive delay because of illness and a "heavy teaching schedule." The Leo Boyland decision was attached.

Leo's grievance was upheld on grounds that the employer had not offered "sufficient evidence to prove that he was under the influence of intoxicants and to provide just cause for discharge." He was awarded reinstatement with seniority and full back pay. I contacted Mark at home to discuss how this might be enforced under present circumstances.

"Leo's claim for back pay will be tossed in with monies owed all of the other unsecured creditors involved in the bankruptcy," he responded. "Somewhere down the road he'll receive the same pennies on the dollar amount as the rest of them."

"What about his job?" I asked. "The award provided for reinstatement."

"Tell Leo to fill out an application with UFI and I'll call Dresser," Mark replied. "I wouldn't get your hopes up."

"Leo's working in Georgia," I told him.

"He'd probably be better off staying where he is then, until we get a better idea where this thing is headed."

The next conversation was with Leo.

"Oh, thank you Jesus! I knew it! I knew it!" he exclaimed before I was halfway through explaining the decision. "The sooner I'm out of this hell hole of a chicken factory the better. Maybe I can be back home for Christmas!"

"You've heard the good news," I said. "You better sit down for the rest . . ."

"So you're telling me that even after what the judge said, that the company did me wrong and all that, I'm not going to get my money? How can they do that? I thought you told me that the company would have to do whatever the judge tells them."

"I did tell you that," I replied. "The problem is, the company is in bankruptcy. No one could have seen that coming. If the arbitrator had been on time, you would have gotten paid before any of this happened. But now that it has, the federal bankruptcy judge has more power over your money than the arbitrator. From his point of view, you're just one of many people that the company has screwed."

"Can't you ask that new judge to make an exception for me?" Leo asked, getting louder and beginning to tremble. "Can't you tell him what I've been through and that none of this was my fault?"

"I promise you that our lawyers will do that," I said, "but it probably won't do much good. The judge is a spoiled rich brat who's more about the company than for us. Even once he's heard your story, it won't be real to him. I'm sorry. I know what a letdown this is. You've had a really awful run of bad luck."

"Well, I know it's not your fault," said Leo, having calmed down a bit. "I really appreciate how hard you and that other guy tried for me. Maybe I'll still get something down the road, as you say. For now . . . could you send me a little something? I'm barely making enough to pay the bills and still have something left over to eat with."

Having just raised and dashed his hopes for a merry Christmas within two minutes, I felt sympathetic and told him to expect fifty dollars in the mail.

I awoke on Monday morning to the sound of rain on my roof. It wasn't pouring but neither was it weather for an all-day picket. I drove to the hall nonetheless, in the event that some of the more stouthearted chose to show up.

Georgia, Donald, and several other committee members straggled in.

"We still on for today?" asked Georgia.

"No," I said. "We need to wait for a day when we can expect a strong turnout and good lighting for the cameras."

We agreed to postpone until Wednesday, allowing for a sufficient interval to reorganize. The names of those we counted on were divided up into phone call lists.

The others seemed in a hurry to leave and make the most of the day, but Georgia stayed behind to chat. I took her to lunch at the buffet, and she invited me to return home with her.

We sat in her living room and, having exhausted our discussion of picket lines and Labor Board charges, began talking on a more personal level.

"How have you been getting by?" I asked.

"I've always had me a second job, part time at a nursing home. I've picked up a few more hours and that, plus the unemployment. . . . I'm doin' better than some. It ain't what I was accustomed to making at the mill, but I don't think I'd be getting along too well with them that are now running things. They're the type that when they say 'jump,' they expect a person to say 'hey, hey.' I don't say 'hey, hey' for no one."

Georgia sipped her coffee and regarded me in silence for a few moments.

"There's something I've been waiting for the right time to bring up," she finally said. "I've been asking around, and those Tankersleys that owns United Foods, they're some bad people. You know they're from Bells, just down the road, right?"

"Yeah, I do."

"Well, the word is they're connected to everyone in these parts, including the wrong sorts of people . . . that they'll stop at nothing to get what they want."

"How seriously do you take that?" I asked.

"All I know is that's what a number of folks been telling. What I can say for sure is that I still got friends left inside the mill. One of them overheard a few of them anti's from Alabama talkin' about how they'd like to put a hurtin' on you, first chance they get. As far as they're concerned, if the union wins, they out a job."

"Jobs they stole from you," I said.

Georgia lowered her cup and stared into my eyes. "You're preaching to the choir, darlin'. Problem is, them boys ain't in no choir. What I'm saying is you need to be careful and watch your back. I'm worried about you. I've got a bad feeling."

Tuesday's edition of the *Jackson Sun* carried a page 2 announcement: *Ex-mill workers to get holiday ham:*

> Former American Mills workers may not be rehired by
> the textile plant, but the mill will give them a holiday
> ham. United Foods Inc., the company that reopened
> the mill after it closed on Oct. 6 is giving free hams to
> those employees who have not been rehired by the mill.
> Don Dresser, executive vice president for United Foods,
> said it was simply a "gift from us to the people in the
> community who need help."

The morning of Wednesday, December 20, dawned clear and cold, and I arrived at the union hall appropriately dressed for picket duty in a leather jacket and woolen hat, with thermal underwear beneath my shirt and trousers.

Thirty-eight people were in attendance as the briefing began, and we were likely to be joined by stragglers once out on the line. It was a strong showing considering how long the mill had been shut and would sufficiently impress the media.

"Did anybody read the newspaper yesterday?" I began.

About half of the hands went up in acknowledgement.

"What did y'all think of the story about the holiday ham? These crooks take away your jobs and think they can make up for it by offering you a ham! They think it's such a great gesture of charity that they announce it in the newspaper."

"I'll tell them where they can go put their ham!" said a woman who was near retirement age. "I'd rather serve my family beans and rice for Christmas dinner than put their ham in my oven!"

"They must think we're still slaves pickin' cotton and will be content with their scraps," said Georgia who was sitting beside me on the stage.

"Pass the word to everyone from the plant you know, that we leave the hams rotting on the shelf!" I told them.

Now that people were relaxed and focused, I turned my attention to the important day ahead of us. "What do you think is the purpose of what we're doing today?" I asked the group.

"To send a message," said Reverend Vandiver.

"That's right. And what is that message?"

"We're telling the company and this whole community that we, the union, ain't going nowhere," said the woman who had previously commented on the ham.

"That's good. That is what we're saying. What else?"

"That we ain't about to take no shit!" said the young man who had expressed a militant viewpoint at the meeting which followed the shutdown.

Several people hooted and clapped in response, and another declared, "If you mess with us, somebody gonna get hurt. Them scabs better think hard about giving us back OUR jobs!!"

"Let's think about that," I said. "How does sending that message help get you back in the plant and United Foods to the bargaining table?"

"It doesn't," said the Rev.

"Why not?" I asked.

"Well for one thing," said Donald, "the people who are working our jobs . . . it wasn't their decision to hire themselves. They just filled out applications like the rest of us."

I had known that this conversation was inevitable and wanted to get through it before we hit the streets.

"There is another message that we're trying to send," I said, raising my voice enough to silence the peripheral chatter. "We're going to run this picket line in a way that shows the company and the whole community of Jackson that we know how to fight like professionals, and not thugs. What's our goal here, anyway? Why are we doing all this?"

"So we can get our jobs back," responded a wiry man in a faded blue jump suit.

"And how do you think we're going to accomplish that?" I asked.

"'Cause the judge is gonna make them do it," a woman answered.

"Is anybody expecting that to happen next week?" I asked, as a few people laughed under their breath.

"The only way you're going to get what's rightfully yours is if we hurt United Foods bad enough to force them to the bargaining table. Read the picket signs you're about to carry. One of them says 'Bargain or Battle.' That's the message we're taking to the company. But think about it. Once they get to weighing their options, I want them to see us as fierce in a fight but reasonable to talk with. If we turn into what they're hoping we already are, which is a bunch of crazy hoodlums, how does that help them reach a decision to sit down and negotiate? How do you think that image will play out with the politicians we're asking for help or the judges who will be deciding our cases?"

There was silence in the hall with faces staring straight ahead, so I knew that my words were getting through.

I reiterated the importance of mending the local and avoiding confrontation with those currently working. Once the initial relief over having a job under any terms had worn off, some of them might begin to realize that this was their fight also.

We walked the several blocks to the mill and assumed a close-knit formation across the street. This was intended primarily as a photo-op, not an attempt to interfere with plant operations, and the picketers were deployed accordingly. I anticipated the arrival of reporters within the hour and planned for a dramatic first impression as they stepped from their vehicles.

I stood facing the group, which now numbered nearly fifty, and shouted, "Are you all ready to send a message to the people who stole your jobs?"

They screamed, "Yes!" and raised their signs.

"Are you ready to let the Tankersleys know that they've come to the wrong town and they're messing with the wrong people?"

Bundled against the cold and with signs rattling, the picket line roared, "Yes!" with increased volume.

"Then let them hear you!" I shouted, and began the chant, "It's Our Mill!"

The mood of the protesters was exuberant and mounting towards frenzy. It was relief to finally be doing something on their own behalf instead of just waiting on people in suits to decide their fate in Memphis. On that afternoon we were invincible, and no force could stand against us.

We chanted the various slogans on our picket signs and, when these had been exhausted, shouted, "Union! Union!" over and over until it made us so hoarse we had to rest for a couple of minutes before resuming.

I was certain that we remained inaudible to the mill's occupants, given the clamor of machinery behind brick walls. This exercise wasn't for their benefit. They would receive the message loud and clear on the evening news. I was building morale that would hopefully carry us into the New Year, after the novelty of protest had worn off and the days had grown even colder.

The van from Channel 7 arrived at a perfect moment, as we were chanting, "We want our mill back!" The cameraman leaped out the back and began rolling tape. A few minutes later, Tom Corwin arrived with a photographer, followed by a reporter from KIX Radio with his recorder.

The journalists received their fill of pictures and sound bites, then departed to write their stories. I didn't observe anyone going through the personnel door in search of comment from management. We were left with a grace period of fifteen minutes before second shift began to arrive. I asked for volunteers to make a lunch run and handed them forty dollars. I positioned three of my more trusted people on each of the employee gates with a stack of leaflets, leaving the remainder of the line in place. The goal was to reach out to workers as they came and went, not make them feel overwhelmed. We had a message tailored for those who'd been rehired (Fig. 11).

I stood at the gate with Donald and Vernette as workers began crossing the street from the parking lot, my collar upturned against an increasing wind, grateful for having grabbed my woolen hat on the way out the door, even though it was inconsistent with my public image.

Some of the workers walked briskly past with their eyes to the ground, ignoring the outstretched hand with a leaflet, afraid of how management would respond to those who carried one inside the plant. Others placed the leaflet in a pocket for later review, or hastily read it where they stood and handed it back. A few were openly hostile, management having inflated their egos and earned their undying loyalty by including them in the chosen few.

"God bless you. Have a Merry Christmas!" Reverend Vandiver would say as our detractors walked past, then smile at me and wink. The distribution was easier with the departing first shift, which had the luxury of reading in privacy within their vehicles.

By 4:00 p.m. the sky was becoming overcast and the demonstration had served its purpose. I thanked everyone for their participation amid handshakes, hugs, and mutual wishes for a Merry Christmas and Blessed New Year.

The news coverage amounted to an open forum for the union's point of view. We had generated an audience-building piece of theater and in turn been granted exclusive rights to center stage. The banner for Tom Corwin's article dominated the front page: *Union fires first salvo with picket line at Bemis mill.*

The story was accompanied by a wide-angle photograph that captured all the picketers with Donald Vandiver out in front, smiling in a leather jacket and sunglasses, holding his sign. My comments about the purpose of the event were accurately reported: "This is a sort of gentleman's shot across the bow to the company and those individuals in the community who supported or acquiesced to this state of affairs. Our focus and our objective is to get United Foods to the bargaining table. This is a measure of last resort. These people without jobs are determined to fight for what they're entitled to."

I loaded my car the next morning to begin the two-day drive home for the holidays, stopping to check the local's box at the post office. There was an envelope addressed to me with a note from Donald written on church stationary.

To Phil Cohen

Hi. Hope you're doing ok. Enclosed is the article
of us Wed. I think he made the attendance a little off,
other than any other ok. Thanks Phil for the hope. I'll
never forget this. Say hi to Coley for me.

I wish Tammy and I could give you something in return. If anybody understands these hard times you do.
The family and I can wish you & Coley a Merry Christmas & Happy New Year, that we love you very much &
may God bless you.

Partners at work & Bro in the Lord
Rev. Donald S. Vandiver V.P.

I headed east with these kind thoughts echoing in my heart, hoping
to reach Knoxville at a reasonable hour.

CHAPTER 18

I knew that if I remained at home for two weeks, the long awaited relaxation and peace would slowly dissolve into a loss of cohesion followed by depression. It was essential to keep moving and remain occupied, though hopefully with activities that would nurture and regenerate.

Colie had spent the year overcoming her own insecurities to journey with me into my world, so I decided to reciprocate with an adventure into hers. We flew to Orlando for a three-day visit to Disney World.

The following afternoon we were walking between attractions in our shirt sleeves, having left behind the chill of winter. I'd taken my daughter on countless rides and filled her with junk foods about which I didn't know better at the time. I realized with a certain amount of guilt that I wasn't enjoying myself. The whirlwind of activity and sensory overload left me exhausted like a long day at work. My only pleasure was experienced vicariously through Colie's laughter and excitement.

I spent thirty-six hours at home, then got in my car and headed up I-85 towards New York City to visit an old girlfriend. Her name was Valerie and we'd met when I was nineteen.

Pushing north, I considered how Valerie had more in common with me than anyone with whom I'd ever been friends. She'd escaped an abusive childhood and made her way as a teenager on the street. Unlike me, she'd taken refuge in drugs, but after hitting bottom, threw herself with vengeance into a twelve-step program. Valerie was a gifted poet and gorgeous in a way that portrayed her unique journey and soul. Soft orange curls flowed around an oval face with piercing turquoise eyes.

As we talked after dinner one night at her apartment on West End Avenue , I shared with her what was happening in Jackson and my feeling that the situation was likely to become even more extreme. She was concerned that I was going to burn out.

"All of us that didn't have a childhood spend our lives chasing something we should have gotten back then," she told me. "For some it's drugs and alcohol, others sex or money. With you . . . it's like you always have to be bigger than life. You always have to be a hero. You have some great victory and it makes you high for a day or two, but then it wears off and you have to do it all over again. A normal day, where nothing spectacular happens, either good or bad, a day that most people would think of as a good day, feels like death to you. You're not happy unless you're living on the edge."

"The thing is," I said, "if you worked in a factory and one day, when you least expected it, you fell through the cracks and got fired for something you didn't deserve, there's nobody on God's earth you'd rather have representing you than me."

"Fuck you, I was trying to teach you something," she said, smiling up at me and laughing like a little girl.

Ernest and I had scheduled a meeting in Greensboro for the morning of January 5 as I began my journey west. He was now spending the majority of his time in North Carolina, laying the groundwork for what would become a major rebuild project involving three Cone Mills denim factories under union contract.

I took a room at the Howard Johnson's on the evening of the fourth. I was learning the wisdom of arriving in town the night before, especially after time off, to align myself with the environment and being back in the field.

I had breakfast in the hotel restaurant and went to Ernest's room, where I found him sitting on a bed strewn with documents and talking on the phone. I paced the floor for half an hour until he finally hung up.

Following the customary New Year's greetings, Ernest got down to business. "The Teamsters are a go. When your contacts in Jackson speak to their International, they'll get the green light. Hit 'em. It's all been wired."

"Good. That's what I wanted to hear."

Ernest was mercurial and seldom stayed on the same subject for long. I often found this frustrating, preferring to methodically exhaust a topic before proceeding to the next. "What do you think of the lawyers?" he asked.

"They're smart and they work their asses off, but they could be a bit more cutthroat for my taste," I answered. "We need something more."

"You're the something more," said Ernest. "But look, if this one doesn't work out, no one's going to blame you. We got dealt a bad hand here. If you get to the point where you feel it's a lost cause, or you're in personal danger, let me know and we'll pull the plug.

"Where I really need you is here with me in Greensboro on this Cone project. We got three plants in different cities with over thirty-five hundred workers. This is going to involve half the organizing staff before it's over, and I'm going to want you to take the lead at one of the plants; I'm not sure which one yet. But I've got some flexibility on when I bring you in. It's your call. I'll back you either way."

I doubted whether Ernest fully comprehended how tempting this sounded. All I had to do was paint the right picture, and I could be working close to home and my daughter within a couple of weeks. I looked Ernest hard in the eyes: "We're not done yet in Jackson."

I'd been confident of Ernest's ability to grease the wheels with the Teamsters at a national level and had prepared a leaflet for distribution to truckers.

I visited every truck stop between Nashville and Jackson, making the rounds at diesel pumps and restaurants. I approached one table after another where tired men with haggard faces swilled coffee in preparation for the next leg of their travels.

"How y'all doing?" I would begin. "Are you guys with the Teamsters?"

If heads nodded, I would continue. "I'm an organizer with the Textile Workers. Our Local 281 has been locked out by a union-busting company in Jackson. This same company has also busted Teamster locals. We're going to be running a picket line, and we need you guys to honor it."

I would hand over a small stack of leaflets printed on bright yellow paper. "You can read more here. Please pass the word and share the extras with other drivers" (Fig. 12).

I awoke from a collage of confusing dream fragments on Saturday morning and after a moment of uncertainty, realized that I was in my Jackson bed. I swung my feet through the covers to hit the floor, wishing that I could be anywhere else but in the same instant knowing that this was where I belonged.

The weekend would allow for a more gradual transition from vacation back into the field. Congressman John Tanner had remained interested in the conflict and requested a detailed chronology and position statement for his office. The next two days provided a relaxed opportunity to work on the multipage presentation.

The Confirmation Hearing in bankruptcy court was scheduled for Monday, January 8. Our attorneys informed me that the judge would instead use the session to review the onslaught of motions that were filed during the past month.

American Mills had prepared a lengthy Disclosure Statement to creditors itemizing its assets and obligations. The seventy pages of micro-print had incurred numerous objections regarding the substance and quality of the information. The union objected on grounds that the statement failed to adequately portray the numerous claims filed on behalf of employees, while providing that United Foods would be reimbursed out of estate funds for legal fees incurred in disputing these claims.

This wasn't a day for witness testimony but rather for polite arguments by litigators about what was already a matter of record. The news media was conspicuously absent, having made the decision that their readers would find this phase of the proceedings as boring as I did. More hearing dates were scheduled, with the Confirmation tentatively set for February 21.

Ernest called me at home that night as I was watching TV after dinner. "We've hit a snag with the Teamsters," he said. "We had the necessary discussions but apparently, maybe because of the holidays, the word wasn't passed along to all the right people. You know how it is in a large organization. The right hand doesn't always know what the left is doing. We're still set, but it may be a few more days before your local guys know it."

"Look, I've already started leafleting the truckers," I responded. "We're going to look kind of lame if word gets passed through the grapevine and then there's no picket line when they show up. I've got a union meeting set for Wednesday to organize the picket going forward, and I think further delays will hurt our momentum."

"I'll take the heat," said Ernest. "Do what you have to."

As with the final union meeting in December, this one was being scheduled through personal contact. I spoke with committee members the next morning to ensure that outreach and commitments were as anticipated and agreed to meet Donald for lunch.

"I appreciate your picking up the tab," said the Rev after we finished our sandwiches.

"Don't thank me. Thank the person who signs my expense check. But you deserve it, with everything you're doing. Without you and a few others, this whole thing would fall apart."

I asked his opinion about the rumors Georgia had shared with me before the holidays and Donald was thoughtful for a moment before responding. "Well, I've heard some things along the same lines. I don't know if the owners of United Foods would actually be involved in trying to harm you . . . but I wouldn't rule it out. They've got a lot at stake and aren't the sort to let someone stand in their way. I have no doubt about how some of those boys from Alabama feel. I've been around people like that my whole life."

"Do you think Georgia's right that I might be in danger?"

"I don't want to disturb your peace of mind more than it already is, but I think you'd be foolish to drop your guard. It would break Tammy's and my heart if anything was to happen to you."

After driving Donald home, I returned to Riverside Drive with a lot to contemplate. There was nothing tangible to support the rumors, but the concern expressed for me was genuine. It had been my experience that the decent and gentle-hearted seldom inspire unsavory folklore.

I concluded my letter to Congressman Tanner that evening as follows:

> There is a growing trend within this country of large corporations seeking to take advantage of existing loopholes in the bankruptcy statutes in order to avoid collective bargaining responsibilities. This is invariably to the detriment of the workforce. The bankruptcy statutes, which were legislated in order to provide relief for the unfortunate, are ever increasingly being used as a tool to exploit the unfortunate.
>
> Clever manipulation of the bankruptcy code, along with delays inherent in the Labor Board process, threaten

to allow United Foods a time window of several years'
duration, during which it can operate with impunity.
One can envision a scenario in which United Foods will
ultimately sell the mill for a profit sufficient to address
its accrued liabilities under the NLRA and WARN Stat-
ues, and then move on to its next project.

In consideration of the fact that situations which are
similar to the one herein described are becoming increasingly prevalent in American industry, the Amalgamated Clothing and Textile Workers Union urges an
investigation by the Labor and Education Committee of
the United Foods, Inc. takeover of American Mills, Inc.

At the union hall meeting on Wednesday afternoon, I counted thirty-
four in attendance, slightly less than our previous gathering. We were
in a war of attrition. The question was whether the number of protesters
would dwindle more slowly than the revenue stream needed to support
the company's bottom line, assuming our blockade was successful.

All rose and removed their headwear as Donald offered the customary prayer. I welcomed the membership into the New Year of our
conflict. I'd given consideration to my discussion with Ernest and felt
that it was an appropriate subject with which to begin.

"I appreciate all of you for showing up on this cold winter day. I'm
sure you've all looked around the room and noticed that there are a few
more empty chairs than last time. There are those who are drawn to
the excitement of a fight but don't have the stomach to go the distance.
Others may have found jobs or now have to stay home with their kids
because they can no longer afford daycare. That's all to be expected. I'm
encouraged to see that this many of you have come through the holidays
and are still with us.

"We have good lawyers, but you all know that people with money
can drag out the legal process for years. How many times have you seen
Mafia bosses on the evening news who were doing just that as they continued to carry on their business? If we want to speed things up, we're
going to have to beat them on the streets.

"But if we're going to do this, we need to go back out on the picket
line and stay there every day, every week, every month . . . until United

Foods is ready to sit down and talk business. We're going to have to stand out there in the cold and deal with whatever comes our way.

"I know that what I'm asking for is a huge commitment and I'm not trying to shove anything down anyone's throat. If this sounds like too much, if you'd rather just let the lawyers handle it and get on with your lives, I'll not only understand but will always respect you for how much you've done already. The union already has another campaign lined up for me.

"But if I'm going to stay here in Jackson, I need to know that we're all in this together. If next time the press shows up they find me standing in front of the mill with three other people, it's all over. The headline will read, 'Union members give up.' I'd rather that we choose our time to walk away than give the company that satisfaction."

"I'm prepared to stand out there until St. Peter calls my number," said Hollis Wade. "But do you think that just seeing the lot of us in front of the plant every day is going to be enough to strike fear into the management of United Foods?"

"No," I answered. "If we go back out there, we're going to be doing more than just holding signs. What does the company need to manufacture cloth?"

The membership stared back in silence as the unexpected question hovered in their midst.

"Do they weave cloth out of thin air?"

Georgia looked at me and then at the assembly. "Cotton," she said.

"And where does the cotton come from? Do they grow it out back of the mill?"

"No," said a man sitting alone toward the rear. "They bring it in on trucks."

"And what would happen if most of those truck drivers turned out to be Teamsters, and they refused to cross our picket line?"

"We'd shut 'em the hell down!" said Hollis.

I watched eyes widen in recognition and facial expressions alter as the discussion sank in. "Some of you might remember receiving a discreet inquiry from Georgia or Donald last month regarding which truck lines serviced the plant. It turns out more than half of the deliveries are made by Teamsters. I've been talking with them in Jackson and Nashville, and discussions have been taking place between the Internationals as well. They're going to back our play if we make it.

"We're obviously not going to all have to stand out there every day for eight hours. We'll make a schedule with four-hour rotations and assign picket captains. On days the press shows up, we'll need everyone. Other than that, we need to maintain enough of a presence, a constant reliable presence, to cut off their lines of supply.

"United Foods can't run the business without cotton and other raw materials. They can't get their goods to market without empty trucks pulling up to the loading docks. They need to understand that it will be impossible to run the mill without our cooperation. I can't make any promises. Maybe this is even a long shot. But if there's a silver bullet left in our gun, this is it. Now, what do you want to do?"

I opened the floor for additional discussion, then put the proposed course of action to a vote. "Please don't vote yes unless you plan to walk the line for as long as it takes," I requested.

Every hand rose as if a switch had been thrown.

It was 2:30 p.m. I planned to unveil the new tactics to reporters with a mass demonstration on Friday, but first wanted to test the waters, given the semiofficial endorsements we currently had from the Teamsters. I asked for ten volunteers to grab signs and join me at the shipping gate.

The rear entrance to the mill was situated on a curving, moderately trafficked road that led out of town. Standing at the gate, one looked up a side street that ended in a "T" intersection at the plant. The decision to migrate to this position had been made in the moment, and I wasn't dressed for outdoors.

The temperature was in the twenties with a biting wind, and within fifteen minutes, my ears and fingers were numb. We strolled about in an effort to stay warm, having as much impact on events as the occasional pigeon that lighted to join us. I wondered if it was too late in the day for deliveries.

A tractor trailer lumbered down the road, slowed, and began its awkward turn toward the entrance. I approached the cab waving a handful of leaflets and stepped onto the runner. "How you doin'?" I asked, as the driver lowered the window. "You with the Teamsters?"

The man nodded his head, "Umhmmmm."

"I'm an organizer with ACTWU Local 281," I shouted over the motor. "We've been locked out and scab labor has been brought in to run our jobs. This company's done the same to the Teamsters in two other places.

We'd be obliged if you'd honor our picket line. Here's a leaflet with more information."

The taciturn driver glanced at the paper, rolled up his window and began to inch backwards. Once he had clearance, the rig made a hard left up the perpendicular side street. My small contingent roared with satisfaction and gratitude, their exclamations of "Thank you!" and "God bless you!" audible only to us.

Twenty minutes later a medium-sized truck, with cargo bay and cab attached, rounded the curve and braked. I approached as it resumed turning but the driver waved me away with an annoyed gesture and accelerated through the gate. The group booed and jeered.

"Forget about him," I said. "He's probably not a Teamster, and if he doesn't make the delivery, he might get fired for insubordination. You can't blame a man for wanting to feed his family. Stay focused on our real enemy."

By the time darkness fell and the cold became intolerable, we had stopped two out of four vehicles. "That ought to give them something to think about," said Donald with a smile.

"It's a good start," I agreed, "if we can keep it up."

A meeting was scheduled for the next day with our attorneys in Memphis. I was tempted to have the picket continue without me but decided against leaving my people exposed to the unknown this early in the venture. We would resume with a vengeance before the TV cameras on Friday.

"They may think that we couldn't get the people to show up for more than one day," said Georgia.

"Good," I responded. "They'll find out different on Friday. Let's keep them guessing."

I entered the sprawling downtown office to be greeted by Sam and Deborah, who in turn introduced me to Lynn Agee, another attorney from the firm who had become involved. Mark strolled through the door a few minutes later, and Sam directed us to an empty conference room, pointing to a freshly brewed pot of coffee in the corridor.

The first order of business was an overview of the bankruptcy proceedings that were far from over. The attorneys were in the process of drafting a battery of motions regarding various aspects of the case. The Proof of Multiple Claims to be filed on behalf of employees would include unpaid vacation money, medical expenses incurred due to loss of insurance coverage, and Leo Boyland's arbitration award of $9,454.

Sandwiches were brought in for a quick lunch before analysis and discussion of other venues began.

Lynn Agee, who was researching a brief to be filed with the National Labor Relations Board, navigated her way around the conference table carrying an armload of materials.

"We're going to be arguing both the 'alter ego' and 'joint employer' doctrines in regard to the relationship between United Foods and American Mills," she began before taking her seat. "These apply to situations where a new employer steps in to run the business on behalf of the first in an effort to disguise continuity of operation and avoid obligations under a collective bargaining agreement."

"Before we continue, there's been an interesting development I want to share with you," said Deborah. "Remember Jimmy Gibbs' testimony about what Dominic Poon said at their meeting, concerning his intent to bust the union? Well, this has been corroborated to me by an attorney for Gibbs who was present, and he's prepared to give an affidavit when summoned."

"I don't believe we have any problem proving animus," Sam interjected. "The question is whether we can meet the Board's standard in directly linking this to the hiring process and what evidence we still need to meet that burden.

"The demographics don't necessarily speak for themselves. At the end of the day, Don Dresser is going to argue that he hired those employees he felt best qualified to turn around an ailing business, based on criteria having nothing to do with union activity. He doesn't have to prove that his reasoning was sound, so long as it provides an alternate theory to our own. We need affidavits that document statements of intent in regard to hiring selection."

"Those are going to be hard to come by," I said. "They've deliberately excluded everyone from the workforce with witness potential."

"What about within the community?" Sam asked. "Members of management live in Jackson. Someone might have been prone to running their mouth at the supermarket, the gym, the neighborhood bar . . . and a union member may have been present, or at least knows someone who was."

"It's a stretch," I said, "but I'm on it. What about this? Most of our stewards, especially the ranking officers, have exemplary work and attendance records. I'm certain that some of the people they hired don't, or at least don't have enough years of service to demonstrate one way or the other. Let's make an information request for the complete personnel file of every employee currently working and those of the stewards who weren't hired.

"I'll prepare an analysis, comparing the work history of each rehired employee with the stewards in whose job classification they're now assigned. It'll disprove Dresser's claim, on its face, that he was looking for the 'most qualified' employees."

"The company might argue that the request is overly burdensome and the Board might agree," said Lynn. "You're talking about providing copies of over two hundred files, some of them thirty years in the making."

"Fine, then I'll go inside the plant, review the files in their front office, take notes and make copies of pages I consider relevant as evidence," I responded. "This isn't a long shot. We can deliver on this one."

"I think it's worth trying," said Mark. "Can someone here at the firm prepare the request for information and see that the Board agent gets a copy?"

"I'll take care of it," said Sam, "but in the final reckoning, it would still help if we had statements to tie it all together."

"You can input the information into the computer," Mark said, turning to me, "correlate it and generate reports."

"That is if I figure out how to turn it on," I replied.

"Call me at the office, and I'll talk you through it again," he offered.

"Let me change the subject here, for a minute," said Sam. "As we mentioned earlier, a claim is being entered regarding the back pay awarded Leo Boyland by an arbitrator. Does anyone know Boyland's current whereabouts?"

"He's working at a poultry plant in Georgia," I said.

"What's he doing there?" asked Deborah.

"Call this going out on a limb," I replied, "but I'd venture a guess that he's engaged in the processing of poultry."

Mark chuckled under his breath, and Deborah retorted, "This isn't a laughing matter. We're engaged in some serious business here."

"Don't talk to me about serious," I said, narrowing my eyes and glaring back at her. "Tomorrow you'll still be here working in your warm safe office, while I'll be freezing my ass off in front of the plant. If the streets of Jackson end up getting painted with anyone's blood, it won't be yours."

"We all have our jobs to do here," said Sam. "The reason we're asking about Boyland is because it's our position that he continues to accrue claims with each passing day, as he hasn't been reinstated as required by the arbitrator. If his hourly earnings are less at the poultry facility than he earned as a weaver, we can argue for the difference."

"They are less," I said. "He's barely making minimum wage."

"There's something else, before we adjourn," Mark said. "I'm going to file a petition with the Department of Labor under the Trade Adjustment Act on behalf of the laid-off workers. When it can be established that a plant closing or mass layoff was at least in part due to foreign competition, the workers become entitled to extended unemployment benefits and additional funding for education, relocation, etc. We're hardly ever turned down when it involves a textile plant.

"The truth is, if it weren't for overseas competition, none of this would be happening. Tennessee Textiles would still be profitable, Dominic Poon would have stayed in China, and United Foods would have been content to remain in the vegetable business."

I awoke on Friday morning with a clear head and sense of purpose. My first official function, however, was both mundane and disheartening. It was necessary to request a suspension of service at the union hall from the municipal water department. Local 281 had been deprived of a revenue stream since American Mills discontinued deduction of union dues back in August and the treasury was now empty. The power company had shut off electricity and the same was now required of the water to keep pipes from freezing.

I arrived a few minutes early to unlock the building, instinctively flicking the light switch in the darkened hallway to no avail. The chill felt worse within the meeting area than on the front lawn in the sunlight. Fortunately the large windows would allow enough light to penetrate for sufficient visibility.

I was encouraged when people began to enter the room as they appeared to be in good spirits. Within thirty minutes, everyone who had been there on Wednesday had returned, along with a few others.

Georgia welcomed, Donald prayed, and I began the presentation. I saw people buttoning their coats and pulling hats down over their ears, and apologized for the unpleasant environment. The membership took it in stride, aware that I was shivering along with the rest of them.

"It'll take more than a little cold to break us!" proclaimed Hollis.

I provided a brief summary of my meeting with the lawyers and the various venues in which we were engaging the company. "Trust me, you're glad you weren't there," I told them. "It was enough to fry your brain."

"So, how do our cases look so far?" asked Betty Trice. "Are we going to win?"

"We have strong cases," I told the group, "but a long and complicated process ahead of us. The thing about the law . . . it cares more about its own technicalities than the human beings it affects."

"But what about the judges who finally decide?" Betty continued.

"They serve the law, not the truth," I answered.

"Remember the parable about a man not being able to serve two masters," counseled the Reverend.

The membership began reflecting upon these matters amongst themselves.

"Listen up," I said with a raised voice. "The lawyers will be happy if five years from now they win the final appeal and it gets published in a law journal. I want to see you back inside the mill before the weather turns warm. We agreed about how at the last meeting. From now on, it's about walking the talk and hanging in there no matter how hard it gets.

"We're going to start out with another demonstration in front of the plant for the media. Then we walk around the block to the delivery gate where the action really is. There are some basics you need to remember when walking a picket line. Always keep moving. If we bunch up in front of the gate we can be accused of blocking the entrance. Stay on the sidewalk. If vehicles slow to look at us, that's they're decision. If we're in the street, it can be said we're interfering with traffic. The company will seize any excuse to take legal action and shut us down. We have the right to ask others to honor our picket line, but not to get in their way if they choose not to. Like everything else in life, this is about appearances, not our good intentions. Does anyone have any questions?"

There weren't any, and I could tell from facial expressions and body language that people were ready. "I hope everyone dressed warm," I said. "Grab a sign and let's do it. It's show time. Let's walk to the mill in tight formation."

We assembled across the street from the front entrance, where reporters would be expecting us. I asked for two volunteers to patrol the rear gate and dissuade deliveries until the rest of us could join them.

A woman named Hazel McBride tapped her friend Alice Johnson on the shoulder and said to me, "That's OK. We got you covered." The two broke ranks, walked down the street, and turned the corner.

The rest of us remained facing the mill with little to take our minds off the biting wind and for the most part unobserved. The demonstrators would perk up and raise their signs at the occasional motorist, taking heart that someone actually knew we were out there. When someone honked in support, further outbursts of enthusiasm were generated. I wondered if the press would actually show up again or if the story was getting old. Perhaps they would just run follow-up pieces based on comments made during my invitation. I began to consider whether too much had been disclosed.

Leading the picketers in spirited chants again felt redundant, especially when there was no one to listen. The best course of action was to remain real and respond to circumstances as they developed.

A car pulled up behind us, and a reporter from KIX Radio emerged with his tape recorder and began asking questions. Within a few minutes Tom Corwin and a photographer joined him. The arrival of news crews was more sporadic than at previous events, and I found myself answering the same questions over and over, doing my best to stay fresh and spontaneous. The print media is simply about content, but television is equally about presence. Our coverage area had begun to expand, including reporters from a Memphis-based TV station and newspaper.

When the last of them had departed to cover their next story, it was still morning, and most of the day lay ahead. I moved the body of picketers toward the rear entrance to engage our primary objective. The parade was over and trench warfare had begun.

Half the group scattered to their cars, driven onward by either the weather or family responsibilities. Some were simply aware that the fun part was over. I thanked them for showing up and standing with us. The most certain way to accelerate attrition within a movement is to criticize people for not having done enough. Two picketers were left at the front office to encounter UPS drivers bearing packages.

Fifteen of us walked in leisurely circles around the wide gate that stood open before the loading docks. It was more than really necessary for the task at hand.

"How'd it go?" I asked Hazel. "I appreciate the two of you holding the front-line position on your own for an hour. That took nerve and I respect it."

"It ain't no thing," she responded. "I ain't afraid of them. We had one truck pull up, and it turned around as soon as he saw us."

A young man in a brown leather jacket approached me, and I recognized him as the hothead who had spoken up at meetings during the fall. "Look, this all well and good," he said, "people showing up with their picket signs, standing out here and all." His voice rose as he continued, and several of the picketers slowed and stood in a group around us.

"This some serious shit we're into," he said, gaining confidence as others paid attention. "We need to let folks know we're for real. We got scabs in there from Alabama working our jobs. I say it's time we start showing up with the baseball bats and getting down to business!"

Two of the men nodded their heads in agreement. This guy needed to be put down, hard and fast.

"And what do you think happens if we do that?" I asked him while addressing those who had gathered around. "I'll tell you what. We just gave Don Dresser a late Christmas present. He calls the police and then his lawyers, and they get an injunction to shut us down . . . permanently! There's nothing the company could do to hurt us half as bad as what you're talking about. You get the satisfaction of bashing in some idiot's head, and after that we can never picket the plant again. Do you think that tradeoff is worth it?"

The instigator just glared at me, but I saw the onlookers shaking their heads as a couple of them muttered, "No."

"I just ain't about taking no shit, is all I'm trying to say," he finally responded.

"If that's the case, then learn how to fight smart. This is a factory we're standing in front of, not a saloon."

The man turned his back and walked away in silence. I never saw him again.

I addressed the several picketers still standing together and reflecting on the interaction. "What would the police say if they pulled up right now and took one look at us?"

There was no response but I waited. Finally one of the men said tentatively, "That we're blocking the gate?"

"That's right," I told him. "We got to get our heads on straight right now. Are we trying to win a tough-guy contest or a labor dispute?"

The men hoisted their signs and began moving. An eighteen-wheeler rolled toward the entrance, and I approached with a leaflet. The driver gave a thumbs-up and reversed his gears.

I turned to the demonstrators. "That is how we draw blood in this fight! Does everybody get that?"

The sun crossed the midheaven and its radiant heat warmed the air on this cloudless day as the wind subsided. It was turning into a perfect afternoon for an outdoor protest. I was obliged to periodically remind the group to remain in motion and on the sidewalk. More than half the trucks reversed course, and the rest passed through us without incident. Traffic slowed to regard us with curiosity while some drivers honked or waved in support. We had dominated the news for three months, and passersby enjoyed their moment of being on the scene.

Donald began stepping to the curb while moving his sign up and down as cars approached, smiling broadly and attempting eye contact with the drivers. I tapped him on the shoulder.

"Rev, I appreciate your enthusiasm, but I don't think that's such a good idea. We don't need to pull people into this who aren't involved. So far, we're getting a good response, but there's no telling if the next vehicle to round the bend is going to be a pickup truck filled with Klansmen. Our job is simple. We're here to stop trucks."

"You're right," he apologized. "Sorry if I got carried away."

"Don't worry about it. You're worth ten men in this fight."

An hour later a police car rolled down the side street perpendicular to us and parked at the intersection. Another pulled in behind him. "Oh no, here it comes . . ." I heard someone behind me say as I walked across the street to greet them, approaching the lead vehicle.

"Good afternoon," I said in a pleasant and upbeat tone, introducing myself and handing the officer my business card.

"How have things been going out here?" asked the policeman. "Have there been any problems?"

"None. Everything's going smoothly. We're all glad the weather's warmed up a bit."

"I need you to keep your people on the sidewalk and out of the road," he said, turning more in my direction. "We need to maintain a normal flow of traffic, and I don't want to see anyone accidentally getting hurt."

I looked over my shoulder and saw several people on the wrong side of the curb. "I apologize for that. I'll straighten it out. I've been trying to teach people the right way to do this, but it's all new to them."

"That's OK. You've got a right to be here. Just don't block the entrance, and we don't want to hear any reports of intimidation."

"You have my word," I assured him before walking back to the picket line.

The patrol cars remained in place as I urged the demonstrators to resume the proper formation.

Another truck turned to enter the gate, and its brakes squealed as I approached with a leaflet. The driver remained stationary for a minute as he read and then slowly inched into reverse. I glanced toward the policemen, but they were unresponsive. It seemed as though an understanding with law enforcement had been achieved, at least for the present.

I was especially impressed with the perspective chosen by Tom Corwin for his coverage in the evening edition. He had driven to the back of the plant and interviewed Hazel and Alice. A large photo of them holding their picket signs appeared prominently on the front page beneath the headline: *Mill picketers call on Teamsters. Truck drivers asked not to deliver goods.*

The behind-the-scenes drama that brought police to the scene was also reported. Management had called Mayor Farmer to complain of our presence, and he in turn had called the chief of police. Chief Ricky Staples told the *Sun*, "We respect their right to picket and will protect that right."

A significant hurdle had been surmounted and I knew this would be even more reassuring to some of the picketers. It was easier to predict the stock market than how police would respond to a union demonstration in a southern town back in 1990.

Saturday morning heralded the weekend lull. The plant was operating on a five-day schedule, which left forty-eight hours to regroup and plan for the coming week. I had a stack of unopened mail from the Memphis law firm sitting on the kitchen table that also served as my desk. I was naturally copied on every motion and piece of correspondence generated by the attorneys. It was dry reading that required no input, and I had taken to reviewing it en masse when an opportunity presented itself.

The documents (or attached cover letters) concluded with the recipient list customary in business correspondence, except that attorneys enhance the formality by including the full mailing address of each party. I'd never bothered to read past the signature line to review the predictable litany. On this occasion, I was drawn to locate my own name.

I was horrified to discover that the attorneys had published my residential address rather than that of the union hall. Given the reputation of our adversaries, it was unthinkably obtuse to inform them of where I slept at night. I trembled with rage that people as sophisticated as our lawyers could in the same instant be so complacently naïve.

I began contemplating my remarks when I called on Monday to cuss them out but realized it would serve no purpose. The damage was done, and fixing it was not in their hands.

I reflected further on what I'd been told about the Tankersleys and the history of labor-related violence in Jackson, and realized the extent of my exposure. I was hours from the nearest union office, operating entirely on my own initiative, having become the rallying point for a determined cadre of resisters. If I were removed, the game would end. It was that simple. There would be no replacement, only years of litigation.

I had survived the streets of New York with a can of mace and a knife. This was different, no longer a question of being prepared for random drug addicts looking to feed their habit. If the need for self-defense arose in Jackson, it would be because I was the target. I needed to be appropriately armed for such an encounter.

I leafed through the Yellow Pages and was surprised at not being able to find a gun dealer within the city limits. There was one listed, however, in a small town twenty minutes away. I called and the store was open.

The owner was standing behind a glass counter as I entered the modest establishment, a stocky man about ten years my senior. He had been following the news coverage and listened carefully as I explained my requirements. "I need something that's small enough to conceal completely, given the way I dress and how I'm built . . . something light and maneuverable but with enough stopping power that if I hit someone once they're going down for good."

The man thought for a moment, reached into the display of hand-guns, and brought out a Charter Arms .38 Special with a five-round cylinder. "This is referred to as an 'Off Duty Special,' because it's what a lot of police officers carry when they're not working. You sacrifice the sixth bullet but it gives you the size and concealment you're looking for . . . and unlike an automatic, it'll never jam when you need it."

He reached down again and placed a box of Winchester Hollow Point +P ammunition next to the revolver. "This is what I recommend you load with. You've got a hollow point round with high velocity. It'll flatten and expand when it makes contact and blow an exit wound through your attacker the size of a grapefruit."

He handed me the weapon. "Here, see how it feels."

The size and weight were perfect, and it was a natural fit in my hands. We discussed holsters, and I settled on a shoulder unit to wear under my winter clothing.

"You're going to have to pay for the gun now, but wait on the results of a background check by the sheriff's department before you can take possession," he told me. "It shouldn't take more than a few days.

"Give me a call when it's ready and I'll come on back," I told the pro-prietor while writing a check.

"There's really no need for you to make the trip," he said. "My son is a police officer with the Jackson Police Department. In fact, he's the department's firearms instructor. He'll call you once we hear from the sheriff and make arrangements to meet you with the gun."

It was time for an "all hands" union meeting now that our strategy was public, with no need for further discretion. I wrote the leaflet on Sunday, glancing wistfully at the silent computer and moving my typewriter into position.

I decided to make the more conservative effort of attempting to uti-lize the contraption to generate the several hundred address labels. I re-viewed the procedures upon which Mark had painstakingly elaborated and pushed the power button. It whirred to life as I prepared to confront my most formidable adversary in Jackson.

I methodically worked my way through the complicated protocols required to access the various programs and databases. The mailing list magically appeared on the screen. I placed label sheets in the printer and began establishing the interface. Suddenly, all that I had so brilliantly manifested crashed and dissolved into a maze of alien symbols.

I pushed my chair back and stood up, wanting desperately to take my coffee cup and throw it through the screen but thought better, knowing that Mark probably wouldn't care much for the gesture. I turned off the power and called Georgia to arrange another envelope party.

Georgia served as picket captain on Monday morning while I engaged the printer in our familiar and tedious routine of layout and copying. I met her at the rear gate with a box of leaflets. She and her crew remained with me, waiting for replacements to arrive, at which time Georgia would join several others at the hall to oversee the mailing.

"How are things going with the trucks?" I asked her.

"They're either for us or they're not. About half of them see us and turn right around. The others keep on coming like they're a bowling ball and we're the pins."

Hazel and Alice arrived in the same car, slowed to wave, and went looking for a place to park.

"We'll be OK from here," I told Georgia and the others. "Thanks for coming out."

During the next hour, we were joined by Rick Hardin and two other men. I had sweated at the printer's in my thermal underwear but was now glad to feel it beneath my clothing. The knit hat pulled down over my ears did little for my public image, but the priority was staying healthy while standing outdoors on a daily basis. Time seldom passes more slowly than when one is both shivering and bored, but then all of a sudden we'd be warmed by a rush of adrenalin as a truck ground its gears to appear around the bend.

Georgia's assessment of the truckers was accurate and there was little need to engage them in conversation. Most of the Teamsters drove their rigs to the factory expecting to see us and reverse direction. The others were in no position to respond, and their private sentiments remained unknown. I knew that missing half of its scheduled deliveries must be taking a toll on the company, but hoped to improve our effectiveness.

One of the several messages on my answering machine that evening was from Ernest, who was staying at the Howard Johnson's in Greensboro. It was ironic to reach my director at a location so close to home from my outpost seven hundred miles away.

"How's it going?" he asked.

"We're hurting them. The question is if we can hurt them bad enough while we still have people to do it with."

"Well, I've got something that I think will help," he said with his usual enthusiasm. "Wait a minute, there's someone at the door."

I waited on the phone for fifteen minutes, periodically saying, "Hello?" and wondering if the line had gone dead.

"I'm here," said Ernest. "Sorry, that was one of my organizers on the Cone campaign. Look, I've gotten the word. It's official from the Teamsters. Their international has issued an endorsement and word is going out."

The next day unfolded with what was becoming my new routine. I spent the morning cultivating my community and political network, spoke with attorneys, and then took charge of the afternoon picket. I had a contingent of eight on this occasion, four for the delivery gate, two awaiting UPS trucks by the front office, and another two for assistance with leaflet distribution.

It remained challenging to get those on their way in for second shift to stop and accept a leaflet. The most profound message was our presence itself. A tall broad-shouldered white man, one of those imported from Alabama in June, took a leaflet from my hand, walked inside the gate and turned to face me. "Do you know what I'm going to do with this? I'm gonna use it to wipe my ass!"

He grinned broadly and laughed with satisfaction at his own wit, then crumpled the flyer and threw it in my direction. I waited until he had passed into the building and entered the gate to retrieve it. Neither the company nor municipality would have the opportunity to accuse us of littering.

The workers emerging from first shift felt more comfortable taking a leaflet to be read discreetly within their vehicles. The brightly colored announcement began with details of the upcoming meeting, followed by an editorial which began:

> The Company is now advertising for workers in
> <u>Nashville and other cities</u>! WHAT ABOUT US?
>
> When United Foods/American Mills decided they
> could make money by playing games with people's
> lives, they chose the wrong group of people. They
> thought that after a while, we'd just give up and
> go away. THEY WERE WRONG! We will continue this
> fight until we gain back what is rightfully ours—
> OUR JOBS, OUR BENEFITS, OUR SENIORITY, OUR RIGHTS
> UNDER THE LAW!

A moderate rain was falling on Wednesday as I circled the plant to the delivery gate, where three of the picketers huddled beneath umbrellas. I grabbed mine from the rear seat and joined them. The ink on our signs had run, and slogans were barely legible by evening; but the weather abated with the promise of better conditions the next day.

I returned to my house after dark and began calling reporters, using home phone numbers for those who had already left the newsroom. The tactic of using union meetings to stage subsequent demonstrations at the plant had been effective, and tomorrow would provide another opportunity.

It was uncertain how much longer the media would remain interested in the same three dozen workers standing in front of the same factory. There's a threshold at which even the most dramatic events fade into redundancy. However, we'd been dealt one new card to play at just the right moment—the formal declaration of support from the Teamsters.

I had finished my calls and was cooking supper when the phone rang. It was the son of the man who owned the gun store. "Good evening, sir," the police officer said. "I have your handgun with me in the patrol car. If you'd care to rendezvous with my partner and I this evening, we could transfer it to your possession."

I finished supper and drove to the deserted parking lot behind a shopping center to which he'd given me directions. I turned in and cruised toward the building where a police vehicle was idling amid rows of empty spaces. The partners were sitting together in front and they invited me to take a seat behind them. The officer who called was behind the wheel, and he reached back to hand me the .38, packaged in a bright yellow box. I thanked him for the accommodation and opened the door to exit.

"Be careful," the policeman said with sincerity. "Call us if you run into problems."

I drove away thinking that this had been a most unusual juxtaposition of players —a union organizer meeting clandestinely with a police officer to receive a firearm. I assumed his superiors wouldn't consider this part of his job description.

On returning home, home I familiarized myself with the weapon, slipping five rounds into the cylinder and handling it with the added weight. I unloaded and got the feel of cocking and releasing the hammer. It took time to properly adjust the shoulder holster to be worn on my left side.

I walked to the bedroom and draped the unit over my bedpost, crawled under the covers with my eyes closed, and reached for the revolver; repeating this maneuver for an hour. In the event of a rude awakening, I would need to know instinctively where to reach.

I parked on the front lawn of the union hall the next day, a few minutes before the noon meeting. There were several other cars already present, and Georgia had unlocked the building. It was a pleasant morning, but a wave of cold, dank air struck me on entering the hallway. There was a sign on the restroom door advising that we no longer had water, but it had obviously been posted too late.

The pace of arrival was sporadic, and we waited until 12:30 to begin the meeting. The turnout was disappointing, as the mailing hadn't generated new participation. The usual group was present and defined the extent of our ground forces.

"I'm all for standing out here as long as my unemployment lasts," said a man who had worked in the card room. "But do you think this is really going to make a difference? We file charges, it's all over TV, and the company seems to keep on doing whatever they want."

"I consider everyone in this room my friend," I replied, "and I'm not going to play games with your hope by making promises I'm not sure I can keep. But I am certain of one thing. A business can function no more effectively than an army when cut off from its lines of supply. The more trucks we keep out, the closer we push them to a breaking point."

"But Phil," asked Hazel, "won't they just start using nonunion trucking companies? I mean, they're wicked but they're not stupid."

"I don't know. It probably has a lot to do with the type of contract their suppliers have with the freight lines. All we can do is push things to the limit and see how they shake out. We've all made a commitment to each other to see this through. That's all we can be certain of right now—our commitment."

We adjourned to assume our station in front of the plant and await the press. I knew it would be highly demoralizing for the protestors if the news vans failed to arrive, but it was a calculated risk I had taken.

This time, the entire press corps showed up within fifteen minutes. Apparently our previous week's performance had generated favorable audience response. There was little new information to gather, so the reporters requested a photo session. The picketers lined up in formation, their signs chest high, touching like the shields of Greek warriors in a phalanx.

"Would you like us to chant?" I asked the newswoman from Channel 7.

"That would be perfect!" she said.

I stood in the road, facing the line from several yards away and began the call-and-response. The cameras clicked and film rolled. Once the photographers had their fill, the exercise ended, and I answered a few questions intended to generate sound bites.

The news crews and most of the demonstrators headed off, while those who remained accompanied me to the rear gate, where we relieved two men who had been maintaining the position.

The staged event was the featured story on the evening news, and the *Jackson Sun* ran the headline: *Picketers stay determined. Union members continue to pressure United Foods to let them work in mill.* Above the print and reaching nearly to the fold was a huge color photograph of picketers with fists raised and signs held high.

The situation had drawn the interest of a U.S. senator though I doubted the extent to which this would translate into meaningful activity on our behalf. I met with his aide the next morning. We were sufficiently high profile that it would have been foolish for any politician to simply dismiss us with a deaf ear. If we won, the union would remain a force to be reckoned with in Jackson and a potential base of support during elections. But granting an audience isn't necessarily the same as becoming an advocate.

I returned home, dressed for outdoors, and strapped on the shoulder holster. Given the level of involvement and media presence the previous day, I hadn't felt the need to be armed. This would be the first of innumerable days during the years to come when I would carry a firearm into the field.

Four of the regulars joined me at the delivery gate. They were all energized by the press coverage, having seen themselves on television, in print, or both. I didn't believe that the management of United Foods had been the least affected by it. They were seeking to turn a profit, not run for office. Their customers were other factories that used their products, not consumers who might have responded to the plight of workers. I dispatched two of the picketers around the block to intercept UPS trucks.

The wind chill had increased from the previous day, cutting through my layers of clothing. I was the only one who walked the line every day, and it was beginning to take its toll. I placed a lozenge in my mouth, hoping that the faint tickle in my chest wouldn't turn into a cough. A semi began its turn into the gate and stopped. The driver honked, waved a solidarity fist, and backed away.

CHAPTER 19

My weekend began with a call from Ernest requesting a status report. He was excited by the initial response we were getting from the truckers and wanted to know if I was still making progress within the political community. I explained that while anyone who held office was pleased to meet with me, I had yet to see these discussions yield positive results.

"It sounds like you're getting cynical," said Ernest.

"I'm beyond cynical when it comes to politicians," I told him.

"It might interest you to know that Mike Zucker has spoken with Congressman Tanner and your position paper is getting some circulation on Capitol Hill. The problem is that Republicans have been running the country for ten years, and it's not a very friendly time in Washington for unions."

"It's not a very friendly time in Jackson either."

"It's all connected. Anyway, you're not going to have to be spending as much time on this as you have been. Mike is sending in someone from his staff to coordinate our community support so you can stay focused on the picket line and holding our people together. His name is Damon Silvers. He'll be arriving on Monday."

"What's he like?" I asked.

"He's a young kid, a couple of years out of college, but he's really smart and hungry to prove himself. Within reason, you can direct him as you see fit."

After lunch I sat down with my pile of unopened envelopes from the law firm. One of the documents was titled, "ORDER ON MOTION TO SUSPEND TEMPORARY APPROVAL OF LIQUIDATING AND OCCUPANCY AGREEMENT," signed by Judge Kennedy.

In response to the union's arguments that the company's collective bargaining obligations hadn't been factored into the court's prior decision, the judge wrote:

> Debtor is not required to comply with the prerequisites of Section 1113 in the facts and circumstances of this case.

That was it. There was no explanation or justification of his decision to dispense with the section of the Bankruptcy Code that had been enacted for the express purpose of addressing these matters. The judge's order would naturally be appealed.

Mark called on Sunday night to make good on his offer to again guide me through the protocols of computer use. But after a frustrating hour of instruction, I had to admit, "This isn't going to work. We can't all be good at everything, and I obviously suck when it comes to this. Why don't you just come and pick the damn thing up?"

"I have a better idea," said Mark. "How about placing an ad in the newspaper for someone who does freelance data entry work on computers? I'll pay them out of my office. You can start by generating reports that break down the people hired and not hired by job classification. If we're successful in getting you into the plant to examine personnel files, the data you provide can be incorporated."

We had a poor showing at the plant gate on Monday, January 22. When I relieved the morning crew, I noted three people with signs, and they were later replaced by only two others. I walked with Georgia to her car.

"We've got to get more aggressive about calling people up and nailing down a schedule," I told her. "If this is what we've got now, what can we expect in a week? I rode by the front office and we had no one there to stop the UPS drivers. Last week I was told they were turning around, but they won't honor a picket line that isn't there when they show up."

"You're right," she said. "I'm sorry for today . . . but you know how these people are. They expect everything in a hurry, and they know ain't nobody getting their picture in the papers again this soon. I'll get with folk. We'll do better tomorrow . . . promise!"

Though lacking in numbers, we succeeded in preventing the majority of trucks from approaching the warehouse entrance. Two trucks simply honked and maintained course without slowing.

Damon, the young organizer and analyst, had driven from the Nashville airport and taken a room at the Ramada. We met at the hotel restaurant for dinner. I had to acknowledge his enthusiasm and passion but sensed little hands-on experience. He was dressed in a long black coat over business clothing, with a neatly trimmed beard and mustache, and conservative haircut. I gave him a typed list of political and community contacts and offered my assessment of each.

"You've got to understand that the real fight is at the plant gate and after that, the evidence we're putting together for the Labor Board case."

"I agree with that," he said. "My job is to build support for your efforts in the community."

"Good luck. I've been whipping that mule for months, and she still hasn't gone anyplace. But hey, knock yourself out with my blessing." I tapped him on the arm and looked in his eyes.

"I'm not prepared to give up on that front," he responded. "Is there anything I can do to assist you with your investigation of the charges?"

"How would you feel about house-calling the union members who've returned to work? Maybe some of the nonmembers who I know aren't anti's? We need statements of union animus from management, especially in regard to hiring, that can be documented."

"I'd love the chance to go out in the community and meet with some of the workers. That's who it's all about, isn't it?"

Welcome to the real world, I thought, but said nothing.

Georgia must have worked her magic because the next day I was joined at the rear gate by eight people, all arriving promptly. Two of the men were sent around front on UPS patrol. A light snow had fallen the previous evening, and we had to avoid icy patches as we circled the pavement, more to stay warm than because of legal admonitions.

Most of the eighteen-wheelers either reversed course or continued down the road without slowing. We fared less well with the smaller rigs, which probably belonged to nonunion fleets, but a couple of them surprised us by turning back at the last moment. I wasn't certain whether their drivers were union or simply intimidated by our presence; or the thought of reprisals from Teamsters. When it comes to organized labor, some people have seen too many movies. In most instances it makes our job more difficult, but on occasion the stereotypes can work to our advantage.

On Wednesday morning I met with representatives of the Postal Workers Union and talked about how UPS drivers were declining to make deliveries at the plant.

"Keep in mind that we're in a different situation," said their local president. "We'll support you any way we can, but for our carriers to do anything other than deliver the U.S. mail is a felony."

"I understand perfectly," I told him. "The thing is, about the mail . . . I know you guys do a great job, through rain and snow and all that. But there are still those times when you're waiting on something really important that never comes. You finally call the person who was supposed to send it, and they swear they put it in the mail ten days ago. Accidents will happen."

I ate lunch in the car en route to the mill, where once again we had sufficient presence to mount a respectable effort. The afternoon dwindled to evening on this overcast day when dampness reinforced the chill. We hadn't seen a delivery vehicle in forty-five minutes; sharing jokes and reminiscing about our lives to pass the time.

A single-unit truck barreled down the main road and slowed as the driver began his turn into the facility. He appeared suddenly to take note of us and reduced his speed to a slow roll, as if uncertain what to do next. I began to approach with a leaflet. Suddenly the truck accelerated toward the open gate. I jumped back and watched as the driver lost control and crashed into the fence, taking out a large section. He paused for a moment on the other side and then headed for the loading docks.

The picketers gathered together looking at the bent metal post and twisted chain-link lying in the parking lot. A couple of them were concerned that we might be blamed.

"Don't worry about it," I assured them. "We didn't do this. It's not our fault the guy can't drive. We're not responsible if he felt threatened for no good reason. Frankly, I appreciate his fine work on our behalf. I wish someone had a camera. It's one more headache and expense for the company."

I privately wondered if I would hear from the police, but didn't. Instead, the next day, reporters began to call. I assumed they were contacted by management, trying to portray us as saboteurs. It worked for me. It was one more news story during a week when otherwise there would have been none.

I provided Donald with transportation the next afternoon as his car was in the shop and he lacked funds to pay for repairs until his unemployment check arrived. He invited me into his home where I exchanged greetings with Tammy as he donned winter gear.

"It's always nice to see your family," I told him as we pulled out of the driveway.

"What about yours?" he asked. "It's been awhile since I've seen your little angel."

"It's been awhile for me, too. This is no longer a fit place to bring a child. If someone tries to jack me, I don't want her in the middle of it."

"Who does Colie stay with when she's not with you? Is she back in North Carolina?"

"She's with her mom."

"What happened between you and Colie's mother, if you don't mind me asking?"

"We were really close once, but it ended badly. The truth is, I'm still hurtin' and trying to sort things out." I was surprised to find myself sharing even this much. "I'm not sure if I'll ever be able to open up and trust in the same way again."

"You know, in the Bible, Jesus says to 'trust in no man.'"

"What do you think he meant by that?" I asked, somewhat taken aback by his response.

"I think it means that we're all human, with our own weaknesses and subject to temptation. We can never know when the imperfections of another are going to interfere with their ability to remain trustworthy. The only one in whom we can place complete faith is the Lord."

I parked my car on the side street facing the rear entrance of the mill, and we joined the picket line. Traffic was light so we stood with our backs to the road admiring the shattered gate. I circulated a photograph of the wreckage that had appeared in the *Jackson Sun* to the amusement of my five comrades.

"When do you think they'll get around to fixing it?" asked Hollis.

"I don't know," I answered. "In the meantime, it's a fine monument to our efforts . . . and there's no way for them to lock up at night. Wouldn't it be a shame if something got stolen?"

"I hope it's something they can't live without," said Alice and every-one laughed.

The temperature had dropped into the twenties, and our spirits numbed within our shivering bodies. With Teamster support at the na-tional level, our efforts had become for the most part limited to remain-ing visible. Very few trucks now passed through our line. I estimated that nearly three out of four deliveries were being curtailed.

The paramount uncertainty was the amount of damage being done to productivity. I had no way of knowing the extent of existing inven-tories remaining to be processed or the degree to which new supplies were required. It all came down to whether our will could outlast their reserves.

I received a call from Mike Zucker after dinner. "What do you think of Damon?" he asked.

"He's got a lot to learn about being in a situation like this," I an-swered, "but he can't be faulted on work ethic. He takes initiative and he's competent."

"Well, one of the things I'd like the two of you to work on is putting together a petition by community leaders to become part of our informa-tion kit as we broaden the front in this campaign."

"That's not a problem," I answered, "but do you really believe that'll help leverage United Foods to the bargaining table?"

"It's another piece of the puzzle," Mike explained. "There's a term I'm fond of using . . . compression. It means that we hit a company in every possible way, from every direction, all at the same time. Eventually we reach a critical mass. There's a tipping point at which a company makes a business decision that it's no longer in their self-interest to continue fighting. That's when we get a phone call and settlement discussions begin, usually off the record at first. We have no way of knowing where that threshold is, only that it exists in every dispute. Our job is to remain relentless on every front until that moment arrives.

"We've been hamstrung up to this point by the good old boys' net-work of West Tennessee, but I guarantee you it doesn't reach as far as Washington."

"The question is," I rejoined, "does Washington give a damn about what's happening in West Tennessee?"

"I don't know. We'll find out."

The next morning I attended a meeting Damon had arranged with members of the City Council and then headed off on my own to meet with representatives of the Communication Workers of America. I ate a homemade sandwich in the car as I drove toward the mill to resume picket duty.

For those who have spent their life working in an office, a day such as this might stand out as a memorable adventure. I experienced only another stretch in a forced march where faith wrestled with exhaustion, and the boundaries between individual days and events became increasingly blurred.

On Saturday morning I had a lengthy phone interview with KIX Radio and was thus able to postpone my descent into the weekend void until midday. I looked forward to the two-day hiatus with increased longing as the week progressed, only to find it disconcerting once it arrived. I remained stuck in high gear and unable to downshift. The abrupt transition from sensory overload to input deprivation left me disoriented instead of relaxed. I feared that if I lapsed too deeply into this ennui I might not be able to regain my edge come Monday.

My shoulders and upper back ached from the tension and felt as rigid as a piece of furniture. I periodically took a massage when back home and decided to find a massage therapist in Jackson. I looked through the local directory and was surprised to find that not even one was listed.

It was impossible to envision when I might next return home and see my daughter. Circumstances were too unpredictable for me to risk being away at the wrong moment. I reflected on how the parallels between my current assignment and the movie *Outland* continued to increase with the passage of time. I was now truly isolated within a remote outpost of my organization, a finger in the dike against corrupt forces that had dominated the landscape from the beginning.

Ernest's open invitation to join him in North Carolina was ever-present in my thoughts. If I told him that I was sleeping with a gun draped over my bedpost, he would likely make the decision himself. He both cared about me as a person and saw me as a resource not to be wasted on a desperate cause.

I realized this was no longer about a job for me. I wasn't putting myself through this for the union or as a career move. The furthest things from my mind were building the labor movement or making a political statement. This was about Georgia, Donald, and thirty other people who had become my friends and to whom I'd made a commitment. It wasn't within me to walk away.

I pulled myself from the throes of melancholic reverie and noted with dismay that it was three o'clock. I decided to force myself to swim laps. Driving to the YMCA, I stopped at a General Nutrition store to buy a bottle of vitamin C. On an off-chance I asked the clerk if she knew of a massage therapist in town and she gave me a number.

The next day was devoted to routine domestic errands from which we are not absolved by even the most dramatic of circumstances. I stocked up at a supermarket, then drove a few miles to a different shopping center for a long overdue visit to the laundromat. As I cruised slowly past the row of small businesses in search of a parking space, someone turned and started to wave at me. Glancing back over my shoulder, I saw that it was Percy. I pulled over to the side and got out of the car to greet him.

Walking in his direction, I mused that we'd not spoken since his phone call about taking medical leave and in the frenzy of the past several months, I'd practically forgotten he existed. The thread of events had been unwinding in fast forward and it felt as though I was encountering an acquaintance from a different reality.

"Hey, it's good to see you," Percy said, grinning. "I been following what you and the others been doin' in the newspaper. I wished I could be out there with y'all, but you know I been on sick leave."

Percy hobbled toward me on a cane, his shoulders slouched and with far more white in his hair and beard than I remembered. He had the appearance of an elderly gentleman out for a stroll on Sunday afternoon.

"How you been getting by?" I asked.

"Not too bad. I got my disability checks coming in, so we're able to make ends meet. If I had to take ill, I'm just thankful it happened while my benefits were still in place."

I shook his hand warmly, gave my regards to his family, and returned to my car.

On Monday morning a young woman named Sandra, who had answered the ad for freelance computer work, knocked at my door. I invited her to sit at my kitchen table and explained the union's objectives concerning the reports to be generated, curious about whether she would be supportive of or offended by our efforts. She seemed utterly indifferent. Digitizing information was her specialty. The ethical ramifications could be contemplated by others.

I asked if she could produce mailing labels from the address list already entered by Mark's secretary. She casually opened the file.

"Not a problem," she said with a smile. I felt like an idiot but relieved at no longer having to wrestle with this area of my incompetence.

I was half an hour behind schedule when I arrived at the picket line but found Georgia holding down the fort with three others.

"Is anyone around front dealing with UPS?" I asked.

"You know I always got you covered," she smiled, punching my arm.

I stacked my sign atop several others against the part of the gate that remained intact. There was no need to hoist them until a truck approached. The temperature remained in the twenties, and hands could remain in coat pockets.

The glory of righteous conflict had quickly given way to the tedium of endurance. I felt a sudden chill penetrate my core which exceeded the effects of winter. I sensed that I was being observed and increasingly at risk . . . from a place within that transcends logic. It's an instinct understood by anyone who has survived dangerous circumstances and is familiar with violence.

United Foods had anticipated the entanglement of litigation and indignant rhetoric in the press. This wasn't their first rodeo and they'd learned from experience. They had also expected a conventional picket line in which the workforce would collapse upon itself in division and hostility.

What they hadn't counted on was me and the alliance with the Teamsters. We had dispensed with frontal assault in favor of exploiting their unprotected rear. I was aware of being engaged with a tactically sophisticated opponent which understood the significance of a lynch pin.

As evening descended, Georgia invited me to follow her home for dinner. Sensing my absence of personal life, she knew that a bit of hospitality might do me good.

We sat on the couch in her living room after eating, and our discussion naturally turned to the campaign. I asked if she had heard any news from inside the plant about how the blockade was affecting operations.

"I've spoken to a few of the people that's working," she answered. "They only running one style of cloth right now—Osnaburg. Do you know what that is?"

"I have no idea."

"Well, it's 100 percent cotton, and it's sold by the roll. It's not good enough to make clothing from; it's more for rags and wiping stuff up."

"You mean it's like a utility cloth. Did you happen to find out who their customers are?"

"No, but according to my friend, there's only one customer for the Osnaburg right now, but they're buying all they can run. It's someone left over from American Mills."

"Is that all they're manufacturing?"

"Except for some yarn and thread which gets sold direct after being spun and doesn't involve the weavers."

"So, here's the big question, Georgia. How's the plant operating? What's the work schedule been like?"

"From what I hear, they started running out of work sometime last week. Looms have been standing and people been getting sent home early."

"We're getting to them. It's working. If we can keep this up and they're unable to find enough scab truckers, we just might pull this off."

"They sure must be hating you, right about now." Georgia shook her head and smiled at me.

I returned home after ten. Sandra had locked the door as instructed but forgotten to turn on the light. The property was too far from the center of town for street lamps, and it was pitch dark in the yard. The nearest house was twenty yards to my right, obscured by a row of trees. I held the .38 in my right hand as I fumbled with the keys in my left, listening for sounds approaching from the side of the house.

There was a message on my answering machine from Damon requesting that I return his call regardless of the hour. He had been introduced to the West Madison County Chapter of JONAH (Just Organized

Neighborhoods Area Headquarters). This was a progressive grass-roots organization that had grown to eleven chapters in West Tennessee, and I'd been invited to address their local meeting the following morning.

JONAH had tentatively agreed to assist with a community-based initiative of letters and petitions to Judge Kennedy, intended to influence his ultimate decision at the Confirmation Hearing. Drained from the day's events, I felt frustrated by this unexpected intrusion into my work schedule.

"Do you really think that a bunch of concerned citizens is going to be able to get through to this judge in a way that our lawyers haven't?" I asked.

"Mike thinks it's a good idea," said Damon with quiet satisfaction.

"Fuck it. I'll be there."

I got Sandra squared away with her assignment on Tuesday morning, reminded her to leave the front light on when she locked up, and drove to my introductory meeting with JONAH.

I offered their members a passionate, unprepared presentation about circumstances at the mill, in which they seemed to take considerable delight. They appeared sincere and energetic, likely to translate good intentions into their best efforts. From a tactical perspective, it would be like unleashing a handful of butterflies against a rhinoceros.

I again tore through a sandwich held in one hand while driving to the plant, where I encountered an unexpected development. Two members of management had approached the picketers, politely distributed a letter, and departed. The one-page document said the Labor Board dispute had been settled and provided an explanation of the terms.

"What's up with this?" asked Donald. "You haven't told us anything about no settlement."

"That's because I haven't heard anything," I told the several people standing with him.

I excused myself to drive to the union hall and call the attorneys. It was somewhat eerie entering the deserted hall. I looked over my shoulder and found no vehicles passing on the street, walked a few steps down the hallway, then turned to lock the door behind me. I instinctively hit the dead light switch and proceeded into the main hall. Mark had fortunately been convinced that paying the phone bill remained a necessity. Comfort is expendable during a conflict, but communication isn't.

I called the law firm and was able to reach Deborah Godwin.

"The Board hasn't decided anything yet," she assured me. "If they had, we'd be the first to know. This is just some kind of company propaganda. I'll give the Board a heads-up as soon as we're done."

"What's the status of our information request to review personnel files?" I asked.

"MacLean says his client is considering our request and that he'll get back with us. I expect their answer will eventually be no. We'll then get with the Board and complain that the employer is preventing us lawful access to information that would be useful in investigation of the charges. It won't cast United Foods in a very favorable light to be seen as obstructing a government investigation. I believe we'll be able to get you inside, but there's still a process to go through."

We hung up; I leaned back to reflect for a moment and began calling my press list. This was another opportunity for coverage in the absence of genuinely newsworthy developments and a chance to discredit management. I gave reporters the Board's Memphis phone number and faxed them a copy of the company letter.

On arriving back at the gate I found the protesters anxiously talking in a group, blocking the entrance and ignoring the road. "Don't worry about it," I told them. "I just spoke to the lawyers. It's all bullshit. There's been no decision. Read the papers tonight. We're about to make the company eat its own words."

Discrepancies in a company memorandum didn't constitute front-page news, but as usual I found Tom Corwin's article to be comprehensive and thorough: *Letter from mill says labor dispute settled.*

Corwin had interviewed Bill Harvey with the National Labor Relations Board. "Let me just tell you that the case is still under investigation," said the assistant director of Region 26. "The Board is prohibited from further comment until a decision is made."

Though unable to fathom the basis of management's inept maneuver, I intended to make the most of it. I postponed dinner to type a brief leaflet, beneath which the article would be pasted.

LABOR BOARD CHARGES

1. Last week, the Company passed out a letter saying that the Board had ruled. The Company misled you.
2. As of this date, the Board has <u>not yet ruled</u>.
3. The Board is still considering the evidence on all charges.
4. If you want the truth, please call the Board at 521-xxxx.

Sandra printed her first set of address labels the next morning, and I careened through the streets of Jackson to the printer. I asked committee members to show up at the plant the following afternoon with as much support as possible. We would leaflet employees while continuing to picket the delivery gate and then hopefully make short work of the mailing.

That evening I eagerly looked forward to an appointment with the massage therapist to whom I'd been referred. It felt as if I had a migraine headache in the muscles of my upper back.

I met the masseuse at his home, discussed my areas of distress, stripped down to my shorts and lay on the table. He lit a cigarette while rubbing oil onto my skin and asked where I was from.

"When I was in the marines back in the late '60's, my buddies and I used to head up to Chapel Hill when we were on leave," he shared to my surprise. "We'd walk around on the college campus until we found us a couple of those hippie types, you know, with the long hair and beads, and then we'd beat the shit out of them just for kicks."

I shut my eyes and tried to relax into the massage, which was hard because his technique was amateurish and he wouldn't stop talking through the ever-present cigarette dangling from his lips. An hour later I departed with less money in my pocket but no reduction in muscle tension.

I arrived at the delivery gate the following afternoon with a box of leaflets and my back still aching. Three picketers were present when I arrived, but during the next hour six more joined us, enough to stop trucks and conduct the other activities we had planned.

As shift change drew near, Donald and I walked around the building to leaflet at the Weaving gate. We passed a lone man stationed by the office in the event of an appearance by UPS. I handed him a stack of leaflets and asked him to cover the other employee entrance for an hour.

As Donald and I awaited the arrival of second shift, the now-familiar but unnatural chill sliced through my body, and I trembled momentarily.

"Are you alright?" asked the Rev. "You're not taking sick, are you?"

"No, I'm just really tired."

A woman walked through the gate without taking a leaflet, then turned back and approached me. "Could I talk to you for a moment in private?" she asked.

We walked about twenty yards down the street until she felt comfortable.

"I'll be honest with you," she began. "I wasn't a union member under American Mills. I wasn't against the union; I just couldn't afford the dues. But there's some things going on inside the plant that I don't agree with and I think you should know about."

"Talk to me. If there's anything you want kept confidential, just ask."

"The last couple of days, there's been a petition being passed around the plant to get rid of the union. I was told by two supervisors that if I didn't sign it, I'd be fired. I finally did sign it but I don't think it's right. I don't think anyone should be forced to sign their name.

"My supervisor told me 'the one's that don't sign this paper are for the union and won't be here very long.' I'm afraid that I'm going to be fired anyway because at first I refused to sign it . . ."

The woman was talking a mile a minute and clearly very agitated. I interrupted and got her to pause by asking her name.

"Libby," she answered. "Libby Strickland."

"It's against federal law for management to solicit employee signatures on a petition like this, let alone threaten them if they won't sign it," I told her. "Would you be willing to meet me at the union hall tomorrow before work to give me a written statement?"

I was aware of how unlikely this was, given the woman's level of anxiety and lack of previous union involvement.

"If I give you what you're asking for, what're you going to do with it?" she inquired.

"I'll fax it to our lawyers and they'll give it to the National Labor Relations Board."

She surprised me by agreeing.

Libby returned to the gate and entered the plant. A few minutes later I heard the buzzer announcing the start of her shift, but the expected exodus of first shift didn't occur.

"Praise God, they must've been sent home early once again for lack of work," declared the Reverend.

We returned to the rear gate, where I left Donald in charge and then proceeded to the union hall to supervise the mailing. Once our task had been completed, we remained to talk until darkness descended both outside and within. I locked the hall as a dozen people headed for their parked cars. Georgia started her engine, turned on the headlights, and got back out.

"Hey, y'all stick around a minute!" she shouted, motioning people to return and positioning them in a horseshoe formation around the front lawn. "Nobody goes anywhere until Phil is safely on his way!"

I wasn't certain this gesture was necessary, but was deeply moved by the concern. The row of workers parted to allow room for my car to back onto the street. They stood vigil until I turned the corner.

I returned to the union hall on Friday at 11:00 a.m. and waited to see if Libby would actually show up. My car parked alone in the front was the perfect invitation to anyone seeking a discreet opportunity for confrontation. I tapped the revolver beneath my coat and then reached inside to unsnap the holster flap. I was no more frightened than when I had driven taxis through bad neighborhoods, but was on equally high alert. I stared at the door to see who, if anyone, would come through.

Libby arrived right on time. She sat across from me at my desk and told her story while I scribbled on a legal pad.

The regulations governing the decertification of union locals are a complex matrix of contradictions. There is a thirty-day window prior to the expiration of a labor agreement during which a local is vulnerable. Absent a contract, there are certain circumstances under which decertification remains an ongoing possibility.

If a third of bargaining-unit employees sign a petition, the National Labor Relations Board will supervise a new election to determine whether a majority still wish to be represented. In the present situation, a voting procedure at the mill would be limited to those currently employed, subject to the daily influence of management and without the presence of elected local officers; rendering the union's chances nonexistent.

The NLRB is strict in its requirement that a decertification petition must originate and be promoted entirely from within the bargaining unit. Management is obliged to maintain neutrality and distance from the process.

The reality is that viable attempts at decertification are generally orchestrated by an employer. Management covertly assembles its own employee committee, from which one is selected as the "petitioner" to present an official request with signatures to the Board. The small circle generally consists of disenfranchised individuals seduced by an opportunity to feel important. The petitioner and other ringleaders are often promised promotions to supervisor and other forms of compensation. They are provided with properly worded petitions, instructions, and increased freedom of movement throughout the work areas. The burden falls on union investigators to prove this.

It appeared from Libby's statement that United Foods' management, emboldened by the lack of union leadership in the plant, was making little effort to disguise their complicity. It was ironic that an effort was being made to decertify a union that hadn't been recognized to begin with; obviously a preemptive move to forestall an ultimate recognition mandate by the Board.

There was another consideration, however, that made these developments less ominous than they might have been otherwise. The NLRB won't act on a decertification petition while charges are pending against the employer. If a complaint is issued alleging a significant pattern of unfair labor practices, the petition will be dismissed on grounds that signers may have been unduly influenced by employer-generated union animus.

Libby signed a detailed affidavit, and I thanked her for having the courage to come forward as we walked to the door. A sandwich and cold cup of coffee awaited me on the passenger seat of my car. I consumed them quickly before taking my position behind the factory.

I experienced a surge of respect and camaraderie as I shook hands with the afternoon's delegation. This had developed into a disciplined picket line in which people knew the schedule and took their turns as expected. Nothing is more intoxicating than victory against a more powerful adversary. Each truck turned away was a black eye dealt the men who had kicked them to the curb and pushed their families deeper into poverty.

I met with Damon for dinner that evening to exchange updates and coordinate the next week's activities. He stumbled over his words, his face haggard with exhaustion, as we sat at a table waiting for service.

Damon had made a few house visits to currently working employees but was concentrating most of his efforts on gathering endorsements for the JONAH-sponsored petition and letter-writing initiative to Judge Kennedy. Armed with a contact list of individuals likely to be sympathetic, he was calling on them at home.

"I believe that we're going to have a strong enough showing of community support by the Confirmation Hearing that the judge is going to have to give it some serious consideration," he shared with enthusiasm.

"Perhaps friendly aliens will intervene on our behalf," I told him. "Anything's possible."

Damon suddenly sat back with a startled look on his face. "I was out visiting people from my list in the western part of the county today, and one of them asked me to come back this evening, when it would be more convenient. I completely forgot about him. I've got to go back and get his signature. I'm sorry. You'll have to order by yourself."

"It's a half-hour drive each way. It's not worth it for one signature. Get some rest and save your strength for what really matters."

"No. I've got to get that signature," he said, getting up from his chair. "I've got an early flight back home tomorrow morning. I'll see you on Tuesday."

CHAPTER 20

There was little to be done in terms of work that weekend. The picket line was running on its own momentum, and there would be few new avenues of investigation regarding legal cases until access to personnel files was granted.

Rick Hardin had invited me to drop by his house for a visit. I tried to call him, but the line was disconnected, so I took a chance on arriving unannounced.

"Hey man, I didn't expect to see you today. Come on in out the cold," he exclaimed while ushering me into his small wooden house. He was in good spirits, his eyes wide and sparkling like someone flying high on a controlled substance.

"I saw your woman the other day," he said.

"Who?" I asked without thinking.

"Your woman. You know, Tina."

I realized she had probably been too embarrassed to admit we had parted company. I'd always had a natural inclination to bolster the confidence of others, but with Tina, all I had done was inadvertently push the buttons that triggered her shame.

"So, how you been holding up?" I asked.

"Well, it's all good," Rick replied. "But way I'm headed, pretty soon I'm gonna to be ending up in jail."

"Why? What's going on? You been busted or something?"

"No, nothing like that. I'm just going to be ending up in jail, 'fore long. That's all. It ain't no thing."

The extent of Rick's intoxication was becoming more evident, but didn't appear entirely responsible for his deep-rooted conviction about his pending fate. I guessed that he was subsidizing his unemployment benefits by trafficking in whatever product he was currently enjoying.

"Look, no matter what you're into, you can cover your ass and be careful," I counseled him. "If you want, you can talk to me about it, and I might be able to suggest some ways to protect yourself. I don't want to see you getting locked up behind this shit."

"I appreciate that, but it ain't no thing," he smiled. "I'm just going to be ending up in jail, is all. The po-lice will come knocking when they do and I'll be here."

I called to speak with Colie that evening, but there isn't much potential for long-distance conversation with a five-year-old. Relationships with a child that age are based on shared experience and affection, not dialogue. Within a couple of minutes, she wanted to resume playing with her friend.

After dinner I was able to watch a movie uninterrupted as there hadn't been any new developments for people to call about. I turned in earlier than usual, hoping to rebuild fortitude for the week ahead. My energy levels were bankrupt with my mind and body as creditors. It was a stormy night, and I fell asleep to the rhythm of pouring rain.

I awoke to a sharp creaking sound, sitting bolt upright with revolver in hand, screaming, "Who the fuck is it?" before being fully aware that I'd done it. I listened intently and strained my eyes through the darkness toward the bedroom door.

It's only me, the old house moaned, and creaked once more.

I lay back on the pillow with my heart racing and remained awake for hours. This wasn't the first occasion I'd been aroused in this manner nor would it be the last. I was hardwired from earlier experience to wake up in fight-or-flight mode at the first hint of the unexpected. It would serve me well in the event of an actual encounter, but was also a liability for one already subject to insomnia.

There was a message on my answering machine from Ernest the next morning. I made breakfast and returned his call to the Howard Johnson's in Greensboro.

"Where have you been?" he asked. "I called you at seven but no one picked up."

I reviewed possible fabricated responses for a moment and answered, "I was sleeping. It's the weekend."

"Oh . . ." he responded, as if this were a concept beyond the realm of his own experience.

"The picket line is holding," I reported. "The gates are manned every day during business hours and very few deliveries are getting through. I don't understand why the trucks keep showing up. Maybe they're waiting for the day our resolve breaks and no one's there."

"When do you see us reaching that point?"

"We won't. Not as long as I'm on the ground. What about my request to pay the utilities at the union hall and put it on my expenses? I feel like I'm operating out of a bunker on the Western Front."

"You got it. Sorry it took me so long to get authorization. You got no idea how many pieces I'm trying to juggle right now. . . . I almost forgot. There's a staff meeting in Atlanta the week after this. You'll need to leave on Sunday night to be there Monday morning."

"How long will it last?" I asked.

"It'll be over sometime Wednesday afternoon . . . depends how long Bruce wants to run his mouth. You know how that is."

"Under the circumstances, it's a really stupid waste of my time," I said in frustration. "I'm in the middle of a war zone and where I'm needed is here. I'm not even going home to see my daughter."

"I'll do my best to explain that to Bruce," Ernest offered. "He won't be happy but I'll deal with it. You do need to at least show your face. No one escapes that. How about driving down on Tuesday night for the last day? I'll try to arrange for us to meet privately with Bruce after it's over."

I decided to celebrate the return of warmth and light at the union hall by scheduling a meeting for Thursday evening. It occurred to me that perhaps the amount of information provided in recent announcements had reduced curiosity and incentive to attend. I prepared a sparse invitation that noted only the topics of discussion. It was a quick turnaround at the printer, and I had no problem joining the picket line prior to shift change on Monday afternoon. Georgia and Alice accompanied me to the weave room gate.

We were in position to greet the occasional early arrival from second shift. The temperature had dropped again but my jacket zipper remained sufficiently open so that the holster could be reached in one move if necessary.

"Someone's coming," said Alice.

The road was empty so I turned toward the mill and observed a man wearing dress shirt and tie emerge and walk toward us. As he drew closer I saw that it was Don Dresser. He passed through the gate and greeted us politely.

"I understand that you're from North Carolina," he said to me. "Whereabouts, if you don't mind my asking?"

"The Chapel Hill area."

"Ah, I understand you have quite the football team there," he noted, attempting to find a topic of mutual interest.

"I don't have much time to follow sports."

"What's the winter been like back there?" he continued.

"I don't know. I haven't been home since the holidays. Normally I find the winters a bit milder than here."

Dresser didn't request a copy of the leaflet nor did he mention trucks or matters of representation. "How have you been getting along?" he asked, addressing Georgia.

"I'm getting along just fine," she replied with a smile, meeting his eyes.

The small talk and pleasantries continued as if we were several old acquaintances well-met in the city park on this clear and brisk winter's day. Dresser did not appear inconvenienced by the weather despite his lack of overcoat. I glanced momentarily at the angle of his gaze, wondering if he could see inside my leather jacket. I had to admire him for walking alone into the midst of his adversaries to engage them and take their measure. It's what I would have done in his place.

When we had finished leafleting, Georgia and I retired to the union hall to assist several others who were already busy with the latest envelope stuffing. We carried the boxes of envelopes, sorted by zip code for bulk mailing, to my car in time to reach the post office before closing. Georgia again instructed those who remained to circle the parking area until I was safely on my way.

I received an early phone call from Libby Strickland. She had been terminated at the conclusion of her shift the previous night. I asked if she would meet me at the union hall to provide a supplemental affidavit and she agreed.

As I turned onto the lawn in front of the hall, I saw Libby sitting on the steps waiting for me. I unlocked the door, throwing the light switch as usual, but this time the fluorescent bulbs flickered to life. I strode to the thermostat and turned on the heat. The one-page statement didn't take long to prepare, and I decided to join the morning shift on the picket line; making a detour to a convenience store and arriving with six large cups of coffee.

The temperature was in the forties on a cloudless day and the sun bathed us with its radiant heat. I removed my knit hat and took a deep breath of fresh air from the Tennessee countryside, laced with the familiar bouquet of industrial fumes. There was little traffic on the road and no trucks. I asked the four members of the picket line how they and their families were getting by.

"At the moment the bills are all getting paid," said an older man named Marvin Rogers, "but I don't know what we're going to do in two months when the unemployment runs out. Who's going to hire me at my age? I'm not looking forward to working for minimum wage after twenty-one years of at least earning enough to support my family like a man."

"Remember that petition the union filed with the Department of Labor," I said, "the one about plant closings and mass layoffs involving foreign imports? We should get a response way before then. You'll get another six months. It's not a permanent solution, but it'll buy you some more time if we can't force our way back in."

"Let's think positive," Betty Trice chimed in. "Maybe right now their lawyer is calling ours asking what they got to do for us to start letting the trucks pass."

We continued to talk and sip our coffee in the absence of activity. Replacements began to arrive, and I slipped away to eat the sandwich waiting in my car.

The afternoon slowly unwound, remaining temperate and uneventful. The damaged section of fence lay where it had fallen, still partially attached to its post by a twisted hinge. A tractor-trailer finally lumbered toward the entrance, and the demonstrators scurried for their signs, grateful for relief from the stupor of inactivity. The driver halted to regard the placards that had just been raised for his benefit. Without acknowledging us, he eased his gears into reverse.

That was our only encounter for two hours. I paced in lazy circles, resisting the occasional temptation to ask those with a watch for the time, not wishing to communicate that I was restless and eager for the release of dusk.

The declining position of the sun indicated that it must be around four o'clock, and a chill was setting in. A yellow dump truck rounded the bend and turned toward the gate. It was loaded with bales of cotton. When we hoisted our picket signs, the driver blared his horn and accelerated past us.

"Hooo-eeeeeee!" exclaimed one of the men. "They must be getting pretty hard up hauling in the cotton on a sorry old truck like that!"

The others roared with the laughter of the bored, starved for a moment's entertainment.

The light was fading, and we were about to call it a day when the small yellow truck once again turned to enter. We could tell it was being driven by the same man.

"What you say there, Bubba?" a voice from the picket line exclaimed, and once again the others laughed.

I didn't share the amusement of my comrades but kept what I was thinking to myself. A new card had been played, the value of which was still undetermined.

Damon had returned from Washington, and we had dinner that evening.

"Mike would like us to prepare another petition," he told me, "this one to all the major creditors and signed by workers. I believe you guys did something similar with ITT a couple of months back. We think it would make sense to expand this approach before the Confirmation."

"Your timing is good," I told him. "We're holding a union meeting on Thursday evening. I'll prepare something. I can get behind this one. If enough creditors become concerned that recovery of their assets is being jeopardized by the labor practices of UFI . . . it won't really matter what the damn judge thinks if the plan gets voted down. It's a bit of a stretch but worth the effort. While you're at it, please try to fit in a few more house calls to working union members. I'd like to see at least a couple of them at the meeting."

I learned that United Foods management was thinking along lines similar to those of Damon and Mike. Workers were being asked to sign forms denoting approval of the reorganization plan and were told that their jobs depended on compliance. A woman named Linda Holmes met me at the union hall the next morning to provide an affidavit about the coercive nature of the solicitation.

I was happy to see Donald standing behind the mill when I arrived. His company would make the time pass more agreeably. I was filling him in on a few of the more recent developments when the yellow dump truck bearing cotton passed through our line. I looked up and saw that the driver was different.

"These guys started showing up yesterday evening," I told Donald. "Who the hell are they?"

"There's a small cotton gin just down the road from here," he answered. "I believe that was one of their trucks that just passed."

"I didn't even know about this place. Where is it? I've never even seen it."

"It's easy to miss. Actually, it's located down a dirt driveway just on the other side of the mill."

"Has the company always done business with them?"

"Not since I've worked here."

That afternoon, another half dozen of these vehicles drove through us on their way to the loading docks.

"When we're done for the evening, I want to check this place out," I told Donald. "Will you come with me?"

"I'm your man," he answered.

We drove in my car around the building, and Donald directed me to a residential street running perpendicular to the plant. We parked and walked back to the driveway at the top of the block.

"This way," he said as we stealthily approached the open gate of what appeared to be a small industrial setting. Darkness was falling, but several of the yellow trucks stood out in the remaining light, adjacent to what appeared to be a storage facility.

"This isn't good," I told him. "Are you free for dinner? We need to put our heads together."

"I'll follow in my car," said the Rev. "Let me just stop at a phone to call Tammy and I'm all yours."

I chose the buffet as it was devoid of music and barroom chatter, and we could choose a private location to sit and talk. I put some food on my plate but ignored it as I regarded my friend.

"This could be the chink in our armor," I said at last. "It could change everything. A bunch of small deliveries equals one big delivery."

"I know . . ." said Donald, as he exhaled slowly.

I met his gaze and held it for nearly a minute. "How difficult do you think it would be to torch this place?"

"It wouldn't be difficult it all," he answered. "A few drops of kerosene and the whole place would go up. It's all cotton and wood in there. It's deserted at night and they're not likely to have any security. It wouldn't be hard to hop over that fence . . ."

I held his eyes. "Would you be willing . . . ?"

"If that's our only chance at keeping this fight alive. I've always got your back. You know that."

"We'd have to plan this really carefully," I said. "Step by step. More recon. Nothing stupid or impulsive."

"I know a place to get some kerosene that couldn't be traced back to us."

"Let's think on this long and hard and talk more tomorrow. We discuss this with no one . . . not even people we both trust. When it goes down, everyone is equally surprised."

I turned to the lukewarm food on my plate and wolfed it down. Donald and I shook hands in the parking lot and went our separate ways.

On Thursday morning I had to shift gears and attend a previously scheduled meeting with Judge Harris and what remained of the Community Task Force that continued to network displaced workers with relief agencies. I hit the pause button long enough for a decent lunch and then assumed my position on the picket line.

The yellow dump trucks were entering the loading area at intervals of forty-five minutes to an hour. A medium-sized rig likewise passed through us, but a tractor trailer reversed gears. I estimated that for every delivery turned away another had simply not been dispatched. United Foods hadn't entirely resolved its supply issues. But the lifeblood which pumped through the arteries of production was cotton and its flow was no longer impeded.

The impact on the morale of the picketers was also becoming noticeable. I anticipated further attrition to the ranks of those willing to endure the elements under these circumstances. The more I considered my discussion with Donald the further I found myself leaning toward drastic action. My footsteps carried me far enough down the road to afford privacy as I deliberated.

Coming to terms with this small, low-volume producer had obviously been the company's last resort when our endurance became apparent. The initiative was ours to seize once more, and eliminating this resource might well be our final hope of outlasting the opposition.

In my mind I replayed the scenario of hopping the fence of the cotton gin at 3:00 a.m., Donald passing over the kerosene and then joining me. We could kindle the blaze and be gone within minutes. I imagined looking back while returning to my car, the darkness giving birth to what would soon be pillars of flame.

After that, it would simply be a matter of returning home and resuming my normal duties in the coming days. I would naturally be a primary suspect, but I had been dealing with members of law enforcement my entire life and wasn't intimidated. They were simply another species which inhabited my jungle whose behavior needed to be understood and anticipated. The same burden of proof that applied to Don Dresser's hiring practices would insulate me as well.

Even if investigators reached the conclusion that I must somehow be directly or indirectly responsible, I was confident of my ability to deny sufficient evidence on which to prosecute. There would be over three hundred possible suspects—displaced workers with shattered lives and viable motive.

The image of sitting in prison intruded upon my reflections, disclaimed by the union and unable to hug my daughter again until she was nearly grown. I eradicated the thought and continued planning. The members of Local 281 were owed every risk and sacrifice necessary to defend their interests. This operation might prove decisive and could be executed in a manner that was unexpected and easy to obscure. I walked back to the picket line with a sense of determination.

"You seem to have a lot on your mind today," said Vernette. "A penny for your thoughts."

"I was just preparing my presentation for the union meeting tonight," I replied.

I was at the union hall by 6:15 to turn on the heat and await early arrivals. People began filing into the hall, and it appeared that some of

Damon's house calls had been to good effect, as there were several currently employed members in attendance.

After the meeting was called to order, I introduced Damon, commending him on his tireless efforts and informing people that petitions would be circulated at the conclusion.

"What about the petition being circulated in the plant?" interrupted a man with whom I wasn't well-acquainted but had encountered while leafleting. "What happens if the union gets voted out? What happens to our money the lawyers are fighting for in court? Is that just lost?"

There was a murmuring of voices against which I raised my own to speak. "The union's not going get voted out. There's not even going to be an election. If a petition does get presented to the Labor Board, it will be rejected because of the antiunion activity.

"But just for your frame of reference in understanding these matters—when a union gets voted out, it loses the right to represent workers in new cases that might arise. Existing cases, which were filed while the union was still certified, are allowed to run their course."

"Do you think the bankruptcy judge is going to rule in the company's favor?" a woman asked.

"Unfortunately, yes, as far as allowing United Foods to continue running the plant the way they want. He's too deep in the company's pocket. I'm not saying he's taking money under the table, because I doubt that. But there's other ways of being influenced. That doesn't mean he's also going to throw out your claims against American Mills. I believe those will go forward."

Instead of a making a formal presentation, I allowed the forum to unwind into an orderly dialogue. I could ill afford to make a public address about an imminent felony. It wasn't difficult to follow the thread of questions into areas that weren't compromising to discuss. Various documents were distributed for signature and we adjourned with the workers appearing satisfied by the information received.

"I'll lock up," said Georgia as she preceded the others through the door and onto the lawn, where she once again arranged people in a semi-circle around the periphery of the parking area to await my departure. The front light of the hall illuminated the human barrier surrounding vehicles densely packed on sparse grass against the backdrop of a darkened street. I entered my own and slowly eased backwards. Donald tapped on my window as I glided past and mouthed the words, "call me."

I allowed sufficient time for Donald to touch base with his family and rang his number at ten. "Have you been thinking and praying about what we discussed last night?" I asked.

"I've been doing little else," he answered.

"So, what do you think?"

"I think we could pull this off if we wanted to," he replied without hesitation.

"How do you honestly feel about actually going through with it? There won't be any turning back."

"Let me put it this way. They chose to get in bed with the Devil, and if they end up getting burned . . . so be it."

"I'll go back out there over the weekend to take another look around with some daylight. I'll talk to you soon."

"Be careful," he said. "Don't let anyone see you."

The next morning I spoke with city officials and members of the Central Labor Council regarding a meeting that Damon was trying to organize. I situated Sandra at the computer on my kitchen table and drove the short distance to the mill.

I assumed my place at the threshold of the loading docks with three stalwart picketers who refused to be deterred by unwelcome circumstances. There were snow flurries in the air, and my hands and face quickly became numb.

I passed the time by rehearsing what I would say during the inevitable police interrogations. Following the advice I'd given in prepping countless witnesses, my responses would remain short, focused, and devoid of opinion, placing the burden of probing further on the investigator.

The small trucks laden with cotton intermittently made their way past us at a casual speed, no longer unnerved by our presence. I occasionally spoke with my comrades in an effort to keep their spirits up.

"What if you went and talked with the man that owns that cotton gin down the road, you know, the way you present yourself?" one of the men asked. "Explain to him what he's doing to our lives and what this means to our jobs. Maybe he'll listen."

"Whoever he is, he doesn't care about your lives," I said. "I wish it wasn't like that. All he cares about is the money he's being paid."

"What are we going to do then? What's the point anymore?"

"Everyday things keep changing. We hold the line and wait to see what happens next."

There is a moment on awakening when all we experience is the essence of our being and the natural joy of existence, unencumbered by the events and sorrow that restrict our lives. The instant fades as we remember and discover ourselves once again draped in the cumbersome mantle of our fate.

I rolled out of bed feeling less rested than when I had turned in, having been jarred from slumber twice by sounds in the night. While I drank coffee and listened to the crackle of frying eggs, the day's mission became clear in my mind as caffeine and adrenaline compensated for the lack of sleep.

There was no set schedule that morning, so I allowed myself the luxury of washing and getting dressed at my own pace. I drove to the plant and turned down the intersection which had been traversed with Donald earlier in the week. A conservative, mid-priced sedan ambling slowly down a quiet residential street on Saturday, its driver perhaps searching for an address or simply wishing to avoid children darting into the road, wouldn't arouse suspicion.

I rolled past the cotton gin on my left. The yellow dump trucks were visible through the locked gate, scattered near the storage building and farther back on the grounds. There was a tower of some sort, the purpose of which I couldn't discern. An unused portion of the property lay between the work areas and a fence, which would offer further discretion in the night.

I continued moving down the block, noting the rows of small mill houses tightly arrayed on either side. They were nearly as old as the factory itself. I imagined the occupants of the dwelling nearest the gin being awakened at three in the morning to stare out their bedroom window at flames leaping and dancing in the night sky. I wondered what they would think or feel.

I envisioned a gust of wind reaching down with its feathery hand to grab a handful of sparks from a fiery pillar and sprinkling them on the roof of the family who watched in awe and confusion. The antique wooden structure would ignite as quickly as the cotton. Perhaps within minutes a few mischievous embers would declare their autonomy from the greater blaze to seek their own nest at a neighbor's house.

This was a potential consequence not previously contemplated and which would need to be addressed. I reached the end of the street, made a right turn at the stop sign, drove at random through the neighborhood for ten minutes, and cruised back up the block from the opposite direction.

I observed two small children playing on a swing set in front of their house and an elderly gentleman raking leaves across the street. We could purchase our materials and then wait for a night when the wind was blowing strongly in the direction I was now driving. It could be a matter of days or weeks, but eventually an opportunity would present itself.

I believed that a decision had been reached in the light of day but returned home feeling ill-at-ease. I lay on the couch and wrestled within. I had sworn to stop at nothing in defense of the local and its members. Now that this course of action had presented itself, I felt an obligation to pursue it. This was the sort of fast, decisive move that had already become and would remain the signature of my career. But fires set with an accelerant can burn for hours, and the wind has been known to shift direction. Putting innocent families at risk was not a line I was prepared to cross.

I lay with my eyes closed and hands on my forehead for another half hour. When I pulled myself up, it was nearly four o'clock. I'd been invited to appear as the guest speaker at a dinner function held by JONAH.

I dressed properly for a formal event and drove toward the address provided, mentally preparing an outline of my remarks. I spoke of politicians, judges, their collusion with corporate interests, and its impact on the lives of working people—much to the approval of those in attendance. I was fully aware of merely putting on a show and preaching to the choir while the lives of mill workers unfolded without the slightest change.

By Monday morning I felt impelled to engage in something proactive. I called the Memphis law firm to pursue our request for access to personnel files and found Sam Morris available.

"I believe that we'll be able to make headway fairly soon," he told me. "I received a phone call late last week, as did the company's attorney. The Board has reached a determination that United Foods is a successor and as such, is required to bargain with the union and provide information. Don't be calling the newspapers quite yet. It won't be official until a decision is reached regarding the charges. This was just the kind of heads-up that a good Board agent will sometimes give the parties."

"So, when will the status quo be ordered back in effect?" I asked. "How will this impact the company's failure to rehire by seniority?"

"That's a whole other question. The Board's position is that when American Mills took over from Tennessee Textiles, there was a contract in force which they chose to terminate, thus initiating the status quo in lieu of a new agreement being reached. When United Foods assumed possession, there wasn't an actual contract in place and under these circumstances, the status quo doesn't automatically transfer from one successor to another. The Board will have to buy our 'joint employer' argument for the status quo to be revived. They're still debating that issue among themselves."

I invited Donald to join me for lunch and we met at a small diner. I was unsure how he would respond to the decision I'd made over the weekend and if he would be disappointed in me.

"Well, I prayed for guidance but I guess that God chose to deliver his answer through you. His ways are indeed mysterious," the Reverend said with a smile.

I felt a wave of respect and affection for this sincere and courageous friend. I decided to take him into my confidence regarding the discussion with our attorney.

"Well, at least we're making some progress," he said.

"How about we go stand in front of the plant and stop those trucks which we can?" I suggested.

Damon had scheduled for us to meet with Mayor Farmer on Tuesday at 1:00 p.m. I resented how this pointless expenditure of time and effort would delay the long drive to Atlanta and regretted having agreed to attend in order to avoid an argument.

The mayor graciously welcomed us into the municipal conference room as if nothing untoward had ever transpired between the union and his office.

"How are your people enjoying their employment with United Foods?" he asked once we were seated.

I was tempted to answer, *Why don't you take a job at the mill for a month and tell me how much you enjoy it? It might make a man of you.* Instead, I simply replied, "The working conditions are less favorable than what they had become accustomed to."

Damon spoke about our growing levels of grassroots support, and I allowed him to carry the meeting.

"I thought that went rather well," he said as we walked to the parking area.

"I'm glad you were satisfied with the reception," I told him.

It was much later than anticipated when I finally headed east on I-40 toward Atlanta. I drove through the night, was stopped for speeding after crossing into Georgia, and wasn't in my hotel room until 2:00 a.m. The alarm blared at seven to rouse me for the final day of the staff meeting that would begin in an hour.

I chose as obscure a location as possible at the conference table and sat with eyes closed and face in my hands through the infinite seconds and minutes of the gathering as Bruce and other speakers regaled the staff with redundant pontifications of the obvious.

"I wish everyone a safe trip back to their assignments," Bruce declared. I looked up at the clock and saw that it was 2:00 p.m.

Ernest tapped my shoulder as I walked to the door. "Get some lunch if you're hungry. Bruce wants to meet with us at the office in an hour."

The Southern Regional office of ACTWU's Textile Division was located within a modest several-story building in College Park, a suburb of Atlanta. I found Ernest and Bruce already in the conference room, talking about locals with which I wasn't familiar.

Bruce sat at the head of a long table with Ernest occupying the first seat along one side. I positioned myself two seats down from him in order to have some space around me. The two of them wrapped up their preliminary discussion upon my arrival.

"Ernest has been keeping me pretty well abreast of what's been going on," Bruce began, "but why don't you fill us in on more of the details."

I rendered a dispassionate and factual report as was expected. The picket line was holding but now limited to about two dozen diehards. The Teamsters weren't crossing, but the company had recently found an alternative source of cotton. The community and political initiatives, though reinforced, did not represent significant leverage. I offered mixed reviews about my expectations within the various legal venues, noting that we might soon have access to personnel files which could prove pivotal in our investigations.

Bruce had the capacity for sustained listening and afforded me this courtesy until I was finished.

"We're done organizing in Jackson," he said.

Ernest looked at me and nodded with the corners of his mouth turned down, as if to say, "Hmm. . . ."

Neither of us had been expecting this.

Time froze for an eternal moment as a barrage of disparate thoughts and emotions cascaded through me. My heart couldn't help but leap with joy and relief. I was going home. The ordeal was over. I would soon be working in proximity to my daughter and able to resume a normal parenting relationship. But my mind, with its strict code and values interjected. I wasn't finished in Jackson. I had stood before the membership and sworn to fight until the bitter end as long as there were those who would join me. Who else would be as qualified to investigate the Labor Board charges once the information became available? I wondered if it would serve any purpose to disagree and request an extension. But no words passed through my lips and the flow of normal time resumed.

"You've done a hell of a job," Bruce continued. "The way things turned out wasn't your fault. We just caught some bad breaks on this one. These people at United Foods are a bunch of fucking war criminals. It's time to leave things in the hands of our lawyers and move on.

"Take a vacation. When you get back, report to Ernest for assignment on the Cone project. Things are about to kick into high gear, and that's where we need you now. Ernest, is there anything you'd like to add about that?"

"As I've already told you, we're running a coordinated rebuild project at our three Cone plants in North Carolina. Do you know where Burlington is?"

"Yeah, sure. I know where it is," I answered.

"Well, there's this little town named Haw River right next to it. Cone Mills has a finishing plant there with about 350 people in the bargaining unit. As of now, that's where I'm thinking of putting you."

I remained deadpan, but my heart again began to race. Burlington is only forty-five minutes from Chapel Hill. This was logistically better than I had dared hope for.

As the meeting continued, I learned that I was being promoted to international representative. I had been authorized to use this title with the media during the past several months, as it had a better ring to it than "organizer," but now it was official, along with the compensation package. It was a long way to have come after only eighteen months with the organization.

"I would like until the end of the month to tie up loose ends in Jackson," I said toward the end. "I can't just disappear without some type of transition."

"Take as much time as you need to do whatever you have to, within reason," Bruce replied.

He walked with me to the door of the office suite, and we shook hands in the hallway. "You'll be working closer to home. You've earned it . . . at least for awhile." There was a funny little Mona Lisa smile on his lips.

Bruce returned to the office, probably to continue meeting with Ernest before getting on the phone until late in the evening. I turned away, feeling hollow and without substance like a wraith. It seemed as though I floated rather than walked down the corridor toward the elevator.

I had not only survived but prevailed personally and professionally. But my friends had gone from the production line to the picket line, and soon all that would remain was the unemployment line. I didn't blame myself or the union. Righteousness doesn't always triumph in this world, and we had done everything possible.

I took the southern route back to Jackson on I-20 and stopped for the night at a motel in Alabama. While registering at the desk, I noted that the premises included a country music saloon. I deposited my luggage in the room and wrestled with exhaustion, deciding to check out the bar in the hope of meeting someone with whom to share the night.

I combed my hair, brushed teeth, exchanged business clothes for jeans, and walked around the building to enter the establishment. My sensibilities were overwhelmed by contemporary country hits on high volume as soon as I crossed the threshold. I stood near the door and scanned the room in all directions, as was my practice in any new environment.

A few of the patrons sat at the bar, while the rest, outfitted in colorfully brocaded and well-pressed country-western apparel, moved up and back in a line dance. The women were all heavily made up, and the men sported cowboy hats, each with the self-satisfied expression of one who believes they are redefining the concept of cool.

The past several months had left me with zero-tolerance for this rodeo fantasy. I departed within five minutes, returning to my room to play guitar and then pursue the elusive angels of sleep through the darkened vestibules of a conflicted soul.

CHAPTER 21

I unlocked the door of my house on Riverside Drive on Thursday afternoon, carried my bags inside and discovered a stack of mail. There was a notice indicating attempted delivery of a certified letter from the National Labor Relations Board. This naturally aroused my interest, and I backed out of my driveway once again to sign for it at the Post Office.

I opened the envelope standing at a counter in the small lobby. The cover letter began:

> Dear Sirs:
> This is to inform you that the petition filed in the above case has been assigned to our Board agent indicated below who will either telephone or call upon you in the near future.

I turned immediately to the attached form and discovered that the decertification petition had indeed been filed. My home address was listed on the document as the office of ACTWU and its Local 281. *This is just great,* I thought to myself. *Even the anti's know where I live. Maybe we should publish my address on the front page of the* Jackson Sun, *in case there's a sociopath in town with an unscheduled evening.*

I concluded the week back on the picket line with three others and learned that the local had maintained this level of presence during my absence. The front office gate had been abandoned as there were no longer many deliveries being attempted through UPS. I noted that the damaged section of fence had been repaired.

It felt like just another winter's day in Jackson, maintaining vigil at the mill's rear entrance. The meeting in Atlanta felt like a dimly remembered dream fragment, utterly disconnected from what had become daily routine.

A tractor trailer began its slow turn toward the gate, and I instinctively moved toward it. The driver squealed his breaks and opened the window as I hopped on the running board. He was a Teamster but hadn't yet heard about the labor dispute, being from out of state and making his first run to the plant. He was happy to honor our picket line and wished us luck as he shoved his gears into reverse.

This briefly raised the spirits of the picketers until a smaller delivery vehicle and two of the yellow dump trucks drove through our position. I had second thoughts about the cotton gin until remembering the basis of my decision. My reassignment was not discussed. The weekend would provide an opportunity to synergize my awareness and formulate an exit strategy.

I slept more soundly that night than anytime during the past several weeks, undisturbed by the inevitable sounds within the old house. I understood with regret, but also an innate sense of relief, that I no longer posed the same level of threat to the company's interests.

My mind cleared as I ate breakfast and sipped coffee at the kitchen table on Saturday. Every moment spent with those closest to me would feel like a lie in the absence of disclosure. As local president, Georgia was owed the courtesy of being the first informed. I invited myself to her house for a visit that afternoon.

I drove toward her neighborhood with uncustomary reserve, appreciative of slower traffic which delayed my progress, rather than darting around it. It was difficult to anticipate what her reaction would be after all we had lived through. The last thing I wanted was to leave disillusioned friends in the wake of my departure.

Georgia welcomed me to her home, brought coffee into the living room, and relaxed on the couch. I pulled up a chair to sit facing her.

"I've been hearing talk that a petition to get rid of the union has been filed with the Labor Board," she said and raised the cup to her lips.

"It has. I found out about it when I got back. I didn't mention it because there ain't much to worry about."

I reviewed the ways in which the initiative was legally compromised beyond serious consideration by the NLRB.

"Well, I guess that will be one for us," she said.

"There's something I need to talk with you about. I don't know an easy way to say this . . . so I'm just going to lay it out. When I was in Atlanta, I met with Ernest and Bruce Raynor. They're pulling me out of Jackson and assigning me to another campaign.

"Bruce feels now that scab trucks have taken over most of the deliveries and cotton is coming into the plant . . . the fight on the street is something we can no longer win. It's not over. We've still got the Labor Board case and all the lawsuits. The legal fees will be paid for as long as it takes. But the union only has so many organizers, and they need to send us to places where we can most make a difference. I know that doesn't do you much good here . . ."

Georgia reached out and held my wrist. "Hey . . . you done fought the good fight. We all have. There's never a time I can remember that you didn't do exactly what you said. You done everything you could and more. I understand how the union is. You can't be blamed for going where they tell you."

"I convinced them to give me another couple of weeks to wrap things up and continue investigating the charges. Hopefully I can find some new evidence to leave with the lawyers. I wish it wasn't like this . . ."

She held onto my wrist and leaned forward slightly, peering into my eyes. "I don't believe you're afraid of the Devil himself."

"Everyone's afraid of something," I told her.

It remained my job to organize while still in Jackson, and I was instructed to present a delegation from Local 218 at the Memphis courthouse on Wednesday for the Confirmation Hearing. I considered it a pointless gesture but began making the necessary calls on Sunday afternoon. Our endeavors in this venue had resembled "The Charge of the Light Brigade" from the beginning, but like the intrepid figures immortalized in verse, I followed orders.

I spoke with Donald as part of this effort and learned that he was scheduled for picket duty on Monday morning. I suggested he stop by the union hall when his shift was over.

There was plenty of time afterward for a leisurely swim at the YMCA, which always gave me a chance to clear my thoughts and contemplate pending activities. I considered how the news should be presented to

Donald, and hoped he'd receive it in the same light as Georgia, given my recent decision to abort what might have been decisive action on our part.

I entered the union hall alone the next day and sat at my desk for fifteen minutes waiting for Donald. I was starting to wonder if he'd forgotten our appointment when he strode through the door, appearing energetic and upbeat as he often did.

"Sorry I'm late," he apologized. "I just got to runnin' my mouth. So, what you got cooking now, big guy?"

He unzipped his leather jacket and pulled a chair to the opposite side of my desk. "I've gotten a few more signatures on the petition, from members of my congregation," he told me, handing over two smudged and crumpled sheets.

"Donald, you're not going to like this," I said. "You know that I was in a meeting in Atlanta last week. They've made a decision to pull me out and send me to another campaign. I wasn't given a choice. Now that the company has found a way around the picket line, they think I could be put to better use elsewhere."

The Reverend exhaled deeply and stared at me from across the desk. "I've kind of been expecting something like this," he said at last. "There's only so long people are going to keep showing up at the gate just to watch the trucks pass through. I know they would have let you walk away from all this after the New Year, but you didn't. . . . We'll just have to leave things in God's hands now, with a little help from our lawyers."

He gave me a wink.

"How are you going to get by?" I asked. "Do you have any plans for after the unemployment runs out?"

"I'm good with my hands and know how to fix things," he answered. "I'm not afraid of hard work. There's always ways for a man like me to take care of his family. I'm more concerned about some of the others."

"I know. If running a loom is all you've ever done, and you can't read or write, where do you go from here?"

"I'm afraid that one of these days when I go into Wendy's for a hamburger, I'll look up and find that I'm being served by one of our members."

"People who are well off seem to think that as long as folks have a job, then all is good in their lives," I replied. "They should all have to work for just one year at minimum wage with no rights, and then see if they still feel that way."

"How long are you going to be with us?" he asked.

"I've convinced them to give me another two weeks. I'll spend as much of that time as possible investigating the charges and sending any new evidence to the lawyers. I'm hoping they can get me back into the plant soon, to go through the personnel records.

"Right now, only you and Georgia know I'm leaving. Let's keep it that way for the moment. If the company gets wind of it, they'll postpone a response to the information request until I'm gone."

I stood up to shake Donald's hand and drove the short distance to the back of the plant, where I found two men in position.

On the morning of Wednesday, February 21, I donned my suit and deftly knotted the second tie that had been added to my collection.

Both Sam and Mark greeted me in the courthouse lobby, along with a dozen people from the local, a respectable showing at this juncture. The attorneys for both the union and Gibbs Machinery had recently filed Amended Objections to the Debtor's Second Amended Plan of Reorganization, which among other matters would be argued on this day.

The union objected on grounds that the plan structure wasn't equitable in regard to numerous employee claims and that it "encouraged and sanctioned" the unfair labor practices of United Foods, noting that our law firm's ability to represent its client had been compromised by the employer's refusal to provide relevant information. The presentations and arguments went back and forth into the evening, and Judge Kennedy continued the hearing until Friday.

I sat with Mark in the empty rows of wooden benches while Sam remained in a caucus with Bradley MacLean and Don Dresser for half an hour following adjournment. The management representatives finally departed, and Sam took a seat in front of us, turning to speak.

"The company has agreed to allow Phil into the front office to review personnel files. I think the judge made it pretty clear today that he found their refusal to provide information to be unacceptable. There are a couple of provisions, however. We won't be allowed to remove documents from the plant nor will we be allowed use of the company's copy machine. Dresser said he was concerned that the potential number of copies might prove excessive and represent a substantial cost."

"I can't commit two hundred personnel files to memory," I said, "and there isn't time to take notes."

"There's an easy solution to that," said Mark. "I can rent a copy machine from an office supply place and we'll bring it into the plant."

"The company is willing to grant access by appointment starting on Monday," Sam added.

"The hearing will probably be over by then," I said.

"Look, this was the best I could work out on short notice. Besides, the real probative value of those files is in regard to the Labor Board case and we have some time on that."

It was after eight by the time I returned home. There was a message on the answering machine from Leo Boyland. The tone of his voice sounded urgent so I dialed the number.

"How you been?" I asked when he picked up.

"Not so good. I slipped while I was in the chicken plant and broke my neck. The doctors got me in a neck brace, and the company says I'm no longer fit to do the work, so they let me go."

"That's awful," I said, unsure of a more appropriate response. "How bad is it? What did you slip on?"

"The floor in there sometimes has blood and other mess from the chickens. I guess I just stepped in the wrong spot. The doctors say I'm going to be alright, just have to wear this damn brace for awhile. The reason I called, and I'm sorry to bother you again, but I want to come home."

"Do you have a place lined up to stay?" I asked.

"A friend in Memphis gonna let me crash . . . that is if I can get up there. Can you send me money for a bus ticket?"

"I'll pay for the ticket up here, and it'll be waiting for you at the local bus station. You'll get it quicker that way."

"Have you heard any news about my money from the arbitration?"

"I just came from the bankruptcy court," I told him. "I feel really bad telling you this, especially after what you just told me, but your money is going to be tied up in the bankruptcy for a long time . . . and if you end up getting anything at all, it will just be a taste. You shouldn't base your life around waiting for it."

"That ain't right . . . for one judge to give me the money and now for another to say I can't have it! You need to do something. That's what I paid my union dues for all those years. Do your job and get me my money!" Leo became increasingly agitated as he spoke.

"The only thing I can do is send you a fucking bus ticket to come back home," I said in a manner intended to effect his return to reality. "The system sucks. It's not my doing. I just work it as best I can."

"I'm sorry," he said, calming down. "I didn't mean to take all that out on you. You been nothing but a friend. I'll just be glad to be coming home."

I took advantage of an unscheduled Thursday morning by visiting a travel agent to plan my vacation between assignments. Like most members of the community, he had been following the news and was eager to provide his best services. I told him that I enjoyed foreign travel and was looking to spend ten days in a place that was warm, beautiful, and had good swimming, where one could unwind surrounded by the natural world. He recommended Cancun, Mexico, extolling its virtues as an island paradise. I told him to make the plane and hotel reservations.

A downsized version of the picket line remained self-perpetuating and I no longer felt the need to make a daily appearance. I scheduled an impromptu committee meeting to discuss my departure and what would transpire afterward. The small group accepted the news with the same gracious stoicism that Georgia and Donald had displayed.

We used the gathering as a springboard to organize a final meeting of the stewards and those who had participated in the picket line. In a sense, I was reverse-engineering my process of insertion into the local a year before.

I returned to Memphis the next morning as the Confirmation Hearing resumed. Following hours of continued argument and last-minute testimony, the Reorganization Plan received final approval. I wasn't distressed by the outcome, as it had been a foregone conclusion in my mind since December. The several hundred community signatures and small stack of letters written in opposition had as much influence on the proceeding as grains of dust scattered on the courthouse floor.

As we exited the building together, Mark told me, "Don Dresser and I spoke when we recessed for lunch. He said he would be willing to sign a contract with me if there was no arbitration clause. If a dispute arose it would be discussed by the employee, with or without a shop steward, and departmental management. If they were unable to work things out, then it would move directly to my level, and I'd fly to Jackson to meet with Dresser. We would try to reach an understanding, but if we couldn't, that would be the end of it."

"You've got to be kidding."

"That's what I told him."

Mark said he would drive to Jackson with a portable copier on Sunday night so that we could initiate the long-anticipated review of personnel files the next morning.

The weekend was perhaps the slowest forty-eight-hour period since my arrival in Jackson. I began arranging personal effects and work files in preparation for my final exodus at the end of the week and prepared an outline for the attorneys of possible candidates for deposition.

Mark and I sat in the front office waiting area of the mill on Monday morning, having presented ourselves to the receptionist. It felt somewhat disorienting to find myself back inside, like visiting a scene from a former life. A member of the office staff ushered us into one of the small rooms adjoining the main conference area, which only months ago had been the site of contract negotiations and frequent grievance meetings.

We were obliged to continue waiting. There was a small folding table in the center of the floor with brochures scattered on top containing pictures of frozen vegetables.

"What do they do in here," asked Mark, "weave broccoli?"

Twenty minutes passed and Bob Knuckles entered the room. I shook his hand as if the past five months had been only a dream. His response was distant but polite. I didn't consider him responsible for the events that had cast us as adversaries. He was simply a man trying to survive and maintain a career in a declining industry.

He led us into a larger room and showed me the filing cabinets where personnel records were stored and arranged alphabetically. Mark was provided with assistance to wheel in the rented copy machine as Knuckles and I continued to talk. He asked for and received my assurances that nothing would be removed from the files or damaged. I could tell that my word was still good with him personally.

Mark excused himself, saying he had to be in Chattanooga the next morning for negotiations. Knuckles left me alone in the filing room, offering his assistance if necessary.

I decided to begin with a comparison of Georgia Bond and weavers hired in her stead. I pulled open a heavy drawer towards the top of a cabinet which had the letter "B" marked in front. I experienced a moment of feeling daunted and overwhelmed, gazing upon the row of thick folders housed within.

The personnel file of a senior employee contains hundreds of pages, documenting every event that has transpired during the course of employment—job transfers, temporary reassignments, long-expired discipline, yearly attendance records, efficiency reports, doctor's notes from the previous decade, etc. The arrangement of these documents is often less than systematic, as management frequently sifts through them.

Once in place, I knew there was barely time to make a dent. The remainder of the day was mine, however, and I plunged into the files. After reviewing Georgia's file, I targeted currently employed weavers with low seniority. As expected, there were individuals whose attendance and work records didn't compare favorably with those of the local president.

I planned to return the next morning, but Knuckles informed me that the conference area was being utilized for two days of "sensitive" meetings and suggested we resume on Thursday. He seemed unaware that I was leaving town, so this didn't appear to be a deliberate attempt at delay.

Mark called during the midday break in his negotiations to find out how things had gone. I shared the progress which had been made but explained that this was an investigation that required weeks of sustained effort.

"I've got a long-term president from a plant that shut recently," he said. "I've been trying to find some work for her that would convince Bruce to put her on the payroll. Let me see what I can do."

I spoke with committee members to coordinate the final union meeting scheduled for the following afternoon. We were using word of mouth to avoid publication of my departure and the opportunity it would provide management to exploit the announcement.

I received an unexpected call from Sam Morris late in the afternoon. United Foods had withdrawn the decertification petition. It had been a futile exercise from the beginning, and this would preclude a formal dismissal and repudiation from the Board.

Mark called again after dinner. He was in his car, driving back to Knoxville. Being more technologically astute than the rest of us, he was first of the Southern Region staff to avail himself of the new cell phone technology, in the form of a cumbersome unit attached within his vehicle. He said he would meet me at the union hall the next evening, accompanied by the person he had earlier mentioned.

On February 28, I had my final conversations with representatives of the NAACP, JONAH, and an aide from Congressman Tanner's office. I then dismantled my living space for departure. My house had been paid for through the end of the month, and the rental agency wasn't disposed to a brief extension as a new tenant had already been found.

I carefully packed my personal effects, including little gifts and drawings from Colie that had helped transform my work residence into a space resembling home. Files and documents from the campaign were stacked in cardboard boxes and all of my clothing, save that for the next day, was tossed into suitcases. It was a bittersweet feeling to tear apart the environment that had served as my nest of privacy and shelter throughout a volatile year, reducing it to the sterile rental property it had been on my arrival.

At 2:30 I had to disengage from this process, retract my personal reflections, and drive to the union hall. I had been uncertain about how the leadership would respond to my departure, but the trepidation was greater as I contemplated the membership's reaction.

Cars were already scattered about the front lawn when I pulled in. I entered the main hall and greeted various members of the committee. Within five minutes of the scheduled start time, all the seats were filled and several empty chairs had to be brought in. The turnout was the largest I'd seen all winter and included a number of individuals who, for whatever reason, hadn't participated in the picket line. The members sat with coats draped over the backs of their chairs, staring straight ahead in silence, their faces showing little emotion.

Georgia called the meeting to order at 3:00 p.m. and Donald offered a brief prayer, standing in front of the area where the committee sat to my left. When his invocation was concluded, he strode to center stage, speaking slowly, with the deep, reverberating tones of a preacher and pointed his finger in my direction. "This man . . . never once stood up here . . . and addressed the membership while drunk!"

The audience rose and exploded into the most dramatic and sustained ovation I'd received during the entire year. I realized that this was perhaps the highest compliment that could be offered by Local 281 of Jackson, Tennessee.

This meeting was primarily personal rather than business. I expressed my admiration and respect for the courage and determination of the union members before me, paying special tribute to the leadership. Without belaboring the details, I provided an update about the ongoing legal campaign and the new phase of investigation that was being initiated.

"I don't know how many of you will end up back in the mill or what the status of the union will eventually be," I told them. "But if you take what you've been through and what you learned from it back into the rest of your lives, then no matter how things turn out, it wasn't all for nothing. There's a spark that will live on through you and touch the lives of other people in ways we can't even begin to imagine."

There were a few brief questions about the economic settlements our attorneys were seeking, and the meeting adjourned. People came forward so that we could shake hands and wish each other well.

I remained in the company of several committee members until Mark arrived an hour later. He introduced me to Mary Evans, the former local president who would continue reviewing the personnel files.

As we sat at one of the folding tables, I began to explain the case theory and evidence needed to support it. Mary's lack of comprehension was immediately obvious. Though she ultimately went on to have a successful career as a union representative, at this stage her experience was limited to presenting second-step grievances and maintaining membership. Building the foundation of a complex Labor Board charge involved a level of responsibility she had yet to imagine.

This was the best assistance Mark had been able to offer on short notice, and it was mine to appreciate and make the best of. I realized that theoretical discussion had little value and that our energies could be best utilized through hands-on training. We arranged to meet in the morning

as she left to get situated at the Ramada. Mark followed me home to retrieve the computer from my kitchen table.

The next morning I ate my final breakfast in Jackson, loaded belongings into the trunk of my car, and deposited keys in the mailbox. I
met Mary at the union hall and she followed me to the plant. A clerical
employee greeted us and made the filing room available.

The investigation resumed with a comparative study of Donald
Vandiver and those currently employed as fixers in the card room. His
supervisor had previously considered him the best mechanic in the department, assigning him the most highly skilled tasks and often requesting his opinion.

I placed his cumbersome file on the table and walked Mary through
the process of sorting its contents, making a small pile of relevant documents to review and copy. When finished, I produced the hard-won list
of current employees and located the files of the first two carding fixers
whose names appeared. We each took one to study.

"If you come across a scab with an exemplary work record, put the
file away and move on to the next one," I told her. "We're not obligated
to include it in the report."

"Why not?" she asked. "Aren't we here to get at the truth?"

"We're here to build a case. You need to understand the difference
because the company sure as hell does. We're looking for the most extreme examples of questionable hiring so we can provide a pattern of discrimination to the Board. I don't want to bury our evidence in a pile of
stuff that doesn't help us. Do you understand me?"

I looked up after a few minutes, saw that Mary wasn't segregating
the documents and selecting exhibits as instructed, and became even
more irritable. She obviously felt uncomfortable, and I apologized for my
manner. I realized that I sounded like a typical boss under pressure, trying to get results from a subordinate, and that wasn't how she deserved
to be treated. My assistant was not responsible for her lack of experience
or the choice of her first assignment.

As the hour approached five, we returned files to their alphabetized
rows and assembled the fruits of our research.

"Please promise me that you'll keep coming back here and finish collecting evidence the way I showed you," I requested before we exited
the room.

"I'll do the best I can," she replied.

I walked across the street to the parking lot and sat in my car for a few minutes watching the daylight begin to fade. I fired the ignition, rolled onto the road, and turned right to circle around the building, unable to resist a final pass by the rear gate.

I observed two men standing before the entrance, with picket signs casually held at waist height, though no trucks were approaching to notice. They appeared joyless but determined, lost in their own thoughts and motionless. Neither of them had been shop stewards or even active in the local while employed at the mill. But they had reported for picket duty on December 20 and thereafter been transfigured by events into these grim soldiers who remained at their post until the end.

They didn't notice me and as the hour was late, I did not draw their attention. I drove around the block toward the thoroughfare leading out of Jackson, turning onto the interstate and heading east through the frozen darkness.

EPILOGUE

Several days later I disembarked at the airport in Cancun and took a taxi to the luxury accommodations my travel agent had arranged. I was soon standing on the balcony of my room, absorbing the warmth of the sub-tropical sun as I viewed the tranquil blue waters of the Gulf of Mexico.

I feasted in the hotel restaurant on a dinner of exquisitely prepared seafood and exotic side dishes, grateful for the agent's recommendation.

I changed clothes to enjoy my first promenade through the village as night fell, wanting to take in each new sight and savor every moment. Despite my best intentions, the mood slowly dissipated. I was in an enclave of gift shops, cafés, and tourist bars. I turned the corner and passed a large discotheque from which loud dance music assaulted the evening as the door opened to allow a young couple to enter.

I strolled for blocks in search of a different neighborhood where I could experience actually being in Mexico, but it wasn't to be found on this island. If there were tropical birds serenading the countryside, their songs were eclipsed by the loud and raucous voices emerging from the various establishments and open-air concessions. I retraced my route back to the hotel and walked out on the beach to hear the gentle lapping of waves, only to discover that the party atmosphere had no boundaries.

The whole purpose of visiting a foreign country is to experience both a human culture and natural world that is different. I've never comprehended the tourist mentality of traveling great distances in order to re-create the familiar. I was back in Gatlinburg, only it was warmer and surrounded by water instead of mountains.

I remained determined to make the best of my respite between campaigns. I slept late the next morning and returned to the beach, where I swam for half a mile to a place of quiet between bathers and the boats.

I went limp to test the currents, relieved that there was little undertow. Two young men on jet skis came speeding by, and I bounced in the churning water.

"Fuck you," I muttered under my breath.

I headed back to the beach, having to navigate through a flotilla of rubber rafts as I drew closer. In 1990, most people were unconcerned about holes in the ozone layer, and I looked forward to renewing my tan. I found my blanket, applied oil, and lay on my back, doing my best to ignore the crowded sands surrounding me.

During the next few days, I visited several different beaches but found them all the same. I rented a motor scooter and circled the island, but this turned out to only be a three-hour excursion. I sampled the various cafés by night, and while the food was excellent, I didn't encounter a single person I was interested in talking to for more than twenty seconds.

I eventually had to accept that I'd come to the wrong place and wasn't enjoying myself. I paid to change my flight and returned home.

The next week I reported to Greensboro, where Ernest briefed me on the Cone Project. I was in fact assigned to the Haw River finishing plant and its Local 1113. The following day I found a hotel room in nearby Burlington. Being integrated into a larger campaign already underway required an abbreviated period of introduction and reconnaissance. I had to hit the ground running and improvise. After several weeks, I was holding mass grievance meetings within the plant. I was ironically rebuilding the union local at the factory where Transit Supervisor John Farrish had once worked—the man who, by looking the other way, had made my entire career possible.

My inner gears were completely stripped, and my nerves were shot on returning from Jackson. Following bursts of intense energy, I would melt into a chair, feeling as though I weighed a thousand pounds, often unable to rouse myself for hours. There were moments when I feared becoming lost in this space, but I always stood up at the appointed time. I was initiating a project within a continuous operation and had to be available throughout the day and night for shift meetings, leafleting, and representation. No one ever had a clue how close to the edge I was.

Several days after arriving, I found a trailer on an acre of land near the outskirts of Burlington to serve as my work residence. Colie was once again able to stay with me three nights a week. I furnished a playroom for her with a plastic cooking range and dinette suite. We would often sit on the tiny yellow chairs as she served imaginary tea.

Once every week we would leaflet the graveyard shift together at 10:30 p.m. The plant was approached via a steep driveway with a security shack on top. After receiving clearance, one proceeded through a gate into the large parking area. The factory itself was surrounded by a second fence with two employee entrances.

Spotlights illumined the otherwise desolate setting. Clouds of steam, reaching ten feet in the air, periodically rose through grating between the entrances. Colie would distribute leaflets with me at one of the gates while stewards covered the other. We would linger after greeting the departure of second shift at eleven.

Once the lot was empty except for parked cars, we would hold hands and leap through the billowing eruptions of water vapor. It was the industrial version of waiting on Old Faithful at Yellowstone. "Here she comes!" I would say. "Close your eyes . . . and . . . jump!" Her little fingers would grasp mine tightly as we sailed laughing through the towering plumes of smoke.

Two weeks after moving into the Burlington trailer, I received a call from Leo Boyland.

"It's good to hear from you," I said. "How've you been doing?"

"Not good," he answered. "I've been shot. A few days ago I went to visit a friend in Memphis, and these two guys pulled up in a car and robbed me. One of them shot me in the shoulder."

"That's terrible. How bad is it?"

"Well, the doctors at the emergency room removed the bullet, got me stitched up OK, and I been released. But I need to be on this medication so it don't get infected, and I can't afford it. I was wondering if you could send me sixty dollars."

I thought for a moment and could only feel inner resistance.

"Leo, I'm really sorry for what happened to you, but I've sent you a lot of money over the past year and I can't keep on doing this. I got plugged into a bunch of relief agencies in your area after the plant closed, and

I could give you the contact information. I'm certain that one of them could help get the medical attention you need. There's no need for me to pay for this."

"Look, please just this one more time," he pleaded. "I really need this medication to heal from the gunshot."

I considered his request again but felt no differently. "Take down these phone numbers. If none of them are willing to help you, let me know and I'll talk with them."

Another ten days passed, during which I was entirely focused on the new project and being a parent. One evening, I got a call from the woman who had lived with Leo prior to his discharge.

"I know that you and Leo were close," she said, "and that you helped him a lot after he lost his job. I thought that you would want to know that he died two days ago."

I expressed my condolences and hung up feeling utterly shaken. As I paced about the kitchen, emotions swelled, spiraling downward into my darkest inner pit. I began to seriously question what sort of person I had become. Had professional success made me similar to the members of management I dealt with, caring more about money than the wellbeing of others? If I had been willing to send sixty lousy dollars, Leo would still be alive.

I needed desperately to speak with someone who could offer some perspective and, after running through my mental index of friends, called Valerie in New York.

"He was a fuckin' junkie," she said after less than a minute.

"Why do you say that?" I asked. "I knew him for a year and there was never any indication of drug use or that he was under the influence."

"Some people hide it better than others," she told me. "Listen, nobody gets fired from their job, goes down to Georgia, gets a job in a chicken plant, slips and breaks their neck, comes back home, and then gets shot, except a junkie. You don't have to believe me now, but when more about what really happened comes out, you'll find I'm right."

"Even if what you said is true, I could have saved him if I'd just sent another sixty dollars."

"It wasn't your fuckin' job to save him. You did ten times more for this guy than anyone else on the planet would have. You offered him a chance to help himself and he didn't take it. This isn't on you. You need to back off and let go."

The next week I got another call from Leo's girlfriend, this time inquiring about the arbitration settlement and whether she could expect to receive any money. I referred her to the Memphis law firm and then asked about the police investigation.

"They don't have any suspects," she answered. "All I know is that they did an autopsy and found cocaine in Leo's blood."

The scattered fragments of the jigsaw puzzle rearranged into a coherent picture. This was a drug buy gone wrong. The outcome, though tragic, didn't rest on my shoulders. I wished her well and hung up.

This was a moment of clarity that remained and guided me through the rest of my career. I had always experienced the emotions of those I assisted as though they were my own, roaring and screaming through my consciousness like a freight train. I considered it my solemn duty to save them from misfortune because I had the ability to do so. The concept of professional distance was something I'd viewed with disdain, but I now began to understand its necessity if one was to survive a career that revolves around the troubles of others.

My passion and dedication never wavered when it came to fighting for and representing the union's members, but I learned to avoid taking responsibility on a personal level for the wreckage of their lives. Though I never turned my back on even the most dysfunctional worker who had an arguable case, their melodramas could no longer find a way inside of me.

Shortly after my relocation to Burlington, the National Labor Relations Board issued complaint against American Mills regarding the first set of charges, alleging failure to bargain the effects of plant closing and unilateral refusal to pay accrued vacation and other benefits, awarding $204,148 to employees. Unfortunately, United Foods wasn't cited as jointly liable, and the judgment was levied on the bankrupt estate.

American Mills chose not to litigate the decision, and NLRB attorneys brokered a settlement between the parties. A portion of the monthly lease payments would be paid into an escrow account until the award had been satisfied, at which time individual payroll checks would be drafted to employees.

In April, United Foods acquiesced to the Board's determination and extended formal recognition to the union. However, the status quo was not reinstated. The agency concluded that as United Foods had assumed control of the bankrupt facility absent a finished contract, the status quo didn't extend between successors, only the obligation to bargain. Several dates for negotiations were scheduled.

United Foods was strategic in its hiring practices as it slowly increased the hourly workforce to 230 employees during the late winter and spring of 1990. A higher percentage of union members and several shop stewards were offered employment, but this naturally didn't include the committee or anyone else with a significant leadership role.

In July, the National Labor Relations Board issued complaint against United Foods for refusal to hire Georgia Bond because of her union activity. The investigators determined, however, that the evidence "did not disclose unlawful discrimination" in regard to sixty-seven other union activists who were not recalled. There was no way to know whether the comparative analysis of personnel files had continued and been argued in a manner consistent with what I'd envisioned.

United Foods contested the complaint regarding Georgia, and a hearing was held before administrative law judge Walter H. Mahoney in September. On December 4, Judge Mahoney upheld the complaint, noting in his decision:

> In short, the Respondent harbored, and continues to harbor, an active and emotional animus, both towards the Union and its active spokesperson, and it has advanced several far-fetched excuses in an effort to explain that it wasn't indulging this animus, when it refused, and continues to refuse, to employ Ms. Bond.

> The series of excuses it has continued to advance in order to prevent an admittedly qualified, experienced, and capable job applicant from being hired . . . compels the conclusion that her union leadership was the real reason for the Respondent's refusal to hire her.

The judge ordered the immediate reinstatement of Georgia Bond with full back pay. He also issued a cease and desist order regarding the employer's coercive discouragement of union membership and activity.

Eight months later, United Foods ceased operations and closed the mill for the last time. Dominic Poon had been right about one thing (according to the testimony of Jimmy Gibbs). United Foods had no idea how to run a textile plant.

The litigation evolved and continued within several venues through the summer of 1994. Georgia's case was further appealed but eventually settled without an admission of guilt. In the absence of funding provided by lease payments, other employee claims were remanded back to the asset pool over which hundreds of unsecured creditors fought for scraps like a band of malnourished hyenas circling a corpse. The insolvent estate of American Mills was closed in 1994 without payment being rendered to those who most needed it.

In the fall of 1991, Ernest invited me to a private meeting at the Greensboro union office and presented a choice. I was offered the opportunity to direct my own team of organizers which would serve as a troubleshooting unit throughout the south. As an alternative, the newly appointed manager of the Central North Carolina Joint Board had requested me as a permanent member of his staff.

"You know which one I'd prefer," said Ernest, "but you've earned the right to decide. Take a couple of days to think it over."

"I don't have to think about it," I told him. "I really appreciate the offer but you know how I feel about staying close to my daughter."

It was the single best decision I ever made. It meant that I was able to remain a real father to Colie throughout her childhood and eventually recover aspects of my life that might otherwise have remained in abeyance forever.

The Jackson campaign represented the last situation in which I allowed others to manage the litigation that ensued in my locals. I developed expertise in arbitration and enforcement of the National Labor Relations Act. The labor movement embodies a unique area of litigation in which a law degree is not required for the presentation of cases. The only thing that matters is the ability to win.

Over the years, I became an asset which was frequently dispatched to the locals of other representatives to arbitrate grievances and develop Labor Board charges, and became a specialist in fighting decertification campaigns. No union local was ever successfully decertified on my watch.

In 1994 my work before the National Labor Relations Board in *ACTWU v. Highland Yarn* established the national precedent for defining "illegal employer assistance in an effort to decertify the union." I remained unaware of the broader implications of this decision until it proved to be the governing instrument in defeating a decertification attempt at a Kmart distribution center in 2003.

I finally learned how to use a computer in 1997. Colie taught me how to cut and paste within a document.

That same year, I became special projects coordinator within the Carolinas and remained in that position ever since. Several locals were assigned to me for ongoing representation, while I continued to perform intervention work in others, and negotiated first contracts at newly organized facilities. Though I was sent into many volatile situations with a high potential for violence, no one ever received a scratch during one of my campaigns.

NAFTA and other free trade agreements legislated in the early 1990s sounded the final death knell for the already troubled textile and apparel industries of the United States. The increased flow of imports from emerging third world economies decapitated domestic competition like a scythe slicing through a field of dry wheat.

I lived through a long succession of plant closings, networking displaced workers with government and relief agencies, at times able to find them jobs at other union plants. There is a cemetery in my mind bearing a cross for every union local at a plant now shut, with whose members I'd once been closely involved. It's a place I share with no one, wandering its desolate pathways alone, on sleepless nights.

The union struggled to survive through a series of reorganizations and mergers, changing its name several times along the way. It diversified into other areas of manufacturing, laundries, logistics, and the growing service sector of our economy. We are now known as Workers United and have become an affiliate of the Service Employees International Union.

Dominic Poon arrived in Tennessee during 1989 and positioned himself at cross-purposes with the tide of history. It was the dawn of an era when American investors would soon be financing textile plants in China. He would have been well-advised to remain at home and wait for the venture capitalists to find him.

Ernest eventually became the union's national organizing director. Several years ago he suffered a stroke, and this once manic and robust figure was forced to retire on disability. In his time he was a great organizer and warrior. He initiated and supervised campaigns across the United States and Canada that touched the lives of tens of thousands of people. He put more money in their pockets and helped them find their dignity. No one can ever take that away from him.

Some might wonder whatever became of a child raised in the unconventional manner of my daughter, with a father who not only never attempted to mold her through discipline, but protected her from anyone else who might try.

Colie graduated summa cum laude from her university and went on to become a successful psychotherapist with a thriving practice. In her application to graduate school, she stated that her travels with me and exposure to the union had instilled, at an early age, the desire to spend her life helping others.

I retired from the field on May 1, 2011, after twenty-three years of service. I was assigned to seven union locals at the time, spread through a wide cross-section of industries. One of my plants was the last remaining Cone Mills facility in America, with 163 workers in the bargaining unit.

APPENDIX

SHIFT MEETINGS

AT THE UNION HALL

AGENDA:

OUR VACATION MONEY!!!

<u>A SHIFT</u> - Wednesday - April 12 - 6 P.M.

<u>C SHIFT</u> - Thursday - April 13 - 6 A.M.

<u>1st. SHIFT</u> - Friday - April 14 - 2:30 P.M.

<u>B SHIFT</u> - Saturday - April 15 - 6 P.M.

<u>D SHIFT</u> - Sunday - April 16 - 6 A.M.

For months we have waited patiently for the vacation money which we've earned and is lawfully due us. We have done everything possible to help the Company through hard times. What have we gotten for our good intentions? One broken promise after another!!!

THE TIME HAS COME

FOR ACTION!

IF YOU'RE INTERESTED IN YOUR VACATION MONEY:

BE THERE!   BE THERE!   BE THERE!

<u>MEMBERS AND NONMEMBERS ARE WELCOME</u>

Figure 1

IT'S YOUR FUTURE!
HOW MUCH DO YOU DESERVE?

On June 8, 1989, the Union and the Company sat down at the bargaining table. Both sides presented their contract proposals in writing:

<u>THE COMPANY'S PROPOSALS</u>

1. WAGE CUTS – eliminate bonuses, incentives, plus other cuts

2. NO MORE 3rd and 4th WEEK OF VACATION

3. CUT SHIFT DIFFERENTIAL TO 5 cents

4. LESS HOLIDAYS

5. INCREASE INSURANCE PAYMENTS - $7 per month

6. CUT OUT UTILITY JOBS

<u>THE UNION'S PROPOSALS</u>

1. A 4% WAGE INCREASE for all employees

2. KEEP ALL 4 WEEKS

3. KEEP PRESENT SHIFT DIFFERENTIAL

4. ADD MARTIN LUTHER KING'S BIRTHDAY

5. KEEP INSURANCE PAYMENTS THE SAME

6. PROTECT UTILITY WORKERS

7. SPEED UP THE GRIEVANCE PROCESS

8. CLEAR UP THE DISCIPLINE AND DISCHARGE PROCEDUE

This is the dawning of a new day for a tired old mill and a group of workers who've been down a long hard road. The new Company has spent millions in buying the plant and will spend much more in repairs and equipment.

In these negotiations, the Union and the Company will be discussing working conditions, health and safety, as well as money and benefits. We have a chance to take one of the sorriest mills in the state of Tennessee and turn it into a decent place to earn a living. But it <u>will only work if the Company comes to realize that there's little point investing in machines if you don't also invest in the people who run them.</u>

SHOW THE COMPANY WHERE YOU STAND!

Figure 2

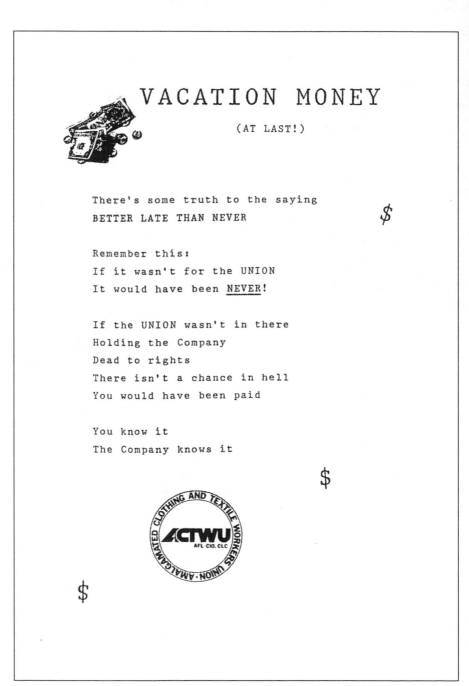

VACATION MONEY

(AT LAST!)

```
There's some truth to the saying
BETTER LATE THAN NEVER                          $

Remember this:
If it wasn't for the UNION
It would have been NEVER!

If the UNION wasn't in there
Holding the Company
Dead to rights
There isn't a chance in hell
You would have been paid

You know it
The Company knows it
                                        $

          $
```

Figure 3

GEORGIA IS PRESIDENT

On July 22, Percy Ray Long resigned for reasons of ill health
and GEORGIA BOND BECAME ACTING PRESIDENT of Local 281. She
will hold office until elections in December.

For years, Georgia has been the grassroots leader within the
plant. She has been the voice of the people, speaking up
against what was wrong, both within the Company and within
the Old Union Leadership.

The New Union Leadership in Jackson strongly supports Georgia
and welcomes her in her new role as President. Together, we
will continue to fight for a good contract and a long overdue
pay raise. With your support, it will go down OUR WAY!

Percy Ray Long served as President of Local 281 through some
very troubled times. His years of dedication and hard work are
deeply appreciated by the Union and his friends wish him a
speedy recovery. Percy will remain active on the Committee and
continue to help in every way possible.

Figure 4

WHAT ABOUT OUR UNION?

The Company has stopped taking dues out of your checks.
They are doing this because we are now without a contract.
They are trying to pressure us at the bargaining table.

IT WON'T WORK!

We will continue to fight for a better contract -
NO MATTER WHAT IT TAKES!

If you're not already a Union member:

JOIN US NOW!

Help your fellow workers win a RAISE, RESPECT and a
BETTER WAY OF LIFE.

REMEMBER:

NO MORE CONCESSIONS!

WE DESERVE A RAISE!

Figure 5

UNION MEETING

AT THE UNION HALL

WEDNESDAY - AUGUST 30 - 5 P.M. - 7 P.M.

AGENDA:

* CONTRACT UPDATE
* OVERLOADED JOBS
* GRIEVANCE REPORT
* VANDIVER GETS SWORN IN

NEW EMPLOYEES ARE INVITED!

VANDIVER IS V.P.

On August 22, the Union Committee elected Reverend Donald Vandiver to serve as Acting Vice President until elections in December.

Donald Vandiver has long been one of the Union Committee's most outspoken members. He has an outstanding track record of resolving grievances on the floor of the Card Room.

Donald is in the forefront of our fight for a better contract and a RAISE!

MEMBERS AND NONMEMBERS ARE WELCOME

Figure 6

EIGHT HOUR SHIFTS!!!

In an effort to make American Mills a better place to work, the Union and the Company are proposing that we go back to 8 hour shifts (6 days per week) for all employees.

DO YOU LIKE IT??

Another idea: Would you like these work schedules?

1st Shift - 8 A.M. - 4 P.M.

2nd Shift - 4 P.M. - 12 A.M.

3rd Shift - 12 A.M. - 8 A.M.

SHIFT PREMIUMS:

Second Shift-15¢ per hour

Third Shift-20¢ per hour

SPECIAL UNION MEETINGS

(AT THE UNION HALL)

FRIDAY - SEPTEMBER 15 - 5 P.M. & 6 P.M.

WE NEED TO KNOW HOW YOU FEEL!!!

MEMBERS AND NONMEMBERS ARE WELCOME

Figure 7

POOR MANAGEMENT
STRIKES AGAIN!

Last week, the Company called Phil and Georgia into an
emergency meeting. The Company is losing money. They are
in deep trouble with the banks. They were suddenly desperate
to change to 8 HOUR SHIFTS in order to increase efficiency.

We put out a leaflet and called a special Union Meeting.
Everyone's spirits were running high.

Just as suddenly, they came up with yet another plan to save
the mill - major style and production changes, which they
say will not fit in with the 8 hour shifts.

The mill is in fact fighting for its life right now, but this
whole mess raises some serious questions:

JUST WHO IS RUNNING THE MILL?

DO THEY KNOW WHAT THEY'RE DOING?

WE KNOW THEY CAN'T DEAL WITH PEOPLE!

DO THEY KNOW ANY MORE ABOUT MAKING CLOTH?

We support whatever policies are really necessary to keep
this plant open. Our representation won't mean much if you
don't have a job. But this whole mess about the shifts makes
us wonder whether we're dealing with businessmen, or a bunch
of chickens running around with their heads cut off!

Figure 8

WORKER'S AID

ACTWU Local 281 is working with the ACTWU Social Services
Department and the Tennessee Department of Labor to provide
the following services for layed off workers:

- Help with Unemployment, Food Stamps, etc.

- Job training and placement

- Child care

- Medical assistance

- Links with all local community and church organizations

If you run into problems with Unemployment or any other state
agency, we will be glad to assist and represent you. If you
have problems or questions, feel free to call:

- Phil Cohen (International Representative) - 424-xxxx
- Georgia Bond (President, Local 281) - 427-xxxx
- Rev. Donald Vandiver (V.P., Local 281) - 423-xxxx

The Union will soon be sitting down with the Company to
discuss both your benefits and ways we can work together to
reopen the plant. We'll be discussing vacation and holiday
pay, pension, insurance, sick pay, etc.

The Company has stated on T.V. and in the newspaper that it
closed due to cash flow problems. They were unable to get
the Sulzer Looms running in time to meet the bank's deadline.

The Company is trying to line up new investors and the Union
will be working with them in every way possible to turn things
around. We are hopeful that through these efforts, the mill
will be able to reopen its gates before too long.

Figure 9

FIGHT FOR OUR UNION!

American Mills and United Foods have put together a plan to
BUST OUR UNION! They plan to reopen as a NON-UNION plant.
They're making their move through lawyers and a bunch of
fancy legal games.

They think that they deserve TOTAL CONTROL over our lives.
They think that all you deserve is to lick their butts,
take whatever they dish out, grin and say, "Yes Sir!"

They've played their little game in court. Now it's time to
ram it back down their throats!

BE ADVISED OF THE FOLLOWING:

1. THE COMPANY IS NOT REHIRING BY SENIORITY!

2. MANY OF THE OLDEST WORKERS WILL NOT BE REHIRED.

3. THOSE WHO ARE REHIRED WILL COME BACK WITH NO SENIORITY.

4. WHAT ABOUT OUR BENEFITS - VACATION, HOLIDAYS, INSURANCE,
    PENSION, ETC?

5. THEY PLAN TO SET WAGES AND BASE RATES WITHOUT BARGAINING.

The Company's actions are ILLEGAL! The Union is going to
take this fight to the screaming limit - in court, in the
shop, in every way possible!

We'll contact you again soon. If you value your freedom,
dignity and right to a decent job - dig in your heels for
a fight!

Figure 10

HOW DO YOU LIKE IT?

- NO SENIORITY

- NO BENEFITS

- WORK RULES LIKE A PRISON CAMP

United Foods had done this in several other cities. Taken over a plant. Busted the Union. Turned it into a slave labor camp.

They won't get away with it in Jackson. They've broken the law and they're going to pay!

The Union has filed charges in court and with the Labor Board. We're going to fight for our rights in every way possible.

The Union wants to see this mill open. Everyone needs a job to live. But United Foods and American Mills are going out of their way to take advantage of this. The workers of our mill deserve a job with seniority, benefits and <u>self respect</u>!

AS SURE AS THE SUN IS GOING TO RISE TOMORROW
THERE WILL BE A UNION AT OUR MILL!!

Figure 11

LOCAL 281: LOCKED OUT!

TRUCKERS:

DON'T CROSS OUR LINE!

The ACTWU International has ordered this action in response to the lockout of Local 281.

On October 6, American Mills shut down and locked its gates with no notice to the Union and 510 workers.

In November, through a Chapter 11 bankruptcy scam, the mill reopened. United Foods is now leasing the plant from American Mills and claiming to be a new company.

They've rehired 160 workers with no regard to seniority. Employees with 15-25 years of seniority are locked out, while employees with 3-6 months of seniority work their jobs. The Union Officers and Committee, as well as most Union members have been locked out!

Those who are working have lost all vacation, holiday and pension benefits, as well as the right to file a grievance.

United Foods has refused to recognize or bargain with the Union.

United Foods busted two Teamster locals in California packing plants in 1987 and 1988. Hundreds of Teamster workers were fired and replaced!

TRUCKERS & TEXTILE WORKERS:
UNITE AGAINST UNITED FOODS!

Figure 12